The Kennedy Doctrine

THE
KENNEDY
DOCTRINE

Louise FitzSimons

RANDOM HOUSE
New York

ISBN: 0–394–46241–6

Library of Congress Catalog Card Number: 75–159343

Grateful acknowledgment is extended to the following for permission to reprint copyrighted material:

Harper & Row, Publishers: From Kennedy, *by Theodore C. Sorensen (New York, 1965).*

Houghton Mifflin Company: From A Thousand Days: John F. Kennedy in the White House, *by Arthur M. Schlesinger, Jr. (Boston, 1965).*

Manufactured in the United States of America by The Haddon Craftsmen, Inc., Scranton, Pennsylvania

9 8 7 6 5 4 3 2

FIRST EDITION

To my father

ACKNOWLEDGMENTS

Special thanks are due Mrs. Margaret Kellog, of the Library of Congress, Washington, D.C., and Mrs. Sylvie Turner, of the John F. Kennedy Library, Waltham, Mass., for assistance in locating research materials.

I would also like to thank Ambassador Llewellyn Thompson for permission to use material in his closed interview in the Oral History Collection at the John F. Kennedy Library; my editor at Random House, Charlotte Mayerson, for perseverance and helpful criticism; my former colleague on the staff of the United States Senate, the late Emerson Hynes, for sharing with me over the years his great insight into government and politics; and my mother, Mrs. Mary FitzSimons, who read the proofs.

L.F.

Contents

The Kennedy Doctrine

One | "Let the Word Go Forth..."

... the same revolutionary beliefs for which our fore-
bears fought are still at issue around the globe. ...
We dare not forget today that we are the heirs of that
first revolution.[1]

In his Inaugural Address, President John F. Kennedy in-
voked America's revolutionary heritage as the inspiration
for his foreign policy, yet under his administration this
nation became the leading defender of the international
status quo. Because we were so strong—militarily, economically, technologically—we became the world's most
effective counterrevolutionary power.

On that bright, cold noon in January 1961 John
Kennedy's words lifted the hearts of Americans and of
millions around the globe. But the brilliance of his rhetoric
masked the belligerence and grandiosity of his approach.
He threw down a challenge and set the nation on a course

3

which, over the decade of the sixties, affected profoundly our image as a world power, our destiny as a nation and, perhaps, the survival of mankind.

> Let every nation know, whether it wishes us well or ill, that we shall pay any price, bear any burden, meet any hardship, support any friend, oppose any foe, in order to assure the survival and the success of liberty.

Ten years later, one looks at the words of President Kennedy's Inaugural Address with an ominous sense of recognition.

Any price? The price to "assure the survival and the success of liberty" in Southeast Asia has exceeded $125 billion and 50,000 American lives, though the objective still eludes us. In 1961 President Kennedy made the basic decision that opened the way to large-scale military involvement in Vietnam when he increased the number of American military advisers above the 685 who were there when he came into office. By the end of 1963, American troops in Vietnam numbered nearly 17,000.

Any friend? The friends needed to carry out this policy have included Spain's military dictatorship, which we have supported under several Presidents by means of an agreement of questionable constitutionality on naval bases. This agreement, and the U.S. commitment to Spain, was originally concluded in the early 1950's without the advice and consent of the Senate required by the Constitution. It was "substantially upgraded" in September 1963 and again in 1968, both times without Senate approval.[2]

Our friends include the military dictatorship in Pakistan which received massive shipments of American arms ostensibly for defense against China. These arms were used in 1965 against India and in 1971 in the civil war against the Bengalis in East Pakistan.

Did "the survival and the success of liberty" require us to undertake in 1962 a unilateral commitment—again without the concurrence of the Senate—to the defense of

Thailand, another notoriously corrupt military government? Did it require the support of Ngo Dinh Diem's increasingly repressive government in South Vietnam?

Any foe? Was the American interest really served by our making an enemy of the hereditary ruler of Cambodia, Prince Sihanouk, a genuine nationalist leader and one of the few Asian leaders with a claim to the affections of his people? Central Intelligence Agency attempts to subvert the neutralist government of Cambodia finally led Sihanouk to expel our embassy and break off diplomatic relations with the United States in 1964.

Was our interest really served by a policy of unrelenting hostility toward Fidel Castro, of attempted subversion, economic boycott and even invasion?

The course of America's cold-war foreign policy, of which these measures were a part, was laid out in 1947, when the British government informed the Truman administration that it could no longer afford to assist the Greek government against Communist-supported rebels. Dean Acheson, then Under Secretary of State, convinced President Truman that Western influence in the eastern Mediterranean must be preserved and that the United States must take up the burden. Congress was convinced of the necessity for an emergency Greek-Turkish aid appropriation after Acheson evoked the specter of Communist corruption spreading out to infect Iran, the Far East, Africa and even Europe.

The memoirs of former Ambassador Charles Bohlen have revealed that Secretary of State George C. Marshall, then en route to Moscow for a conference, had reservations about the language of President Truman's message to Congress on the Greek-Turkish aid request, the message that became known as the Truman doctrine. Marshall suggested that the President was overstating the case in presenting the program primarily as an anti-Communist measure. But he was told that that was the only way the bill could be gotten through Congress.[3]

So the anti-Communist crusade was launched for reasons of political expediency. Over the years, that medium —anti-Communism—was to become the message as the American people were persuaded that the struggle with the Communists was a matter of national survival.

The concerns of the first generation of cold warriors are perhaps easier to understand and explain than are those of President Kennedy's generation. Those who were, in Dean Acheson's felicitous phrase, "present at the creation" of the postwar world viewed with great alarm the possibility that the United States might revert to isolationism, as it had after World War I. The leaders of the foreign policy establishment argued eloquently and persuasively that America must accept the responsibilities of world power and world leadership. They did their work well. The nation did, in a certain sense, accept those responsibilities.

Once it had become clear that the cold war would prevent the United Nations from assuming the peace-keeping role its founders had intended, the idea became prevalent in this country, perhaps without ever being consciously acknowledged, that the United States should assume the role of world policeman, that it was our mission to preserve world order. Dean Rusk was to remark many times during his tenure as Secretary of State under two Presidents that we did not seek or particularly relish the role of watchman at the gate, but that there was no one else.

In the most significant part of his historic message to Congress, President Truman declared,

> I believe it must be the policy of the United States to support free peoples who are resisting attempted subjugation by armed minorities or by outside pressures.[4]

Little attention was paid to whether the "free peoples" we aided were indeed free or whether their governments were repressive. It did not matter that the armed minority we were opposing might be a more authentic expression of national aspirations than the government that was repressing it—with our help.

But despite John Foster Dulles's policies of brinkmanship and massive retaliation during the Eisenhower years, American foreign policy before 1961 was essentially a reactive effort. It aimed at maintaining the status quo around the world by military containment of the USSR and China through American involvement in a string of military alliances: the North Atlantic Treaty Organization (NATO); the South East Asia Treaty Organization (SEATO); the Central Treaty Organization (CENTO);[5] the Australia, New Zealand, U.S. pact (ANZUS); and bilateral pacts with the Philippines, the Republic of China (Taiwan), Japan, and Korea.

In pursuance of this policy we fought against what we thought was a clear case of Communist aggression across agreed international boundaries in Korea. In more complex situations, our activities remained under cover. Thus the CIA sponsored or supported the overthrow of the governments of Iran in 1953 and of Guatemala in 1954 when it was feared that those countries might "go Communist." And in Indochina, we supported with money and arms the French colonial war against the Indo-Chinese nationalists because they were led by Communists.

Although President Truman's original statement had not made a distinction between Communist armed minorities and other armed minorities, such a distinction was made in practice. Latin American military coups were numerous, but were not the occasion for American concern.

The means for carrying out our policy in the 1950's were primarily military, in response to what was conceived to be a basically military challenge. As President Kennedy recognized early in his administration, the purely military challenge had faded. The lesson of the Bay of Pigs failure, Kennedy thought, was that the conventional military response was no longer adequate and that we must learn to best the Communists at their own game. The contest was now for the hearts and minds of men and women throughout the world.

The link between the policy Kennedy was to develop and the policies of Eisenhower and Truman in the past was the presumption that the challenge was overwhelming; it was still "them or us." "In the long history of the world," John Kennedy said in his Inaugural Address, "only a few generations have been granted the role of defending freedom in its hour of maximum danger. I do not shrink from this responsibility—I welcome it."

President Kennedy's policies were as dominated by cold-war thinking as were those of his predecessors. But he added new ways of doing things, new tools to do the job. America's anti-Communist mission was to be strengthened by the benefits of advanced technology and justified by our high moral purpose. We now had the capacity and we could therefore develop the means—as well as the will—to affect significantly the course of events around the world and, in effect, reshape the world in our image. Economic development, industrialization, a higher standard of living, consumer goods, Western-style democratic elections, good government, and his own land could be the lot of every man. "Freedom," not Communism, would bring it to them.

After 1961, as a result of decisions made early in the Kennedy administration, our reactive policy of military containment became an active counterrevolutionary or counterinsurgency policy that involved not only military efforts against irregular forces seeking to overthrow established governments, but also a full range of political, economic, psychological, and sociological activities. The military objective of counterinsurgency is to maintain or restore internal security so that the other elements of the counterinsurgency program can operate. These "other elements" attempt to win the "hearts and minds" of the people for the government we are supporting. Vietnam, of course, has been the great laboratory experiment in counterinsurgency techniques, although, as we shall see, the massive commitment of American troops in 1965 violated the tenets even of good counterinsurgency theory.

The adoption of a strategy of counterinsurgency by President Kennedy in early 1961 constituted an enormous expansion of the American role on the world scene. Indeed, the word "expansion" hardly conveys the change in approach, which was qualitative as well as quantitative.

At one point, on President Kennedy's grave in Arlington Cemetery lay a collection of Green Berets, a tribute to the late President's special interest in and sponsorship of the U. S. Army's elite Special Forces, the vanguard of America's counterinsurgency effort.

The assumptions that led President Kennedy to espouse counterinsurgency, or "special warfare," recall the great debate of 1950 over how we had "lost" China. There was, first, an assumption that we could substantially or decisively affect the course of history—a mistaken assumption in the case of China in the late 1940's and hardly a certainty when applied to revolutionary or insurgency situations in the early 1960's.

Second, and perhaps less evident at the outset, was the assumption that because we *could* control events we *ought* to control them. These assumptions about the world and about history are at the root of the Kennedy doctrine, the Kennedy view of America's role in the world: We *can* and, therefore, we *should* affect the course of events around the globe. Cuba, for example, is only ninety miles from our shores. But once it is accepted that it is a proper concern of the United States to affect the course of history in Cuba, it becomes difficult to set the limits. Where does one draw the line? In Berlin? Laos? The Congo? Vietnam? At ninety miles or nine thousand?

Transposed onto the world scene, as they were during the Kennedy administration, these assumptions became the basis for the globalist American policy for which President Kennedy devised the means. This policy, which rose to its high-water mark in Southeast Asia under his successors, was a full swing of the pendulum away from the isolationism of the years between the world wars.

John Kennedy was a President in the cold-war tradition of postwar American foreign policy. He differed from his predecessors more in style and method than in philosophy. In spite of the hopes raised by the New Frontier, there is no evidence that Kennedy or any of his principal advisers ever questioned the basic American ideological scheme for the cold war: that the world is divided into two hostile camps; that the "free world" is the area synonymous with U.S. strategic interests; that every "outpost of freedom," no matter how insignificant in itself, must be denied to the Communists or the entire "free world" would be threatened.

In contemporary terminology the outposts may be called "test cases for the theory of wars of national liberation." The adoption of the idea of counterinsurgency, not only in its paramilitary but in its economic, political, and social programs, was one of the most significant steps taken by the Kennedy administration in foreign policy. It dictated our military posture as well as our diplomatic stance.

After the interval of a decade, we may question whether President Kennedy's Inaugural Address describes an appropriate, rational, and prudent role for the United States in the world; whether it is an outline for an era of negotiation and accommodation and friendship; or whether it is a prescription for an untenable globalism, leading inevitably to increased areas of conflict, to a heightening of the arms race, and to American concern with and involvement, to one degree or another, in the affairs of almost every country in the world.

To the nations of Latin America, he pledged

> to convert our good words into good deeds, in a new alliance for progress, to assist free men and free gov-

ernments in casting off the chains of poverty. But this
peaceful revolution of hope cannot become the prey
of hostile powers. Let all our neighbors know that we
shall join with them to oppose aggression and subversion anywhere in the Americas.

Yet he tried to subvert and overthrow the one genuine
revolution—in Cuba—the Americas have seen in the last
generation.

To the Soviet Union, he said

we offer not a pledge but a request: that both sides
begin anew the quest for peace, before the dark
powers of destruction unleashed by science engulf
all humanity in planned or accidental self-destruction.
. . . *Let us never negotiate out of fear. But let us never
fear to negotiate.*

Yet he chose confrontation instead of negotiation over
Berlin in 1961 and over the question of Soviet missiles in
Cuba in 1962.

To Europe,

those old allies whose cultural and spiritual origins
we share, we pledge the loyalty of faithful friends.
United, there is little we cannot do in a host of co-
operative ventures. Divided, there is little we can do
—for we dare not meet a powerful challenge at odds
and split asunder.

Yet he sacrificed our relations with Britain and France to
pursue an anachronistic vision of an "Atlantic partnership" dominated by Washington and Bonn.

His message to the third world set the stage for his
policy of seeking to assure that the new nations would be
allowed to go their own way, unless their route would
lead them outside American influence—a prescription for
interventionism.

To those new States whom we welcome to the
ranks of the free, we pledge our words that one form

of colonial control shall not have passed away merely to be replaced by a far greater iron tyranny. We shall not always expect to find them supporting our view. But we shall always hope to find them strongly supporting their own freedom—and to remember that, in the past, those who foolishly sought power by riding the back of the tiger ended up inside.

He called on "both sides," the United States and the Soviet Union, to "formulate serious and precise proposals for the inspection and control of arms." Yet he acted on the excuse of a missile gap he knew did not exist and he inaugurated the military build-up that led to a renewed arms race with the Soviet Union.

When President Eisenhower left office the United States had a $40-billion military budget. Ten years later the military budget approached $90 billion, an increase only partly attributable to inflation. In the early 1960's, new weapons systems were chosen to carry out the strategic doctrines that were the muscle of the Kennedy foreign policy: flexible response, the 2½ war capability, the capacity for instant intervention, a nuclear strategy of assured penetration (including MIRV), and ballistic missile defense. Today's enormous military budget will not decrease substantially with the ending of the Vietnam war largely because of the bills now coming due for decisions made early in the Kennedy administration.

Any Inaugural Address may attempt to be all things to all men, and John F. Kennedy's obviously had a few words for the activists as well as for the reactivists, for those who supported an increase in arms and for those who wanted new steps towards arms control. The most important aspect of the address, perhaps, is what it does *not* say. John Kennedy devoted his Inaugural Address entirely to foreign affairs, a reflection of his conviction that "that's what's really important these days."[6]

Foreign affairs are, of course, more important than

ever before in our history. When man harnessed the power to obliterate all life on earth and developed the capacity to place that power in the hands of two or three individuals, the world was no longer the same. The checks and balances of the American Constitution became, for practical purposes, irrelevant. The decision whether or not to push the button releasing our nuclear missiles in case of a surprise attack cannot wait for Congress to declare war.

Yet in spite of this somber responsibility that has fallen on every American President since 1945, foreign policy, in a democratic society, is not and cannot be an end in itself. We have a foreign policy for purposes outside itself. It is the means by which we protect and secure our democratic institutions and values. These values are, to a large extent, the processes, the *way* we do things; the way justice is administered; the way the government deals with the individual citizen. In overemphasizing foreign concerns at the expense of domestic needs—a trend that did not begin with but was greatly accelerated under President Kennedy—we have moved a long way toward putting our values at the service of our foreign policy, instead of the other way around. President Kennedy does not appear to have appreciated this distinction between ends and means. Indeed, much of the nation began to appreciate it only in 1968, when the debate over national priorities became the major issue in American politics.

We find in John F. Kennedy's Inaugural Address no mention of America's pressing domestic problems, no expression of concern for the nation's poor, existing, or subsisting, amid her affluence; no sense of the great moral force of the movement for black freedom, the civil rights struggle that was to reach a peak in the summer of 1963 in the March on Washington led by Dr. Martin Luther King, Jr.; no hint of understanding of the aspirations of all Americans for some measure of individual dignity and worth amid the increasingly depersonalizing pressures of government and technology on their lives.

President Kennedy was certainly not unaware of these problems and movements. But one is moved inexorably to the conclusion that he did not really understand movements or great moral issues. He did not think them very important until they pressed on him too closely, or when a smoldering fire like the situation at the University of Mississippi flared up.

In some areas of foreign policy John F. Kennedy was superb. During the early 1960's, much of the continent of Africa achieved independence from colonial rule. President Kennedy's appreciation of the importance of ceremony, his sense of his office, the style and sophisticated courtesy with which he received important visitors lent an atmosphere of dignity and warmth to our relations with the new African nations. His sympathetic attention to the problems of the new nations and their leaders, his sensitive choice—in most cases—of ambassadors to African capitals, his ability to make small nations feel that the United States valued their friendship and their contributions to the international community resulted in a substantial storehouse of good will in Africa toward the United States.

In Latin America, although the Alliance for Progress, did not, in the long run, come near to achieving the goals set for it, President Kennedy's articulation of the needs and aspirations of the masses of Latin America gave to those people, for almost the first time, a sense of hope in the future.

These were perhaps achievements of style rather than of substance. Yet they suggest the real paradox of Kennedy's Presidency. His actual, tangible impact on history was not significant enough to explain his enormous psychological impact, the indefinable way in which John F. Kennedy touched people throughout the world. In the humblest villages of India one still sees three photographs side by side in a place of honor: Gandhi, Nehru, and Kennedy. In the most depressed areas of the rural southern United States one sees similar displays of photographs: Martin Luther King, Jr., Senator Robert F. Kennedy, and President Kennedy.

Here was a man with a fantastic potential for leadership, both in his own country and throughout the world, a man who somehow captured the imagination of millions, a man who could have used that ability to move the nation, and possibly much of the world, in new directions. Through the force of his own personality and his own charisma, he might have surmounted the strictures of the cold war, might have made us see that power and weaponry are no longer synonymous, that the United States is not best served by those who would maintain a Pax Americana, that negotiation and accommodation are the only means to halt the arms race and reduce the danger of nuclear war, that men's and nations' interests must be accommodated so that they can live in peace.

John F. Kennedy failed to understand and use his own potential for greatness. Because he had the ability to touch people, he could have inspired and led them to accept the need for fundamental change both at home and abroad. Yet he did not. George Kennan, President Kennedy's ambassador to Yugoslavia and expert on Soviet affairs, feels that if Kennedy

> failed anywhere in his approach to foreign policy, it was in the fact that he did not do enough to teach the American public the basic facts about the world.

Kennan considers President Kennedy's American University speech in June of 1963, in which he began to move toward a new direction in relations with the Soviet Union, "important and constructive." But, says Kennan, "one speech is not enough. I think he should have done more."[7]

President Kennedy could not lead the nation away from its traditional fixation with competition, combat, and victory because his own background and training were of a piece with that tradition, because he was taught from an early age to believe that only winning matters—not how you play the game. His sister Eunice Shriver once said that their father, Joseph P. Kennedy, "always kept telling us that coming in second was just no good. The important thing was to win. . . ."[8]

President Kennedy's failure to use his great potential was also the result of his view of leadership. He sought to manipulate the people rather than to guide them and give them direction. He did not sense the difference between the two kinds of leadership.

Kennedy seems to have had no overall political philosophy, no general conceptual outlook, no long-term view of American self-interest. He understood that individuals can move history; his heroes were its activists, Marlborough and Churchill. He appreciated as well the extent to which man is the victim of history, caught up by forces beyond his control. But he really did not understand the nature of the historical process, that it ebbs and flows, that it may sometimes be directed but that only tragedy results from the illusion that it can be controlled. His greatest failure resulted from that illusion—that the outcome could be controlled, through the use of the Green Berets and CIA agents, through specially tailored foreign-aid programs, through nation-building, through techniques of counterinsurgency, through alarmist rhetoric about the need for fall-out shelters.

President Kennedy had little patience with idealists and visionaries, those whom he considered impractical or sentimental. Arthur Schlesinger wrote that Kennedy found it difficult to understand why historians rated Woodrow Wilson a greater President than Polk or Truman, and observed that "his measure of presidential success was concrete achievement; thus people who educated the nation without necessarily accomplishing their particular purposes rated, in his judgment, below those . . . who accomplished their purposes without necessarily bringing the nation along with them."[9]

As observers have indicated, President Kennedy was the essence of the practical man, the consummate pragmatic politician. State Department official U. Alexis Johnson has noted that Kennedy was reluctant to deal with long-range issues: "he liked to deal in hard realities . . . the immediate, specific issue that required decision at the time . . . without trying to look too far ahead."[10]

James Reston of *The New York Times* found him incapable of responding to a question about what he hoped to achieve during his Presidency, or to a question whether he "did not feel the need of some goal to help guide his day-to-day decisions and priorities . . . It was only when I turned the question to immediate, tangible problems that he seized the point and rolled off a torrent of statistics."[11]

Mastery of the techniques of achieving power does not necessarily equip a man to use power wisely. President Kennedy approached the great issues of his Presidency as problems to be solved, or at least managed. He tried to manage foreign policy as he did his rise to the Presidency, by careful planning, by mastery of all the facts, by leaving as little as possible to chance. While a case can be made for this approach, it leaves no room for intangibles, for factors that cannot be quantified. In concentrating too heavily upon problem-solving, he fell victim to the fallacy that so often has plagued American pragmatists: they have frequently failed to recognize that great decisions are made not on the basis of facts but on the basis of principles, that the facts are important but may be deceiving. In the first of his foreign policy crises, neither facts nor principles served President Kennedy well.

Two | The Bay of Pigs

By the time John F. Kennedy moved into the White House, preparations for what was to prove his greatest mistake were well under way. Within a few weeks of Fidel Castro's entry into Havana at the beginning of 1959, the Eisenhower administration had begun considering measures that might be taken should his triumph not prove to be a blessing. It was not until March 1960, however, that President Eisenhower decided to approve the Central Intelligence Agency's plan to recruit and train a Cuban exile force for use against Castro. That decision marked the end of a long period of increasing U.S. disenchantment with the Cuban revolution.

Though many had welcomed Castro's triumph, illusions quickly disintegrated. The CIA had suggested as early as the end of 1958 that a Castro government in Cuba might not be in the best interest of the United

States.[1] By March 1959, it was reporting that Communists were operating openly in Cuba, infiltrating labor unions and the armed forces, but the CIA did not feel that Castro had as yet committed Cuba to communism.

Apparently, Vice President Richard Nixon was forming a different opinion. During Castro's visit to Washington in April 1959, the Vice President met with him for three hours—an encounter that left Nixon convinced that Castro was "either incredibly naive about Communism or under Communist discipline."[2]

In Cuba, pledges for elections were broken, the press was muffled, hundreds of members of the old regime were hauled before firing squads, hundreds of others were imprisoned awaiting trial, their property and businesses confiscated. During the first year of Castro's rule the old order was destroyed.

Mass trials and executions continued, and the victims were not only the associates and followers of Batista. Suspicion began to fall on those who questioned Castro's methods and the direction in which he appeared to be leading the nation. Many Cubans who had hailed Castro's victory, who had worked and fought with him, began to fear that the revolution they had helped to bring about would give way to a new dictatorship.

President Eisenhower himself by now suspected that Fidel was a Communist and he was "deeply disgusted at his murderous persecution of his former opponents."[3]

Thus, while at first it had been feared only that Castro might "go neutralist"—into that unaligned condition decried by John Foster Dulles as immoral—now the ultimate nightmare of the cold war threatened: the Communists were at the gates, or in any event, they were only ninety miles from American shores.

Various suggestions were advanced within the Eisenhower administration for dealing with Castro. Cuba might be quarantined to starve him out. Less onerous economic sanctions, such as reduction of the amount of sugar the United States would buy from Cuba at an inflated price, were considered, as were military measures.

By early 1960 the administration was convinced that "something would have to be done," although at that time it was apparently not committed to unilateral action. But efforts to interest other nations in the hemisphere in joining us in opposing Castro foundered; they had no particular fear at that time of a threat from Cuba.

In February, Soviet Deputy Premier Anastas Mikoyan visited Cuba, where he and Castro signed a commercial and political agreement under which the Soviet Union would purchase five million tons of sugar over a five-year period and Cuba would receive a $100-million credit at 2½ percent interest over a twelve-year period. Secret agreements for military assistance may also have been made at this time.

Against this background, on March 17, 1960, Eisenhower secretly ordered the CIA to begin organizing and training Cuban exiles for guerrilla warfare against Castro. The training was conducted outside the United States—mainly in Guatemala—to facilitate denial of U.S. involvement. Plans for use of the exiles were not specific at that time because the various political factions among the Cuban refugees had not been able to agree on a leader for a government-in-exile.

From the point of view of the administration, the situation continued to deteriorate. During the summer of 1960, an Army attaché at the U.S. Embassy in Havana came into possession of photographs of Cuban soldiers with Czech semiautomatic rifles in their hands.[4]

By September, plans were under way to shut down the U.S. government-owned nickel-processing plant in Cuba, to abolish preferential tariffs for Cuban imports to the United States, and to speed up the evacuation of U.S. citizens. The Eisenhower administration also cut the 1960 sugar quota by 700,000 tons. Later the quota for the first three months of 1961 was set at zero.

The U.S. government stated officially that it would never permit the seizure of our naval base at Guantánamo, on the southeastern tip of the island of Cuba, and U.S. marines were sent to reinforce the base.

Fear now arose that "Castroite groups" were fomenting trouble in Venezuela and El Salvador. In November 1960, when a revolt broke out in Guatemala, President Eisenhower "decided that if we received a request from Guatemala for assistance, we would move in without delay."[5] With the Cuban exiles training under the CIA in Guatemala, there was fear that although the training was supposed to be a secret, Castro would send his forces against the Guatemalan government. On a request for assistance from Nicaragua, U.S. naval vessels were directed to patrol the coasts to head off any Cuban invasion attempt.

Finally, on January 2, 1961, Castro ordered the U. S. Embassy in Havana to reduce its staff to eleven within forty-eight hours. (The staff totaled eighty-seven, half of whom were Cubans.) This, says former President Eisenhower in his memoirs, was the "last straw," and the United States broke off diplomatic relations with the Castro regime.

Like many other Americans, John F. Kennedy welcomed the overthrow of Batista and the accession of Castro. Writing in *The Strategy of Peace* in early 1960, he called Castro "part of the legacy of Bolivar" and suggested that the bearded revolutionary might have taken a less anti-American course had the United States not remained so long a supporter of Batista. But as he moved into his Presidential campaign, Kennedy began accusing Fidel of betraying the ideals of the Cuban revolution.

During the campaign, Kennedy repeatedly referred to the presence of Communism "ninety miles off our shores; eight minutes by jet." He told a veterans' convention in Miami Beach on August 26, 1960, "For the first time in the history of the United States an enemy stands poised at the throat of the United States."[6] It is difficult to discern whether his highly anti-Castro rhetoric reflected strong personal conviction or whether it was the inevitable political reaction of the challenger to the administration in power.

The strongest statement of his position came on October 6, 1960, at a Democratic dinner in Cincinnati. Cuba, Kennedy said,

> was the most glaring failure of American foreign policy today . . . a disaster that threatens the security of the whole Western Hemisphere . . . a Communist menace that has been permitted to arise under our very noses, only 90 miles from our shores. . . . The once friendly island that our own shortsighted policies helped make communism's first Caribbean base. . . .

He reviewed Castro's struggle against the Batista regime and the initial promise of the revolution. But, he continued, "those promises have all been broken" and Cuba "is in the iron grip of a Communist-oriented police state. Castro and his gang have betrayed the ideals of the Cuban revolution and the hopes of the Cuban people." He then raised the specter of the possible spread of Castroism beyond the shores of Cuba—most important, as a spearhead for Moscow and Peking,

> [Castro's] ambitions extend far beyond his own shores. He has transformed the island of Cuba into a hostile and militant Communist satellite—a base from which to carry Communist infiltration and subversion throughout the Americas. With guidance, support, and arms from Moscow and Peiping, he has . . . rattled red rockets at the United States, which can hardly close its eyes to a potential enemy missile or submarine base only 90 miles from our shores.
>
> He has transformed the island into a supply depot for Communist arms and operations throughout South

America—recruiting small bands of Communist-directed revolutionaries to serve as the nucleus of future Latin revolutions. . . .

The American people, he continued, wanted to know the truth about how this "critical situation" had been permitted to occur. The Eisenhower administration must "accept full responsibility for this disaster," which it had brought about through its lack of leadership, imagination and compassion. It had ignored warnings that "international communism" was behind Castro.

Although heavy-handed in fixing the blame, Kennedy was less specific in suggesting what the Eisenhower administration might have done to avoid the "disaster." It had erred, he charged, in four respects: first, it had "refused to help Cuba meet its desperate need for economic progress"; second, "in a manner certain to antagonize the Cuban people" the United States had used its influence to advance the interests of private American firms in Cuba; third, "and perhaps most disastrous of our failures," we gave "stature and support" to the Batista dictatorship; fourth, "we did nothing to persuade the people of Cuba and Latin America that we wanted to be on the side of freedom."

Yet in spite of all this, he said he had "no basic disagreement with the President's policies of recent months—for the time to save Cuba was some time ago."

Kennedy concluded on an ominous note. "Hopefully events may once again bring us an opportunity to bring our influence strongly to bear on behalf of the cause of freedom in Cuba." But his only suggestion for the present was that we "constantly express our friendship for the Cuban people—our sympathy with their economic problems—our determination that they will again be free."

Finally, he felt that

if we are to halt the advance of Latin communism, we must create a Latin America where freedom can flourish—where long enduring people know, at last, that they are moving toward a better life for themselves and their children—where steady economic advance is a framework for stable, democratic government—and where tyranny, isolated and despised, eventually withers on the vine.

Although short on program—expressions of sympathy and friendship hardly seem adequate if the disaster and the menace are as great as depicted—there is much in the Kennedy speech that foreshadows the future, not only in relation to Cuba and Latin America but to the world.

It was a tough speech, as tough as any of his Presidential campaign. Even allowing for the usual excesses of campaign oratory, it is difficult not to conclude that the dimensions of the "disaster" were grossly exaggerated. Then, the presumption that we could have substantially or decisively affected the course of events in Cuba is dubious, at best. Clearly, Kennedy was not suggesting that we should have propped up Batista to prevent Castro's coming to power. The only alternative, which was clearly impractical, would have been the possibility of converting Castro into an American puppet while he was still in the mountains.

Third, and less evident, is the assumption that not only could we have controlled events but that we *ought* to have controlled them. Through some kind of political-economic intervention, Kennedy seems to be suggesting, we ought to have created a climate in which Castro could never have happened. And for the future, we should *"create* a Latin America where freedom can flourish. . . ."[7]

It is ironic, in the light of the view history has taken of the candidates of 1960, of Nixon as the "hard-liner" and of Kennedy as more conciliatory, that in fact it was Kennedy who took the tough line on Cuba. One writer, Arthur Schlesinger, has suggested that to some extent this was the product of overzealous advisers who were concerned that the candidate might appear "soft." On October 20, 1960, the Kennedy campaign headquarters released a statement in Kennedy's name that had not, according to Schlesinger, been seen in advance by the candidate himself.[8] Generally provocative in tone, it suggested that the next administration would have to do better "if it intends to wage a serious offensive against communism on our very doorstep." It concluded with a call "to strengthen the non-Batista democratic anti-Castro forces in exile, and in Cuba itself, who offer eventual hope of overthrowing Castro. Thus far these fighters for freedom have had virtually no support from our Government." Schlesinger reports that Kennedy later told him that he would have changed the phrase "fighters for freedom" to "forces for freedom" but that otherwise he approved of the statement.

Press reaction to this saber-rattling was generally harsh and Kennedy dropped the matter for the remainder of the campaign. Dean Acheson, the former Secretary of State, had advised him to stop talking about Cuba. Acheson told Kennedy he thought that trying to solve important foreign or domestic policy problems in campaign rhetoric was dangerous and warned him against getting "hooked into positions which would be difficult afterwards."[9]

The subject arose again, however, in the final television debate between the two Presidential candidates. Nixon knew that Kennedy had received an intelligence briefing and therefore presumed that his opponent knew of the plans for the use of the exile guerrilla force. In an attempt to neutralize the effect of Kennedy's militant statements on the Cuba issue, Nixon accused him of irresponsibly advocating support for Cuban exile groups and thus implicitly advocating the overthrow of another government. Of course, this was the secret policy of the Eisenhower administration, as Nixon was well aware, but Kennedy could hardly admit that the Eisenhower administration was doing what he had been advocating all along. Whether Kennedy knew the whole scheme or not, he later maintained that he learned of the plans for the use of the exile brigade only *after* he had won the election.

The original CIA plan approved by President Eisenhower had included a military program under which the CIA would train a Cuban exile force for guerrilla action against the Castro regime along with a political program under which the disparate groups of Cuban exiles would be brought together in a broad political coalition which would, however, exclude both pro-Batista and pro-Communist elements. The idea was to use the exiles as small guerrilla bands which would operate under the control of the Cuban refugees' coalition and would be assisted by CIA supplies, communications equipment, and provisions for transportation. The CIA was planning, in effect, to use against Castro the same general tactics he had used against Batista.

Shortly after the plan was approved, CIA agents, representing themselves as employees of a group of wealthy capitalists who were ardent anti-Communists and who had influence with the U.S. Government, began to recruit among the Cuban exiles in the Miami area. They insisted to the Cubans that they did not represent the government of the United States. There is some question as to whether the Cubans accepted that story from the beginning. Some apparently felt all along that the government of the United States was behind the effort and this strengthened their conviction that the United States would not fail to back them fully. Others apparently believed the CIA operatives in their cover story; they had no place else to turn for help in their desire to liberate Cuba from Castro. Some of these Cubans later considered their blind trust in the Americans to have been misplaced. Yet everything about the Americans who contacted the Cuban exiles suggested a large organization and a great deal of money. (President Eisenhower had approved a $13-million budget for the operation.[10]) The exiles were impressed by the manner in which their new American friends had spirited Manuel Artime, who later became one of the leaders of the Brigade, out of Cuba and through U.S. immigration. Artime himself was convinced that the American government was involved in the training. The Americans offered each man who left for the training $175 per month plus $50 for his wife and $25 for each other dependent.[11]

By June, a camp was established and training begun on the U.S. island of Useppa, off the west coast of Florida. There the first group of exiles was tested and screened to select those who would learn to train members of the army of liberation. During the testing each man was given a serial number; the numbers began with 2500, to confuse the enemy.

On June 22, 1960, twenty-eight men were chosen as the initial cadre and were told that they would leave immediately for the next base. They returned to the mainland and boarded a plane whose windows were taped so that they could not see their route. After a very slow flight of six or seven hours, they arrived at night deep in a tropical jungle. They soon learned that they were at Fort Gulick in the Panama Canal Zone, at the U. S. Army jungle-warfare training area.

For seven weeks the Cubans received intensive and rugged training in guerrilla warfare and on August 22 were flown to their third training camp, part of a large coffee plantation in the 5000-foot Sierra Madre mountains of Guatemala. The plantation belonged to Roberto Alejo, brother of the Guatemalan ambassador to the United States, and its use as a secret training base for anti-Castro Cubans was the result of an understanding or agreement between the United States and the government of Guatemala; the terms of the agreement have never been made public.

Near the town of Retalhuleu, on the plains below the

plantation, an airstrip was to be constructed. Two thousand feet above the plantation the Cubans, under American supervision, constructed their camp, which became known as Base Trax. For the next six months, under difficult conditions, they prepared for their mission.

In Washington, planning for the operation was in the hands of the "special group," composed of representatives of the State Department, the Defense Department, the CIA, and the White House. Shortly before the 1960 election, the "special group" was considering abandoning the guerrilla campaign in favor of a direct assault—an invasion of Cuba. The guerrilla operation appeared increasingly unattractive for several reasons: it was felt that supplying the guerrillas by airdrop would be too difficult; Castro's military strength was growing; and his control over the island had tightened.

On November 4, 1960, four days before the American Presidential election, the CIA advisers at Base Trax in Guatemala received word from their superiors in Washington that the guerrilla operation had been scrapped in favor of invasion. An infantry assault landing of a few hundred men was planned.

It appears from his memoirs that President Eisenhower was not personally involved in the decision to change tactics. He later claimed that although he had approved the training for guerrilla operations, no invasion was planned while he was in office. Since, according to many accounts, President Eisenhower did not usually become involved in the working out of policy decisions, it seems likely that he did not know of the change in tactics. The decision to change may well have been made at a lower level, without specifically consulting or even advising President Eisenhower. His subordinates may have felt that, in any event, the new President would have to make the final decision on whether or not to go ahead.

Conditions and training at Base Trax improved markedly after the decision to change tactics. The CIA's motley group of European and Asian guerrilla-warfare instructors gave way to new American instructors, of professional military bearing, who arrived to train an assault force. The core of the assault force was to be drawn from the 430 men who were in camp at that time; they were later supplemented by additional recruits, many of whom received little or no training. The assault force decided to call itself Brigade 2506, adopting the serial number of one of their comrades who had been killed in a training accident.

Within the camp, as within the larger group of Cuban exiles in the United States, there were three main factions: the former Castro rebels; the former supporters of Batista; and the students, who were opposed to both of the other factions. Within these factions political sentiments ranged from extreme left to extreme right, with the CIA tending to favor former Batista officers who had had some previous military training. There was much political infighting among the Cubans at Base Trax.

Concurrently, the Cuban political leaders in the United States were being urged by the CIA to put aside their differences and unite in a political front that could provide the basis for an anti-Castro government-in-exile. President Eisenhower had suggested in December the formation of a "front" which could be recognized as a government-in-exile and the legal government of Cuba. He had hoped to be able to recognize a Cuban government-in-exile before leaving office.[12]

Thus matters stood when, on November 18, 1960, President-elect Kennedy was briefed on the plans and learned—possibly for the first time—of the plan for the invasion.

That same day, the State Department made public the details of the military assistance supplied to Cuba by the Soviet Union and other Communist countries. It noted that "Since Fidel Castro came to power, Cuba has created and armed a military force 10 times the size of that of ex-

President Fulgencio Batista and far larger than any army in Latin America." In addition to the weapons of Castro's own fighters from the Sierra Maestra, the Castro government had accepted delivery from various sources of arms ordered by Batista. Castro had also sent arms-buying missions to Europe. He had announced that he now had a sufficient supply of small arms to equip his 200,000-man militia as well as large amounts of heavy equipment. Recent arms shipments to Cuba, the State Department continued, came exclusively from Iron Curtain countries, and the Cubans had announced their intention to rely on that source for further build-up to their war matériel. "The bloc nations apparently desire to contribute to Caribbean tensions by burdening the Cuban economy with excessive arms purchases and by supporting the aggressive policies of the Cuban Prime Minister."[13]

The State Department list of the arms and ammunition estimated to have been acquired by Castro in the twenty-two months of his rule included: 93,000 automatic rifles, 11,000 submachine guns, 200 machine guns (including those of .50 caliber), 254 mortars, 55 tanks, 60 armored personnel carriers, 100 rocket launchers, 80 anti-aircraft guns, 10 Soviet helicopters, 8 MIG aircraft (not yet delivered), and over 58-million rounds of ammunition.[14]

Ironically, the State Department's impressive list, because it was limited to Cuba's arms acquisitions from Communist countries, did not mention what were probably the most crucial weapons at the Bay of Pigs battle: two T-33 jet trainers equipped with rocket launchers—these had been supplied to Batista by the United States and later confiscated by Castro.

At a briefing by the outgoing administration on the day before the inauguration, President Eisenhower told his successor that U.S. policy had been to aid the anti-Castro forces "to the utmost" and that they were training such forces in Guatemala; he recommended that the effort be accelerated.[15]

On January 21, 1961, John F. Kennedy assumed responsibility for the Castro problem and the force of Cuban exiles being prepared to deal with it. His Inaugural Address did not mention Cuba, and oblique warnings were couched in terms of joint action with other American states.

> Let all our neighbors know that we shall join with them to oppose aggression or subversion anywhere in the Americas. And let every other power know that this Hemisphere intends to remain the master of its own house.

In his first press conference, four days later, in response to a question of whether he was considering restoring diplomatic relations with Cuba, President Kennedy set forth what he felt were the dangers Castro presented. Although the United States was interested in those movements in Latin America that offered a better life for the people, he said, it was concerned about "external forces . . . directed . . . towards imposing an ideology which is alien to this hemisphere." He was particularly concerned when such "intervention" took the form of "military support which threatens the security and the peace of the Western Hemisphere," and he also warned that the "peaceful revolution" we were fostering could be "seized by aliens for their purposes. . . ."

In his first State of the Union Message, on January 30, Kennedy sounded the same theme.

> In Latin America, Communist agents seeking to exploit that region's peaceful revolution of hope have established a base on Cuba, only 90 miles from our shores. Our objection with Cuba is not over the people's drive for a better life. Our objection is to their domination by foreign and domestic tyrannies. Cuban social and economic reform should be encouraged. Questions of economic and trade policy can

always be negotiated. But Communist domination in this Hemisphere can never be negotiated.

In this emphasis, he was reflecting the traditional cold-war mythology that denies the possibility of any indigenous Communist revolution; all Communists are automatically "alien" to the soil in which they are found; all are, by definition, Soviet puppets. Dean Rusk, Kennedy's newly appointed Secretary of State, had voiced the same attitude as early as 1951 in a speech forgotten in 1961 but frequently quoted in recent years. In that speech Rusk described the Chinese Communist government as "a colonial Russian government—a Slavic Manchukuo," which was "not Chinese" but rather "driven by foreign masters. . . ."[16] In the traditional cold-war view, Castro was no more Cuban than Mao Tse-tung was Chinese, for in espousing Communism the enemy sheds his national origin and becomes a tool of the "international Communist conspiracy."

Kennedy had been briefed on the full details of the CIA plan for the invasion of Cuba on November 28, 1960, by Allen W. Dulles, director of the Central Intelligence Agency and brother of the late Secretary of State. Months later President Kennedy told Theodore Sorensen that when he had first heard the details of the plan he had been "astonished at its magnitude and daring." He told Sorensen that "he had grave doubts from that moment on."[17] Nevertheless, in late January 1961, Kennedy instructed Dulles to proceed with the plans, reserving the right of final decision on putting the plan into operation. At that time he considered it a contingency plan. But, as Arthur Schlesinger noted, the Bay of Pigs operation had taken on a life of its own and Kennedy had not yet realized how contingency planning "could generate its own momentum and create its own reality."[18]

Meanwhile political dissension at Base Trax in Guatemala remained a serious problem. It finally led to a mutiny which the CIA managed to put down when, in a particularly sordid episode, it carted off twelve of the alleged ringleaders to a remote and inaccessible—except by helicopter—spot in northern Guatemala where they were held prisoner under deplorable conditions until after the invasion.

Members of the new Kennedy Cabinet were briefed on the operation over the next few months by Allen Dulles and by Richard Bissell, the CIA official directly in charge of the plan. Bissell was the official who had been responsible for the CIA's most successful, though ill-fated, intelligence-gathering operation, the U-2 flights over the Soviet Union.

Much of what has been written about President Kennedy's decision to go ahead with the Bay of Pigs adventure has emphasized the wide disparity between the actual situation and the plan's prospects as they were presented to the President. These accounts, most of them written by former officials of the Kennedy administration, understandably blame the CIA for deceiving the President. As a result, Kennedy, who assumed personal responsibility for the failure, is pictured as the victim of a heedless bureaucracy over which he had not yet had time to establish his authority—deceived by the CIA, badly advised by the Joint Chiefs, let down by his associates.

The CIA does bear particularly heavy responsibility, but all involved were guilty of poor judgment. And, with one or two exceptions among major advisers, all the advice the President received was bad.

It is difficult to avoid the conclusion that, on the one hand, the CIA officials deceived Kennedy about the prospects for the success of the operation and, in their enthusiasm, glossed over some significant details; and on the other hand, they also misled the Brigade members specifically with respect to the details of the invasion itself, and generally with respect to the restraints President Kennedy had placed on the U.S. role, in that he was determined not to commit U.S. forces.

The plan and the prospects for success as presented

to the President must be considered against the background of what a former CIA official has described as "almost a frantic desire in Washington to get rid of Castro."[19] Kennedy himself discussed with George Smathers, his close friend from the Senate, the possibility of having Castro assassinated. The former senator from Florida has stated that he frequently brought up the subject of Cuba with the President, at least until early 1962. They discussed what the reaction to an assassination might be:

> would the people be gratified. . . . He was just throwing out a great barrage of questions. He was certain it could be accomplished. I remember that. It would be no problem. But the question was whether or not it would accomplish that which he wanted it to. Whether or not the reaction throughout South America would be good or bad.

They also discussed the possibility of a false attack on Guantánamo which would give an excuse for U.S. intervention in Cuba.[20]

The intervening years have brought to light an incredible miasma of misunderstanding and sloppiness in coordinating the CIA plan for the invasion. In an operation as large and as complex as what the CIA was undertaking, there is an enormous amount of detail, and many aspects that cannot be discussed here. But the gap that developed between illusion in the White House and reality on the beaches of the Bay of Pigs may be illustrated by three important areas of misunderstanding.

The first was the question of whether mass uprisings on the island were expected, and if they were, whether their occurrence was essential to the success of the operation. Roger Hilsman, then director of intelligence and research for the State Department, reports that he learned of the existence of the assault force through newspaper accounts, and inadvertently found out the plans for its use. He says that he went to Rusk and told the Secretary what he had learned. Hilsman reminded Rusk that an invasion on a hostile shore was one of the most difficult of military operations, and that if it was expected that a brigade of a thousand Cubans could defeat Castro's militia of two hundred thousand, the CIA must be assuming that the Cuban population would rise to support the invaders. Hilsman asked for permission to put his own intelligence people to work on the matter but Rusk replied, "I'm sorry . . . but I can't let you. This is being too tightly held."[21]

Some of the exiles, on the other hand, apparently believed that, as Castro's band of less than 1500 had prevailed over Batista's 40,000-man army, their small group would be able to defeat Castro's 200,000 men. Of course, this optimism overlooked the fact that Castro had not defeated the Batista army in battle. Actually, Batista's position had been rapidly deteriorating, and this, combined with the difficulties of direct confrontation with Castro's guerrillas, led to his fall.

Allen Dulles has claimed that the press—and presumably everyone else—mistakenly assumed that the CIA was counting on an uprising: "I know of no estimate that a spontaneous uprising of the unarmed population of Cuba would be touched off by the landing."[22] Arthur Schlesinger maintains that this view "certainly did not come across clearly in the White House meetings." The White House Staff, the Joint Chiefs, and, it was thought, the CIA considered uprisings essential to success. Dulles's later statement reflects the CIA belief that the invasion could win by attrition, and it is not strictly inaccurate if one puts sufficient emphasis on such words as "spontaneous" and "unarmed." As Schlesinger has pointed out:

> Obviously no one expected the invasion to galvanize the unarmed and unorganized into rising against Castro at the moment of disembarkation. But the invasion plan, as understood by the President and the Joint Chiefs, did assume that the successful *occupation*

of an enlarged beachhead would rather soon incite *organized* uprisings by armed members of the Cuban resistance.[23]

Actually, the CIA was planning what they called an Anzio style of operation: a continuous build-up and enlargement of the perimeter around the initial landing site. The beachhead would provide a base for the establishment of the government of Free Cuba, whose leaders would be flown in from the United States. They felt that once the Free Cuba government was established, there would be many defections from Castro's forces. The Free Cuba government could then request assistance from the United States and could urge all Cubans to rally to its support.[24]

The Joint Chiefs of Staff, in their initial approval of the first proposed landing site, told the President that success would depend on either a substantial uprising on the island or substantial support from the outside. Later, after Kennedy had reiterated his absolute ban against participation by U.S. forces, the Joint Chiefs considered Cuban resistance indispensable. How else could fifteen hundred men conceivably overcome two hundred thousand? Schlesinger also reports that Dulles and Bissell, in their briefings, reinforced the White House impression that there would be mass uprisings by claiming that over twenty-five hundred persons belonged to resistance organizations in Cuba, that twenty thousand more were sympathizers, and that, once established on its beachhead, the Brigade would be supported by at least 25 percent of the Cuban population.[25]

Only afterward did it become known that the intelligence evaluation side of the CIA was never informed of any aspect of the operation, and, as noted, the State Department's intelligence apparatus was also kept in the dark. Estimates about the possible success of the operation and the effect the landing might provoke in Cuba were being made, therefore, not by disinterested evaluators in the traditional intelligence machinery, but by those same men who were planning the operation and who were most committed, personally and professionally, to it. As Hilsman has said, "CIA's excessive security restrictions" required Rusk to make a judgment without the benefit of advice from his own intelligence staff and the President was also denied "the judgment of CIA's own estimators on the research side of the organization."[26]

The importance of this misunderstanding is illustrated by a remark the President made on March 28, a few days before his final decision to go ahead, that the critical point in his judgment was the idea that the landings would touch off a mass insurrection.[27]

A second area of misunderstanding was the alternative available to the Brigade should it be overwhelmed and fail to secure the beachhead. The CIA planners proposed originally that the landing take place at the town of Trinidad, at the foot of the Escambray Mountains on Cuba's south-central coast. The State Department objected, fearing that taking a town of 20,000 would create too high a "noise level" in world and United Nations reaction. The alternative site at the Bay of Pigs was more isolated, surrounded by practically impassable swamps and marshes, and it offered an airstrip suitable for the exiles' B-26 bombers that were to control the air over the beaches while the Brigade dug in. Dulles and Bissell assured the President that if the beachhead failed to hold, the men could "melt away" into the mountains. "I don't think we fully realized," says Schlesinger, "that the Escambray Mountains lay *eighty miles* from the Bay of Pigs, across a hopeless tangle of swamps and jungles."[28]

This is a serious admission. The President may not have been aware of the nature of the intervening terrain, but it is difficult to imagine that he could have failed to realize the importance of the fact that the distance was eighty miles. Even if he was under the impression that the escape route was as solid and clear as the New Jersey Turnpike, what did he expect Castro's forces to be doing while the remnants of the Brigade, depleted and exhausted from their ordeal on the beaches, were making their way over those eighty miles? Not specialized or expert knowledge, but common sense should have prompted him to ask about this enormous loophole in the plan.

There is considerable evidence that, far from telling the Brigade that in case of difficulties they were expected to melt away into those mountains eighty miles distant, the CIA told them that they were to fall back on the beaches, where American forces would come to their aid, openly if necessary, and prevent their defeat. One of the Brigade leaders told author Haynes Johnson that the Brigade was not told that if they failed they were to go to the mountains as a guerrilla force; rather, the Americans told them, "If you fail, *we* will go in."[29]

Contrary to what President Kennedy had been told or allowed to believe, most Brigade members were not prepared for guerrilla warfare and indeed had been given no guerrilla training after the decision, the previous November, to abandon the guerrilla operation in favor of a direct assault. Theodore Sorensen has noted that melting away into the mountains was

> . . . never a realistic alternative. It was never planned by the CIA officers in charge of the operation, and they neither told the President they thought this option was out nor told the exiles that this was the President's plan.[30]

In spite of the "grave doubts" he had felt, Sorensen reports that Kennedy told him afterward:

> "I really thought they had a good chance" . . . explaining that if the exiles, without overt U.S. help, could establish themselves, proclaim a new government and rally the people to their side and eventually oust Castro, Latin America would feel safer and if they

were forced to flee to the mountains and carry on guerrilla warfare, that would be a net gain too.[31]

The third major area of misunderstanding was the estimate of the "noise level" the operation would produce and the degree of the culpability of the United States in the eyes of the world. It seems unlikely that President Kennedy could have failed to realize that the United States would bear the responsibility for the invasion in world opinion. Despite the State Department's concern to lower the "noise level," a landing force of half a dozen ships and some 1500 men, supported by a company of paratroopers and a force of antique though serviceable bombers, was bound to attract the attention not only of Castro but of Khrushchev and of the rest of the world. The President must have realized this, yet he acted as though he did not, and this was probably his most serious error in judgment. "Obviously," Schlesinger reminisces:

> . . . no one could believe any longer that the adventure would not be ascribed to the United States—news stories described the recruitment effort in Miami every day—but somehow the idea took hold around the cabinet table that this would not much matter so long as United States soldiers did not take part in the actual fighting.[32]

Strong advocacy by the CIA was certainly an important factor in the decision. They were not only presenting the plan and evaluating it for the President, but they were urging it upon him—a role not marked out for the agency in any of its authorizing legislation. Allen Dulles assured the President that the Brigade would be able to carry out its mission and that Castro could be overthrown without "actual aggression" by the United States, and with no risk of involvement and little risk of failure.

"I stood right here at Ike's desk," Dulles told Kennedy, "and told him I was certain our Guatemalan operation would succeed, and, Mr. President, the prospects for this plan are even better than they were for that one."[33]

The President was told that he had to move against Castro very soon because the Brigade was ready; Guatemala was asking that the camps (whose existence was becoming increasingly public) be closed; Castro's forces were being built up by Soviet arms. Was he, Kennedy, willing to let it be said that he was less determined than the Republicans to get rid of Castro? Further, Dulles strongly emphasized that if the Brigade was not used against Castro, there would be a "disposal problem." The men would spread out all over the United States, possibly over the whole hemisphere, with the story that Kennedy had pulled the rug out from under the plan to overthrow Castro.

The CIA plan which began as a contingency was becoming a reality. Schlesinger notes that the CIA, "having created the Brigade as an option . . . now presented its use against Cuba as a necessity."[34]

From almost the beginning of the recruitment and training of the Brigade, leaks about the operation were horrendous. The men were anxious for action against Castro, and rumors of the existence of the training camps spread throughout Miami. In Guatemala, too, the "secret" was well known. A story in the Guatemalan paper, *La Hora*, on October 30, 1960, described preparations for the invasion as being "well under way."

The first indication in the American press was an editorial in *The Nation* on November 19, 1960, expressing concern over a report by Dr. Ronald Hilton in the *Hispanic American Report*, a Stanford University publication, that the CIA had acquired a large tract of land in Guatemala and was training Cuban counterrevolutionaries for an eventual invasion of the island. The editorial expressed concern that the U.S. press seemed unaware of the public commotion the subject was arousing in Guatemala.

Correspondent Richard Dudman of the *St. Louis Post-Dispatch,* one of the most respected and influential newspapers in the United States, later confirmed the existence of a "secret 1,200-foot airstrip" cut out of the jungle and of barracks that could house five hundred men. Guatemalans told Dudman that the soldiers at the base spoke with a Cuban accent. "What is going on in Guatemala?" asked the *Post-Dispatch.* "Who is trying to conceal what, and for what purpose?"

In January 1961 an article in *The Nation* by Don Dwiggins told of the airstrip and plans for a coming air attack, for which pilots were being offered $25,000.[35]

On January 10 a lengthy article, written from the air base at Retalhuleu, appeared in *The New York Times.* While the article avoids saying directly that the operation is U.S.-controlled, that fact is made clear by implication, for the forces are described as being drilled by "foreign personnel, mostly from the United States," and Americans are said to be assisting with "matériel and ground and air facilities." The story does not mention the nationality of the men being trained, but does report the rumors—and the denial by the Guatemalan authorities— that the men were being prepared for an offensive against Castro. There is no suggestion in the article of CIA involvement.

At the same time, the New York *Daily News,* the largest-circulation paper in America, began a series of articles that described the Guatemala activities as a preparation for an invasion of Cuba, although it laid the responsibility at the feet of "American and Cuban industrial interests." And the *Miami Herald,* on January 11, opened a series of articles on the operation, beginning with a description of the recruitment activities in Miami. Finally, on January 27, *Time* magazine laid the operation at the door of the Central Intelligence Agency. There were other reports.

By the end of January 1961, preparations for the invasion and the deep American involvement were an open secret, if not a matter of public knowledge. Even as he assumed the Presidency, John F. Kennedy, an avid reader of newspapers and magazines, must have been aware of the extent to which the United States was already implicated.

Stories appeared more and more frequently as spring came. As the President moved toward the day of decision, he heard few dissenting voices. Arthur Schlesinger was opposed to the plan, but confined himself to a private expression of his views to the President, feeling that his was too junior a position around the Cabinet table to oppose the august Joint Chiefs and department heads. Schlesinger's opposition was not based on moral or even legal grounds. He apparently would have been content with the operation if Castro's overthrow could have been achieved "by a swift, surgical stroke." Furthermore, he was concerned about damage to the new image of America that he felt was embodied in John F. Kennedy.[36]

A similar concern was expressed by Under Secretary of State Chester Bowles, who strongly opposed the project, although Bowles's views apparently did not reach the President before the invasion.

Bowles learned of the invasion plans while acting as Secretary of State in Rusk's absence. On Rusk's return to Washington on March 31, the Under Secretary gave him a memo expressing his "deep concern" over the plan, which he found "profoundly disturbing." Bowles wrote that his concern stemmed "from a deep personal conviction that our national interests are poorly served by a covert operation of this kind at a time when our new President is effectively appealing to world opinion on the basis of high principle." He noted that the Cuban operation would violate the "fundamental obligations" the United States had assumed by treaty and he added, "We cannot expect the benefits of treaties if we are unwilling to accept the limitations they impose on our freedom to act." He felt that "this operation will have a much more adverse effect on world opinion than most people contemplate." Finally, Bowles wrote, "We should not . . . proceed with this adventure simply because we are wound up and cannot stop."[37]

Bowles asked Secretary Rusk to permit him to take his objections to the President personally should the President appear determined to proceed.

Senator J. William Fulbright, chairman of the Senate Foreign Relations Committee, had become alarmed over the news stories, and on March 30 he gave the President a memo in which he strongly opposed the invasion. In his memo Fulbright assumed that the invasion would succeed; he also assumed that because of the advance publicity the United States would be blamed despite whatever disclaimers were issued. Fulbright argued:

> Such an action would be denounced from the Rio Grande to Patagonia as an example of imperialism and as the conclusive answer to those who felt that the 1960 elections presaged a change in U.S. policy . . . So far as insulating the rest of the Hemisphere is concerned, the United States would not find the overthrow of Castro, in the manner described above, a pure gain. It might even find it a net loss.

Fulbright also warned of the possibility of encountering such resistance in Cuba that the United States would be faced with the question whether it could let the attempt fail. He also suggested the possibility, which does not appear to have occurred to anyone else at the time, that Castro might eventually become an expensive liability for the Soviet Union.[38]

Senator Fulbright also suggested that the attempt to overthrow Castro would violate at least the spirit, and probably the letter, of the Charter of the Organization of American States as well as other treaties and federal legislation. He warned that if the invasion appeared on the point of failure, we would be heavily tempted to use American forces directly, and even if the illegitimacy of this action was papered over, it would undo thirty years' work of trying to live down the onus of previous interventions in the Caribbean.

> To give this activity even covert support is of a piece with the hypocrisy and cynicism for which the United States is constantly denouncing the Soviet Union in the United Nations and elsewere. This point will not be lost on the rest of the world—nor on our own consciences. . . . The Castro regime is a thorn in the flesh; but it is not a dagger in the heart.

Haynes Johnson and Bernard Gwertzman, in their authoritative biography of Senator Fulbright, have reported the Foreign Relations Committee chairman's recollections of the decisive meeting on April 4. Fulbright did not feel that his March 30 memorandum had made much of an impression on the President; Kennedy had read it hurriedly and had appeared to dismiss it. He did, however, ask Fulbright to attend "a meeting I'm having on this." When Fulbright arrived at the Senate Department on April 4, he was surprised to find not a small group but the full array of senior administration officials, including the military. Those present included the Secretary of State, Dean Rusk; the Secretary of Defense, Robert S. McNamara; the Secretary of the Treasury, Douglas Dillon; the chairman of the Joint Chiefs of Staff, General Lyman Lemnitzer; the chief of Naval Operations, Admiral Arleigh Burke; the director of Central Intelligence, Allen W. Dulles; the CIA's chief planner for the project, Richard Bissell; Latin American expert Adolph Berle; former Assistant Secretary of State Thomas Mann; the Assistant Secretary of Defense Paul Nitze; the Latin American affairs advisers Arthur Schlesinger and Richard Goodwin; Fulbright; and President Kennedy. It was the final, full-dress review for the Bay of Pigs; it set the stage for the first, and in many ways the most significant, foreign policy decision of the Kennedy administration.

The CIA representatives made a strong presentation, ending with an impassioned advocacy of the operation. The President then went around the table, pointing to each man in turn, asking whether he supported or opposed the invasion. He did not call on everyone present; Fulbright recalls that Rusk, Goodwin, Schlesinger, and Dillon did not speak.[39]

The CIA had placed heavy emphasis on the "disposal problem," but, says Senator Fulbright, "this didn't appeal to me a damn bit."[40]

The chairman of the Senate Foreign Relations Committee, who had himself almost been selected as Kennedy's Secretary of State, was excited and unprepared for such an august occasion and he was facing overwhelming contrary opinion from all of the experts. No one else opposed the invasion. Fulbright spoke emphatically, eloquently, and with deep feeling, denouncing the whole idea, calling it wholly out of proportion to the threat it was supposed to meet. "He gave," Schlesinger remembers, "a brave, old-fashioned American speech, honorable, sensible and strong; and he left everyone in the room, except me and perhaps the President, wholly unmoved."[41] Others present felt that the President was "visibly shaken" by Fulbright's presentation; they were sure that his view would prevail and that the President would scrap the operation.[42] But he did not. Later the President was to tell Fulbright, "You're the only one who can say I told you so."[43]

After the meeting Secretary Rusk told Bowles that the plan had been modified greatly and that "he did not feel it was necessary for me to see Kennedy." Bowles writes that he does not believe Rusk deliberately deceived him because key Defense Department officials also gave him the impression that the plan had been considerably reduced in size.

Some time shortly thereafter, probably at a meeting

the next day with Rusk, McNamara, and Dulles, Kennedy made his final decision to proceed. Yet he still insisted that the operation be set up so that he could call it off as late as twenty-four hours before the Brigade hit the beaches. Plans were made for diverting the ships, if necessary, to Puerto Rico. "With heavy misgiving," according to Sorensen, Kennedy decided to go ahead.

Why? Certainly no one factor was wholly responsible, but the following appear to have been significant. First, John Kennedy's general anti-Castro posture. Sorensen says that he was not committed or forced by his campaign pledges, "but he did feel that his disapproval of the plan would show a weakness inconsistent with his general stance."[44] The distinction is difficult to grasp.

Second, although he did not feel Castro was a direct threat to the United States, says Sorensen, yet he did not see why he should "protect" Castro from other Cubans. He was also influenced by his fear of adverse public reaction, by his concern that he would be criticized for stopping an attempt to get rid of the Cuban dictator.[45]

Third, he was apparently convinced that he had "pared the invasion plan down from a grandiose amphibious assault to a mass infiltration."[46] If this had been correct, then it would have been the first "infiltration" in the history of warfare to be accompanied by a bomber assault, a paratroop landing and a provisional government waiting in the wings. Kennedy apparently felt that both the military and political costs of failure had been reduced to a tolerable level. He remarked to Schlesinger, "If we have to get rid of these eight hundred men, it is much better to dump them in Cuba than in the United States, especially if that is where they want to go." Schlesinger feels that this statement illustrates the influence of Dulles's emphasis on the "disposal problem."[47] It was also a serious indication, if the remark is correctly reported, that either through his own misunderstanding or through CIA misrepresentation, the President was understating by *almost half* the number of men to be put ashore—nearly fifteen hundred. Was this a factor in his judgment that the assault could be considered only an infiltration? It is a fine line; but the magnitude of the error is troubling.

Fourth, Kennedy was new in office. His term had now run less than ninety days. He tended to be intimidated by the experts, particularly the CIA and the military. He remarked:

> If someone comes in to tell me this or that about the minimum wage bill, I have no hesitation in overruling them. But you always assume that the military and the intelligence people have some secret skill not available to ordinary mortals.[48]

The cult of expertise is a trap into which many have fallen and the experts always presume on it. There is a kind of aura of "If you knew what I know" which is intended to intimidate the uninitiated. Thus the Joint Chiefs of Staff use this technique to influence Presidents; senators and congressmen with access to "special inside material" use it to influence their colleagues; Presidents use it to influence the people.

But the Bay of Pigs, insofar as this factor affected Kennedy's decision, is an illustration of the fallacy of expertise. With the exception of certain esoteric technical matters, many of which never reach the President, foreign policy decision-making is not an arcane art to which only the inner circle has access. George F. Kennan once remarked that except for technical areas, which may be only marginally significant, all of the "secret facts" necessary for an intelligent and proper decision in the field of foreign policy are usually available to any careful reader of the newspapers within about three days of an event. Thus, any reasonably well-informed American is probably as well qualified as is the President of the United States to make general foreign policy judgments. Foreign policy decisions are, in essence, political, and depend more on judgment and long-range vision than on secret intelligence or military factors.

Fifth, Kennedy was overconfident. Schlesinger suggests that the President was influenced by his "enormous confidence in his own luck . . . everyone around him thought he had the Midas touch and could not lose."[49] This is, of course, a subjective judgment by a close observer, but it suggests the existence of a trait that is highly dangerous in one who controls the nuclear trigger.

Sixth, there is another psychological factor related to the Kennedy style. Theodore Sorensen, who knew nothing about the invasion until it was over, reports a remark that may shed light on Kennedy's motivation.

> When I asked the President a few days earlier about the bare hint I had received from another meeting, he replied with an earthy expression that too many advisers seemed frightened by the prospects of a fight, and stressed somewhat uncomfortably that he had no alternative.[50]

Since nearly all of his advisers were urging him to go ahead, Kennedy was probably overstating the lack of combative instinct he sensed in his staff; yet the remark illustrates the much-discussed Kennedy activism and aggressive spirit, the legendary "toughness" and pragmatism of the New Frontiersmen. Was the President more concerned about not appearing to shrink from a fight than about the danger of setting a belligerent tone in his first major foreign policy move?

With the decision to go ahead, the administration moved to try to protect the security of the operation, although it was really already too late for secrecy. Once the plan had been changed from a guerrilla operation to a direct assault, the size of the Brigade had to be substantially increased; the final total was 1443. The CIA was able to supply all the matériel the invasion force would need, but delivering it to ports of embarkation without attracting attention was more difficult. American involvement became more and more difficult to conceal as recruitment efforts picked up, particularly in Miami, and were reported in the press. In early April, recruiting efforts among Cuban exiles were so out in the open that the addresses of local recruiting stations appeared in the New York *Mirror* and in *El Diario*, a New York Spanish-language paper. Recriminations among the exile factions and one or another faction's complaints of treatment by the United States filled the press.

On April 7, *The New York Times* printed a long story from Miami by Tad Szulc, an experienced Latin American correspondent, confirming that the training was going on in Florida and Central America. On April 8 the *Times* reported that the Florida camps were closing down as the recruits left from supposedly abandoned airfields for their staging areas in Central America. Publication of the April 7 story was the subject of consternation and uproar within *The New York Times* management. In a speech over five years later, Clifton Daniel, the *Times'* managing editor, revealed that the story as originally written had been toned down "for reasons of national security" to eliminate reference to the CIA and the suggestion that the invasion was imminent. A planned four-column head was reduced to one column over the objections of editors who claimed it was the first time that the play of a front-page story in the *Times* had been altered for policy reasons. The *Times* management thought they were performing a patriotic service, and although President Kennedy later complained about their exposure of the plan, he also told a *Times* official, "If you had printed more about the operation, you might have saved us from a colossal mistake. . . . I just wish you had run everything on Cuba. I am just sorry you didn't tell it at the time."[51]

Perhaps most damaging of all was a front-page story by James Reston in the *Times* of April 11 which told of the conflicting advice being given the President on how much assistance the United States ought to provide the exiles trying to overthrow Castro. Reston implied that the Defense Department and the CIA favored giving enough aid "to enable the refugees to establish effective control over at least part of Cuba." The State Department was pictured as being concerned about the consequences in Latin America and in the world at large of the use of military force by the United States to achieve political ends. Reston reviewed all of the moral and political concepts at issue, and the major arguments for and against: the right of anti-Castro rebels to try to overthrow a despotic government, the possibility of Castro's increasing his influence and poisoning the hemisphere, the possible encouragement—if he was left untouched—of Soviet and Chinese activities in Latin America; and, on the other hand, the view that our assistance was a clear violation of our treaty commitments, that a U.S.-backed invasion would undermine our efforts to prevent Communists from doing the same thing in Laos and Vietnam, that our prestige would be damaged and our moral credit lowered in the United Nations by our use of force in clear contravention of the U.N. Charter which prohibits the use of force in the settlement of international disputes.

Those opposed, said Reston, recognized that Castro could crush all opposition if he received modern weapons and might even try to extend his influence, but "large-scale clandestine arms for invasion would revive Latin fears of American interventionism." He noted that if Castro used arms against, for example, Haiti, we could legally oppose him, but the clandestine aid to the rebels would be illegal. The point of decision, he emphasized, was near. The possibility of a spillover into the delicate situation in Laos, or a threat to Berlin troubled the State Department. The essential questions appeared to be: Are we going to live up to our treaty commitments, or are we not? Are we going to condemn the use of force in international disputes only when the Russians use it?

An account in *The New Republic* magazine accurately describing CIA activities among the exiles was withdrawn as a patriotic gesture after President Kennedy had expressed the hope that its publication could be stopped.[52]

To prepare an ideological framework for the invasion, the administration, on April 3, issued a White Paper outlining U.S. policy toward Cuba. The document was prepared by Arthur Schlesinger under the close supervision of the President. With a surge of cold-war rhetoric, the White Paper called upon Castro's Cuba to "sever its links with the international Communist movement." The Castro regime, it said, offered a "clear and present danger to the authentic and autonomous revolution of the Americas."[53]

As the day for the invasion approached, rumors reached the White House that the Cuban Revolutionary Council, the coalition of exile groups that was officially sponsoring the invasion, expected almost immediate U.S. recognition as the legitimate government of Cuba and possibly the assistance of U.S. troops. Concerned that the United States might be drawn in irresistibly, Kennedy dispatched Adolph Berle and Arthur Schlesinger to New York to advise the council members that there would be no U.S. recognition until they were well established and that, under no circumstances, would American troops intervene openly. Berle and Schlesinger returned convinced that the Cuban leaders simply did not believe that the United States would not support their efforts to the utmost. Alarmed, the President directed the CIA to make absolutely clear to the council that, unless they agreed to going ahead with the clear understanding that there would be no U.S. military support, the invasion would be called off. The Cubans in New York gave formal assent, but it is not certain whether they fully believed that the President would let them be defeated.

To foreclose further the possibility that he might be drawn in deeper, and possibly with the intention of sealing himself off against bureaucratic pressures for deeper involvement that might develop should an emergency arise, President Kennedy, on April 12, told his news conference that

> . . . there will not be, under any conditions, an intervention in Cuba by United States Armed Forces. This Government will do everything it possibly can, and I think it can meet its responsibilities, to make sure that there are no Americans involved in any actions inside Cuba.[54]

Although Kennedy was determined that U.S. forces would not intervene, Fidel Castro was by no means certain. By early April—and probably much before—he must have known about the training camps in Guatemala, and he must have been expecting a significant attempt against his government. All known and suspected members of the opposition in Cuba were rounded up. Nearly a hundred thousand people were arrested or detained, the very elements that might have come to the support of the invaders.

Haynes Johnson interviewed the survivors of Brigade 2506 at length and reported their stories in his book *The Bay of Pigs*. He reports that the Brigade members, preparing to move to their embarkation points, were unaware of the restrictions placed by President Kennedy and that many if not most of them went ahead confident that their American friends would not let them down. The CIA operatives apparently encouraged and strengthened this misguided belief. CIA representatives had assured them that there would be no problems. The provisional government would be recognized, they were told; help would come from the United States and from other nations; the Cuban underground was ready.

There was one chilling note. Early in April the head of the CIA advisers in Guatemala told two Brigade members that "forces in Washington" were trying to block the operation and that if he, the CIA man, received orders to stop it he would advise the Cubans secretly. The

Cubans were then to take over the camp by force, make prisoners of their advisers, cut off their communications with the outside, and continue their training; and the CIA advisers would reveal the entire invasion plan to them in secret so that they could carry it out even over the opposition of Washington. Some of the Cuban officers were disturbed by this obscure warning since they knew that most of the men had joined the Brigade because they were convinced that the Americans were conducting the operation. But the Cuban officers went along because it was evident to them that only a rich and powerful organization would be able to move the Brigade to another secret base and place them on ships for Cuba.

The CIA deceived the Brigade about several different aspects of the operation: first, the CIA told them that the Brigade at Base Trax was only part of the total invasion force, that other units were training in other bases and would be landing with them; second, they told the Brigade, or at least encouraged them to believe, that they would have full United States military support, including air cover; third, it was suggested that the invasion would take place even if "forces in Washington" tried to stop it at the last minute; and fourth, they were given the clear impression that the effort would not be allowed to fail.[55]

They were deceived on all of these points. In the first place, while a small diversionary landing of less than two hundred men was planned, it failed to take place; there were no other camps like Base Trax, and the Brigade was the only invasion force. The U.S. role had been highly circumscribed by President Kennedy; no U.S., as opposed to Cuban-exile, air cover was *ever* planned. The U. S. Navy was under orders to intercept the ships if the President decided to call off the operation at the last minute. Most important, President Kennedy had publicly committed the United States not to intervene directly "under any conditions." His words probably did not reach the exiles training in the remote Guatemalan jungle. It may have been that the CIA advisers were unaware of the orders given to the Navy; it may also be that the advisers thought that, faced with the possibility of the defeat of the Brigade, the President could be persuaded to permit direct U.S. military support. But with respect to the existence of any other elements of a landing force or a plan for U.S. air cover, it is unlikely that the CIA was ignorant of the real situation.

The Brigade at Base Trax received its mobilization orders on April 9, and on the next day they moved by truck down to the air base at Retalhuleu. There they boarded transports, again with the windows taped, which carried them high over the mountains to their port of embarkation, Puerto Cabezas, on the Atlantic coast of Nicaragua. There they found their fleet, old cargo ships in poor condition; their landing craft, 14-foot open boats with outboard motors and no protection—they had expected LST's; and the Brigade air force of sixteen World War II B-26 bombers. Some of the Cuban officers expressed concern about the open boats and what they felt was the poor placement of the machine guns on the cargo ships, but they were told not to worry about the defense of their vessels, as they would be supported at all times from the sea and from the air.

Finally, on April 14, came the final briefing when the details of the invasion plan were revealed to them. The Brigade was to land at and defend for three days beachheads at the Bay of Pigs and Playa Giron in the Zapata Swamps on the southern coast of Cuba. The area they captured would serve as a base for ground and air operations against Castro. After they had held the beach for three days, the chief CIA adviser told them in a stirring speech, described by one of the survivors to Haynes Johnson, "We will be there with you for the next step. . . . But you will be so strong, you will be getting so many people to your side, that you won't want to wait for us." With a sweeping gesture of his arm, vividly recalled by all present, he concluded, "You will go straight ahead.

You will put your hands out, turn left, and go straight to Havana." The Brigade cheered.[56]

Then they were told that they were to have air superiority. Although it was apparently not explicitly stated that this would be U.S. air support, the Cubans were assured that Castro's forces would not be able to get to them. Castro's air force, such as it was, was to be destroyed in advance on the ground. The intelligence upon which the operation was predicated considered Castro's air force disorganized and lacking in experience. The few planes that were thought to be operational were not considered to be in combat condition.[57]

Two air strikes were planned to neutralize Castro's air force. One, flown by Cuban exile pilots, was to be carried out two days before the landings. After the raid, to avoid revealing U.S. complicity, the pilots would say they had just defected from Castro's air force. The second strike was to be coincident with the invasion at dawn on Monday.

On Saturday morning, eight Brigade B-26's flew from their base in Nicaragua and attacked Cuba's three main airfields. An additional plane flew direct from Nicaragua to Miami to act out the cover story of the "defectors." While the first air attack did inflict considerable damage, a few of Castro's B-26's were still operational, and, more important, the two T-33 American jet trainers originally supplied to Batista, which the CIA had apparently overlooked or ignored, escaped damage.

The Saturday morning air attack caused an immediate uproar in the United Nations. Cuba accused the United States of aggression at an emergency meeting of the Security Council. Although President Kennedy had given instructions that nothing be done to undermine the credibility of Adlai Stevenson, the U.S. Ambassador to the United Nations, the State Department had not apprised Stevenson of the invasion plan and he unwittingly repeated the Castro-defector cover story which the State

Department was handing out. But the cover story did not hold up and the uproar mounted.

The point of no return for the invasion fleet was reached on Sunday noon, and President Kennedy gave orders to let them proceed. By late Sunday, however, the international uproar had heightened. Soviet statements were threatening; a countermove in Laos or against Berlin was feared. It became clear to all in the administration that if the second strike, scheduled for dawn, occurred, there would be no doubt that it came from Nicaragua, not from the beach at the Bay of Pigs as the President had anticipated. Therefore, in line with the policy of not allowing the invasion to jeopardize larger U.S. interests, President Kennedy ordered the second strike canceled. The assurances he had been given that the invasion had a chance even without this kind of American support apparently were a factor in the decision to call off the dawn strike.

No other element or decision in the whole sorry Bay of Pigs affair has caused as much controversy and recrimination as has the cancellation of the second air strike. It is sometimes claimed that the invasion failed because Kennedy "canceled U.S. air cover," although, of course, no U.S. air cover was ever planned.

When the word was passed to the CIA to call off the dawn strike, consternation arose. Allen Dulles was en route to Puerto Rico as part of the cover plan to demonstrate CIA's innocence by his absence from Washington. General Charles P. Cabell, CIA's deputy director, and Richard Bissell met with Dean Rusk late Sunday night. Rusk confirmed that the President had called off the air strike because of the United Nations protest and because the "noise level" of the first strike had been higher than anticipated. Rusk told the CIA officials that they could appeal to the President directly if they chose. They decided not to appeal and returned to the CIA operations center, where, among the officials, angry comments such as "criminally negligent" were applied to the President's decision.[58]

An article in *Fortune* by Charles J. V. Murphy in September 1961, possibly inspired by the CIA and the military, since they are the two elements that escape criticism in the article, considers the cancellation of the second strike to have been the turning point responsible for the defeat. This view scornfully attributes the President's decision to "political considerations" that were allowed to prevail over military needs. It claims that the plans were that "should the T-33's escape the first surprise blow, there would be ample opportunity to catch them later on the ground."[59] If this was the assumption, it is difficult to imagine why the CIA would have expected Castro to leave the planes out to provide ready targets. He had, in fact, already grouped his out-of-service planes by threes on open airfields, while the more valuable aircraft were hidden or camouflaged.

It is, of course, impossible to prove the case one way or the other. Would the invasion have been successful had the second strike gone on as planned? Castro's control of the air was perhaps the single most important factor in the decisiveness of the defeat the Brigade suffered.

Even among the CIA officials, opinions differed. Lyman Kirkpatrick, former inspector general of the CIA, has stated:

> If there had even been a moment during the battle when the Brigade had been near to achieving victory, then we might be able to say that it had been close. In my opinion, the outcome was never close and even to this day there is serious question whether it would have succeeded even if the H-hour air strike had been permitted, and even if Castro had no airplanes and tanks to put into battle.[60]

On the other hand, Richard Bissell, who directed the operation, has stated, "If we had been able to dump five times the tonnage of bombs on Castro's airfields, we would have had a damned good chance."[61]

The President himself later came to view the cancellation as a mistake but not decisive in the defeat.[62] In the unlikely event that the second strike had succeeded in eliminating all of Castro's air power, there was still the problem of 1500 men against 200,000.

At about the time the President was calling off the dawn air strike, the men of Brigade 2506 were preparing to disembark at the Bay of Pigs. The evening before, the Brigade's ships had reached the point thirty miles south of the Cuban coast where they were to rendezvous with their supply ships, large landing craft from the U.S. naval station on Vieques, which carried the tanks and other heavy equipment. In the darkness the convoy moved up the coast into the mouth of the Bay of Pigs, and at about eleven o'clock Brigade frogmen began to move in toward the shore to mark the landing points.

Using interviews with survivors of the assault force, Haynes Johnson has described in detail incredible failures of intelligence and planning on the part of the CIA. The men on the Brigade flagship, the *Balagar*, first became concerned as they moved up the coast when, instead of the dark, deserted, half-constructed resort houses the CIA had told them they would find, they saw a shore blazing with lights (the houses were occupied by construction workers and their families). Then as the frogmen moved to the beach they encountered rocks and razor-sharp coral reefs, not the sandy beach they had expected; the area was not at all suitable for a landing, particularly at night.

The CIA had assured the Brigade that the area was deserted and that it would be hours before their presence was discovered. But by the time the frogmen had placed their first landing light, they had been discovered by a local militia patrol. The militia patrol car turned its lights to sweep the sea, the Brigade frogmen opened fire, and the alarm was sounded. Thus the element of surprise, the only justification for risking a dangerous night landing on an unfriendly coast, was lost almost immediately.

As the landing boats moved in they were illuminated by the patrol-car lights, and the unprotected boats came under direct fire. The men were forced to jump into the water as shots hit their boats and make their way to shore through the dangerous coral.

The men moving to the second landing point at Playa Larga also struck coral offshore and had to abandon their boats as well; as they reached the shore they were attacked almost immediately by Castro's militiamen. Word went back to the task force lying offshore that they had been discovered and that the rest of the Brigade must land immediately.

Nothing went according to plan or prediction. The landing proceeded over innumerable obstacles; the outboard motors on the small boats failed and some of the men were left adrift in the middle of the bay. The Brigade quickly captured a small radio station, but it had already been able to transmit a call for help. By 3 A.M. Fidel Castro had been informed of the invasion, and he moved to take personal charge of the defense.

Castro moved quickly; he knew that he must crush the invasion on the beaches before a provisional government was able to land. An old rebel himself, Fidel knew all the moves.

By 6:30 A.M. the frogmen had managed to chart a route through the reefs, and the large landing craft with the tanks and heavy guns began moving in.

Then Castro's B-26's and two rocket-equipped jet trainers appeared. The landing continued under fire from the air, the men abandoning their boats when they cracked up on the coral reefs a hundred and fifty yards from shore and wading and swimming in, carrying their equipment and ammunition. They ducked under water when the planes swept overhead. One survivor recalled, "It was a nightmare."[63]

A Brigade B-26 appeared to try to provide cover for the landing, but it was no match for the faster jets and was soon shot down. The *Houston*, one of the large ships of the task force, was carrying the Brigade's 5th Batallion which had not yet disembarked. As the men tried to launch their boats, the *Houston* was hit and began taking on water. The captain headed her for the shore, grounding her about three hundred yards from the beach. The men leaped into the water, many without weapons, and twenty-eight died without ever having reached the beach —drowned, strafed by Castro's jets, or attacked by sharks.

Shortly after 7 A.M. a tremendous explosion was heard and a ball of black smoke appeared offshore; some of the men already on the beach wondered if an atomic bomb had been dropped. It was the *Rio Escondido*, victim of a direct hit by a rocket from one of the jets. On the *Rio* were virtually *all* of the Brigade's supplies for the first ten days—ammunition, food, medical supplies, gasoline, and communications equipment. Why the CIA concentrated so much vital equipment on one ship has never been explained.

After the sinking of the *Rio Escondido*, the task-force commander radioed ashore that he had been ordered to withdraw to the open sea, and the remaining ships quickly departed. Only 10 percent of the ammunition had been unloaded. Meanwhile, the Brigade paratroop batallion had landed, but its equipment had been lost in the swamps and was never recovered.

Thus, by midmorning of the first day, Brigade 2506 was stranded on the beach, without supplies and under constant air attack, and Castro was moving up his main strength.

That afternoon, President Kennedy received an angry message from Khrushchev pledging "all necessary assistance" to Cuba.

All day Tuesday, reports filtered in. In his reply to Khrushchev, Kennedy stressed that in the event of intervention by "outside force we will immediately honor our obligations . . . to protect this hemisphere against external aggression."

Late Tuesday night, after the annual Congressional reception and into the small hours of Wednesday morning, the President and his advisers, still in full dress, met at the White House. The news was still fragmentary, but all bad. The CIA and the military urged an air strike from the U.S. carrier *Essex,* lying off the coast of Cuba, to knock out the T-33 jets which were creating such havoc on the beaches and among the Brigade's slower B-26's. Finally the President agreed to authorize a flight of six unmarked U.S. fighters from the *Essex* to provide cover for a Brigade air attack from Nicaragua on Wednesday morning. Their mission would be to defend the Brigade bombers from air attack, although they would not initiate combat.

The B-26's left Nicaragua Wednesday morning, some manned, despite the President's prohibition, by CIA pilots as replacements for the exhausted Cubans. But that effort, as all else in this unfortunate adventure, was doomed. By some still not fully explained mishap, the vulnerable bombers arrived over the beaches an hour before their escort from the *Essex.* They were quickly disposed of by Castro's fighters, and four American pilots were killed.

Meanwhile, at Opa-Locka airport near Miami the Cuban Revolutionary Council, which was theoretically sponsoring the invasion, was being held incommunicado by the CIA. The council was awaiting transportation to the beaches as the government of Free Cuba. Several members of the council had sons and other relatives in the Brigade. As the bad news began coming in, one council member threatened suicide. Others insisted on being taken immediately to the scene of the fighting.

As the meeting at the White House went on into the small hours of Wednesday morning, President Kennedy was apprised of the situation at Opa-Locka. He had not been aware that the CIA had made virtual prisoners of the council members. Kennedy dispatched Adolph Berle and

Arthur Schlesinger to Miami to try to calm the council members. But the distraught council told the President's emissaries that all they could ask now was to be permitted to go to the Bay of Pigs and die with their comrades. They were vehement in their denunciations of the CIA and its betrayals. They begged for U.S. support. Manuel Ray, an exile leader ignored by the CIA as too leftist to be trusted, was particularly bitter at the CIA's failure to bring his underground movement in Cuba into the operation.

By the time Berle and Schlesinger left the meeting with the council and called Washington, they were informed that it was, in effect, all over. Even evacuation was impossible. All that was heard from the beaches were SOS's.

The council members were brought back to Washington that afternoon, and in a somber meeting at the White House, President Kennedy tried to explain to the distraught and embittered Cuban leaders why he had expected the invasion to succeed and why he could not now intervene to save it—or their sons.

For three days, as they had been asked to do, the Brigade fought bravely, with no rest, hardly any food or water, and with little ammunition. Then the fighting was over. Those who survived the beaches faced even greater ordeals. Some perished in the swamps trying to reach sanctuary in the mountains. Others drifted for weeks at sea in a small boat without water; the boat was finally picked up with a few men barely alive off the coast of Louisiana. And 1199 members of the Brigade endured nearly two years of unspeakable conditions in Castro's prisons before their release was finally effected in December 1962.

In the aftermath of the disaster, the President appointed General Maxwell Taylor, Allen Dulles, Admiral Arleigh Burke, and Robert Kennedy as a commission of inquiry. As two of the members of the commission were among those most directly concerned, it is hardly surprising that the inquiry was confined to a study of the details of the operation; the basic premises were apparently never questioned. Robert Lovett, who was called to testify before the commission, recalls the "somewhat embarrassing setup" of having to present to the head of the CIA and a member of the Joint Chiefs criticism of their operations and judgments.[64]

The commission dealt extensively with whether or not the CIA could reasonably be expected to carry out an operation of such size. While the commission's findings have never been made public, it has been reported that they found that the Brigade suffered from a shortage of ammunition and that the plan itself was militarily marginal. The Brigade was too small and there were too many unforeseen obstacles. The conclusions, as summarized by Theodore Sorensen, were the following:

> Even with ample ammunition and control of the air, even with two more air strikes twice as large, the brigade could not have broken out of its beachhead or survived much longer without substantial help from either American forces or the Cuban people.[65]

A more damaging investigation was made by the CIA's own inspector-general. He found that, despite Dulles's injunction that their best men, best planners, the very best of everything that the CIA had ought to be available for this project—the largest the CIA had ever undertaken—this was not the case. Rather, the CIA people working on the invasion were of varied and not particularly relevant experience. Most of them had no knowledge of Spanish and had to deal through interpreters. Many of them had no feeling for the political sensitivities among the Cuban exiles. A former CIA official has noted, "I think we could have had an A team instead of being a C— team. . . ."[66]

In the long run, the many failures and errors of the CIA compromised whatever chance for success the invasion might have had, and they probably hastened the final defeat of the Brigade. But those errors were not crucial. There was never a reasonable chance for success. The new President had been caught in the cold-war illusion that the Cuban people would be so anxious to rid themselves of Castro that they would rush at the opportunity no matter the risk.

The two arguments that appear to have influenced the President most were that he, and through him the United States, would be considered a paper tiger if he called off the invasion, and that the "disposal problem"—what to do with the trained Cuban forces—would create a difficult situation. But if he feared the world would think him faint-hearted for canceling the operation, he must have assumed that the world knew of it already. And if the operation developed a momentum of its own and grew to its eventual scale over the course of time—as it apparently did—it is difficult to understand why it could not have been stopped before it got out of hand. If he did have the "grave doubts" attributed to him, the time for calling off the invasion was the moment the President took office. The decisive factor was as evident then as it was later, although apparently President Kennedy did not appreciate it; the question was never whether the plan was feasible, whether it had a chance of success in overthrowing Castro, but whether it was *politically justifiable*, whether the proposed response was reasonably proportionate to the challenge and threat Castro represented.

Yet, President Kennedy apparently failed to realize that political justification was the issue. He permitted himself to be swayed by too great a respect for his own image. Most important, he failed to assess properly the significance of the open knowledge of U.S. involvement. Once it became evident, from the advance publicity, that the United States would be blamed for either success or failure, then to avoid a major blow to American prestige he would have to have been willing to guarantee success even by direct American participation. Since, and rightly, he refused to consider this course, the whole operation should have been scrapped. Why should a group of Cubans, however brave and well motivated, be allowed to jeopardize larger U.S. interests in such a risky venture?

It would have been bad enough, as Senator Fulbright pointed out on March 30 in his memo to the President, for the United States to have intervened to overthrow Castro and succeeded. It would have been our Budapest. But, for the United States to intervene to overthrow Castro and bungle the job showed us up before the world not just as imperialists but, worse, as *incompetent* imperialists.

As was to be the the case in his later foreign policy decisions, President Kennedy approached the question of the invasion of Cuba as a problem to be managed, when he never should have considered it at all. As Chester Bowles has put it, when the CIA was proposing to sponsor an invasion in clear violation of American treaty commitments, "there was no need, in my opinion, for a series of endless White House meetings to examine the proposal from a hundred different angles. The answer to Mr. Dulles' proposal should have been promptly and firmly negative."[67]

Within a few days, it became clear that the Kennedy administration's first major foreign policy decision had led to a major disaster, an enormous loss of respect and prestige for the United States. Apart from the display of bungling and poor judgment, the long-run consequences of the Bay of Pigs were that Castro was strengthened, not weakened. Khrushchev, in responding to our actions, appeared as a protector of small nations. World confidence in the quality and wisdom of U.S. leadership was severely shaken, and in Latin America there was a serious revival of the fear of Yankee interventionism.

Perhaps the most important result was not the damage, great as it was, to American prestige, but the lesson the new President thought he had learned from the experience and the new direction in which he moved American foreign policy because of it. President Kennedy himself described this reaction in a speech on April 20, 1961, before the American Society of Newspaper Editors. Characterizing the decision not to intervene with our "armed forces" as being in line with the nation's tradition and obligations, he went on:

> But let the record show that our restraint is not inexhaustible. Should it ever appear that the inter-American doctrine of non-interference merely conceals or excuses a policy of nonaction—if the nations of this Hemisphere should fail to meet their commitments against outside Communist penetration—then I want it clearly understood that this Government will not hesitate in meeting its primary obligations which are to the security of our Nation!

Nor would we accept, he continued, the outcome that had befallen the Brigade. It was not "by any means the final episode in the eternal struggle of liberty against tyranny anywhere on the face of the globe . . ." The exiles felt that Cuba could not be abandoned to the Communists. "And we do not intend to abandon it either!"

The lessons he had learned from "this sobering episode" were:

> *First,* it is clear that the forces of communism are not to be underestimated, in Cuba or anywhere in the world. . . . If the self-discipline of the free cannot match the iron discipline of the mailed fist—in economic, political, scientific and all the other kinds of struggles as well as the military—then the peril to freedom will continue to rise.

Second, all the nations of the hemisphere must be aware of the "menace of external Communist intervention" in

Cuba and its potential "for subverting the survival of other free nations. . . . It is for their sake as well as our own that we must show our will."

Third, and finally, it is clearer than ever that we face a relentless struggle in every corner of the globe that goes far beyond the clash of armies or even nuclear armaments. The armies are there, and in large number. The nuclear armaments are there. But they serve primarily as the shield behind which subversion, infiltration, and a host of other tactics steadily advance, picking off vulnerable areas one by one in situations which do not permit our own armed intervention. . . .

We dare not fail to see the insidious nature of this new and deeper struggle. We dare not fail to grasp the new concepts, the new tools, the new sense of urgency we will need to combat it—whether in Cuba or South Viet-Nam. And we dare not fail to realize that this struggle is taking place every day, without fanfare, in thousands of villages and markets—day and night—and in classrooms all over the globe.

The message of Cuba, of Laos, of the rising din of Communist voices in Asia and Latin America—these messages are all the same. The complacent, the self-indulgent, the soft societies are about to be swept away with the debris of history. Only the strong, only the industrious, only the determined, only the courageous, only the visionary who determine the real nature of our struggle can possibly survive.

No greater task faces this country or this administration. No other challenge is more deserving of our every effort and energy. Too long we have fixed our eyes on traditional military needs, on armies prepared to cross borders, on missiles poised for flight. Now it should be clear that this is no longer enough—that our security may be lost piece by piece, country by country, without the firing of a single missile or the crossing of a single border.

We intend to profit from this lesson. We intend to reexamine and reorient our forces of all kinds—our tactics and our institutions here in this community. We intend to intensify our efforts for a struggle in many ways more difficult than war, where disappointment will often accompany us.

For I am convinced that we in this country and in the free world possess the necessary resource, and the skill, and the added strength that comes from a belief in the freedom of man. And I am equally convinced that history will record the fact that this bitter struggle reached its climax in the late 1950's and the early 1960's. Let me then make clear as the President of the United States that I am determined upon our system's survival and success, regardless of the cost and regardless of the peril!

In some ways, this statement was as important a departure in American foreign policy as that embodied in the proclamation of the Truman doctrine; it parallels the Truman doctrine in its counterrevolutionary flavor, and it brings in new, modern, and—it was thought—more effective means to help non-Communist or anti-Communist governments control their discontented peoples.

Public reaction to the new tough line was swift and overwhelmingly approving. Editorials around the nation, almost without exception, hailed the new cold-war strategy. Americans in 1961 still felt that cost must be no object when it comes to combating Communism. Perhaps they still saw the cost primarily in financial terms; not in social terms—in the neglect of our problems here at home; not in terms of the lives of Americans to be expended when conscript armies were sent abroad to carry out what was clearly announced to be the Kennedy doctrine.

Far from showing any concern with the appeal to the

decent opinion of mankind on which the United States was founded, the *Los Angeles Times*, for example, on April 21 cheered the inauguration of

a policy whose implementation is not conditional on the reaction of "world public opinion" or polls of friendly foreign governments. It is a policy in which other nations have been invited to participate. But, if need be, it is a policy the United States is prepared to pursue alone. . . . There may be those . . . who will find the President's remarks too tough, too radical a departure from traditional treaties and collective action, too dangerous a doctrine to employ. But for our part we are glad to hear this clear and forceful expression of anti-Communism from the President.

Finally, a word must be said about the hoariest myth of all—that the Bay of Pigs was a cheap-at-the-price lesson in crisis management which gave the new President valuable experience that enabled him to save the world from nuclear destruction in 1962. While there is no evidence that Kennedy himself believed this, it has been widely reported that his father, his brother, and his closest advisers all stressed to him the value of the Bay of Pigs as a lesson for the future. The cheapness of the price might be disputed by the 1119 men who spent nearly two years in Castro's prisons as well as by the bereaved families of those who never returned from the Bay of Pigs.

It is also frequently stated that the most important characteristic of President Kennedy was the capacity for growth. But however valuable the experience was for Kennedy and however much he may have grown from it, the Presidency of the United States provides little room for on-the-job training. While no amount of experience can prepare a man for the Presidency, the American people are entitled to expect from their President a mature and balanced judgment from the day he enters the office.

It is said that Kennedy regarded the Bay of Pigs as

an "incident, not a disaster."[68] Yet it was heavy with portent for the future.

At that full-dress post-mortem at the White House late Tuesday night, on April 18, Robert Kennedy remarked that his greatest concern was that now nobody in the administration would be willing to stick his neck out and to take a chance on bold or aggressive moves against the Communists.[69]

There is much to suggest that John F. Kennedy, consciously or unconsciously, spent the rest of his administration and his life trying to recover from and make up for that initial colossal error. He was determined to undo the damage done to his own image and that of the nation, and that determination colored most of his important decisions in the area of East-West relations. According to one interpretation,

> President Kennedy's decision to increase American advisers in Viet Nam seems inseparable from the sequence of events leading from the Bay of Pigs through Vienna, Laos and Berlin. There was a strong feeling that the line had to be drawn somewhere, even if that means "the wrong war. . . ."[70]

Haynes Johnson and Bernard Gwertzman, who based their biography of Senator Fulbright on extensive tape-recorded interviews as well as on Fulbright's files, wrote:

> Fulbright always believed that the Bay of Pigs accounted for many of the ills that afflicted America throughout most of the 1960s. He and others felt that Kennedy's poor handling of that situation caused Khrushchev to misjudge the young President as inexperienced, unsure, and perhaps weak. Conversely, the shock of defeat strengthened Kennedy's determination to prove that he could be as tough as any leader. Subsequently, Kennedy moved to bolster

American forces in Berlin and in Saigon. The emphasis of the administration switched to paramilitary operations and a harder line was manifested. Now, one heard expressions of desire to beat the Communists at their own game.[71]

By noon of Tuesday, April 18, 1961, when it was already evident that the invasion could not succeed, and as appreciation of the magnitude of the disaster grew in the White House, President Kennedy appeared "free, calm and candid" and "spoke with detachment about the problems he would now face. . . ." At a private luncheon attended by Arthur Schlesinger and James Reston of *The New York Times,* Kennedy was asked whether U.S. prestige might not be injured if the invasion was allowed to fail. "What is prestige?" he asked in reply.

> Is it the shadow or the substance of power? We are going to work on the substance of power. No doubt we will be kicked in the can for a couple of weeks, but that won't affect the main business.[72]

He was wrong. That kick in the can was felt in Vienna and further on. In the conduct of foreign affairs the shadow is important as well as the substance, and the Bay of Pigs affected "the main business" very much indeed.

Three | Summit at Vienna:
Preparation for
Confrontation

John F. Kennedy was not particularly disposed to summit meetings, but like all modern American Presidents, he succumbed to the temptation of dramatically confronting other heads of state. No amount of reading of cables from ambassadors or briefings by advisers can substitute for the sense of confidence a President derives from taking the personal measure of his Communist adversary. Sooner or later, he would meet with Soviet Premier Nikita Khrushchev and the sooner the better.

In the past, John Kennedy had been somewhat critical of summit meetings and, in 1959, had regarded with caution the prospect of attending such meetings.

> Without grounds for hope of success, I would be reluctant to go to the summit unless it were the only way to avert war. To go to a summit which merely

provided the Soviet Union with a backdrop for propaganda would, of course, be ridiculous.[1]

In his first press conference as President, responding to a question about the possibility of a summit meeting, Kennedy expressed the desire to work through "more traditional exchanges" toward common ground with the Soviet Union.

The recent history of summit encounters had been checkered. President Eisenhower's 1959 meeting with Khrushchev at Camp David led to a general détente in U.S.–Soviet relations. But when Eisenhower went to Paris the following spring for a Big Four summit, the meeting ended in disaster. On the eve of that meeting the Soviet government announced that an American U-2 spy plane had crashed in the Soviet Union, and its pilot, Francis Gary Powers, had been captured. In violation of the traditional practice whereby nations deny all incidents of espionage, no matter how blatant, President Eisenhower publicly acknowledged the U-2 flight and took personal responsibility for the incident.[2] Khrushchev used the "insult" to break up the summit conference and to denounce the American President. Soviet–American relations suffered a severe setback. The inauguration of a new President offered an opportunity to repair, or at least paper over, the breach of international etiquette and the personal estrangement between the American and Soviet leaders caused by the U-2 affair.

Premier Khrushchev had sent President Kennedy a cordial message on his election and again on his inauguration. Shortly thereafter, Khrushchev ordered the release of two U. S. Air Force officers who had been held virtually incommunicado in the Soviet Union since July 1, 1960, when their plane was shot down near the Soviet border. In exchange for this gesture of good will, although without specifically indicating that a quid pro quo was involved, President Kennedy announced that U-2 flights over the Soviet Union would not be resumed.[3]

. . .

After his 1958 visit to the Soviet Union during which he had been granted an unusually extensive interview with Khrushchev, Walter Lippmann commented on the difference in the world view between the two superpowers. The United States, he wrote, regards the status quo in international affairs in traditional, static terms—things as they are at any given moment. For Khrushchev and for Communists in general, however, the status quo is a dynamic, "the process of revolutionary change"—the continuing struggle of oppressed and colonial peoples against imperialist domination; struggles for national liberation are the status quo, and any attempt to suppress wars of national liberation, any counterinsurgency action, is a violation.[4]

The Communist view is not a contrived rationale. Rather, for the Soviet leadership, it is a belief that has its foundations in the doctrine of the inevitability of the class struggle and the eventual triumph of communism. When Khrushchev says, "We will bury you," he is not necessarily making a threat. He is expressing his confidence in the predestined outcome of the historical process. Attempts by the capitalist countries to hold back the natural forces of history are regarded as futile and foredoomed; the doctrine states that the socialist camp will win the cold war because it is on the side of history. The Soviet leadership is determined that the West accept their view of this essential nature of the historical process.

An opposed yet equally determinist American view is that formulated by Walt W. Rostow, a principal adviser to both Presidents Kennedy and Johnson. In his *View from the Seventh Floor*, Rostow sees the forces of history favoring the West. "If we succeed in defending the present frontiers of freedom," he writes,

> the outcome of that test of strength [with communism] will be determined by the slow moving forces

of history. . . . Are these underlying forces now working for us or against us? I would put it to you strongly that they are working our way, if we have the wit to work with them.[5]

Rostow claims that advanced democratic societies, by which he appears to mean exclusively capitalist societies, have demonstrated that they can avoid the pitfalls of the business cycle; further, the American pattern of high standards of consumption for the mass of the people is now the general pattern sought by all peoples. Rostow appears to view communism entirely as a Moscow-directed or Peking-directed conspiracy and he sees the Communists checked in the industrialized countries and moving into what they hope will be more fertile territory, the underdeveloped countries.

Yet this, too, he finds, is unsuccessful. "The Communist states are drab and hungry." China, he claims, is incapable, even with oppression, of forcing men to grow enough food while

India and certain other underdeveloped nations have begun to demonstrate that real momentum and steady progress can be obtained in an underdeveloped area by mobilizing the energies and loyalties of the people by consent and normal human incentives.[6]

There are many who would quarrel with these conclusions, particularly with the optimistic picture of India. Many starve in democratic India; while information about Communist China is much less exact, it appears that virtually no one starves there, although control, regimentation, and oppression surely exist. (The question remains: In which country would you rather take your chances as an anonymous human being?)

Rostow maintains that the reason "The Communist offensive in the underdeveloped areas will fail . . ." is that "We can honestly align our policy with . . . the drive for independence," and the Communists cannot. This, too, is a mixed case. We have persisted in defining communism anywhere as inimical to American interests and therefore impermissible, and such a practice can hardly be equated with permitting independence.

Rostow's analysis does not seem to have much more historical validity than that of the Communists. The record does not sustain the judgment that democracy and freedom will always triumph. We may hope that democratic systems may be sufficiently flexible to make necessary adjustments, but they may not be. Democratic Greece, republican Rome, and democratic medieval city-states all disappeared.

Apart from its questionable presumptions about the development process—whether underdeveloped countries can be persuaded under democratic rule to make the sacrifices and accept the degree of discipline required for accumulation of capital in primitive societies—Rostow's analysis is probably as much a misreading of history as is the Communists'.

By early 1961 it was evident that Soviet foreign policy was undergoing a basic shift in strategy. Direct conflict with the United States was no longer considered inevitable or even probable. Emphasis was shifting to support for wars of national liberation in the third world.

At the beginning of 1961 Khrushchev delivered a major foreign policy address, setting forth the Soviet position in response to the dynamic process of revolutionary change. He said that his analysis of the world situation showed him unmistakably that time and history were on the side of socialism. Soviet missiles and the Soviet industrial growth rate outdistanced America's. The third world was in ferment and would soon pass inevitably into the socialist camp. Everywhere, capitalism was in retreat and socialism on the march. Wars of national liberation, just wars of colonial peoples rising against their oppressors—

as in Algeria, Cuba, and Vietnam—would be supported wholeheartedly.

President Kennedy considered Khrushchev's statement carefully, read several paragraphs aloud at a National Security Council meeting, and commended it to the attention of his staff.[7] He was alarmed at the confident and bellicose tone of the Soviet leader's remarks, but felt that Khrushchev would not push his support for revolutionary wars to the point of nuclear confrontation.[8] This judgment was shared by Walter Lippmann, who had another extended conversation with Khrushchev in April 1961. Lippmann concluded:

> The USSR is not contemplating war and is genuinely concerned to prevent any crisis, be it in Laos, in Cuba, or in Germany, from becoming uncontrollable. On the other hand, there is no doubt that the Soviet Government has a relentless determination to foster the revolutionary movement in underdeveloped countries. The relentless determination springs from an unqualified faith in the predestined acceptance of Communism by the underdeveloped countries. The Soviet Government has great confidence in its own military forces. But it regards them not as an instrument of world conquest, but as the guardian against American interference with the predestined world revolution.[9]

Llewellyn Thompson, the U.S. ambassador to the Soviet Union, had been called back to Washington for consultation in February 1961. He advocated an early meeting between Kennedy and Khrushchev because he felt it impossible to convey a full picture of the personality of the Soviet leader and felt that President Kennedy should have the opportunity to find out for himself.[10]

In February, President Kennedy sent a personal letter to the Soviet Premier suggesting a meeting later that spring in Stockholm or Vienna. Khrushchev seemed pleased at the possibility of a summit meeting.

The early months of the New Frontier, for all their glitter, exuded an aura of random though feverish activity. Congress was deluged with nearly fifty special messages and proposals covering such matters as airports, the balance of payments, distressed areas, education, feed grains, health and hospital care, highways, housing, a national cultural center, the Nile Valley monuments, oceanography, veterans' compensation, and watersheds. Foreign VIP's descended on Washington en masse: the Prime Ministers of Canada, Australia, New Zealand, and Greece; the leaders of the West, Adenauer and Macmillan; the leaders of the third world, Presidents Nkrumah of Ghana, Sukarno of Indonesia, and Bourguiba of Tunisia. James Reston of *The New York Times* noted that the new administration appeared to be having difficulty telling the difference between what was more important and what was less important.[11]

During the first months of the Kennedy administration, U.S.–Soviet relations deteriorated markedly. The Soviet achievement of placing the first man in space, the strengthening of the Communist position in Laos, and the Bay of Pigs were major blows to American prestige, and, in the case of the last, to the prestige of the new President himself. Europe was somewhat fearful at the apparent absence of realistic policy priorities that was demonstrated by the Cuba fiasco. General De Gaulle in particular was skeptical of U.S. leadership, and Kennedy's performance in the Cuban affair can hardly have assuaged his concern. President Kennedy was anxious to meet with the French President, whose historical role and great sense of history he had long admired. Protocol dictated that the meeting take place in Paris; De Gaulle had visited the United States during the Eisenhower administration.

Kennedy's first meetings with the other leaders of the

Western alliance, Macmillan and Adenauer, did not go well. His first meeting with the British Prime Minister, at Key West at the end of March, was devoted entirely to Laos. The British were distressed—as was President Kennedy himself—at the depth of U.S. involvement in Laos, but since it had not been possible to bring about a cease-fire, felt they had no choice but to support the American position.

A week later, Kennedy and Macmillan met again in Washington for full-scale talks on a range of matters. These discussions were plagued by excessive formality and were bogged down by ever-present platoons of advisers. Macmillan was not impressed with the new President, whom he found uncertain and overly dependent on his advisers.[12]

The following week, Chancellor Adenauer of West Germany arrived in Washington. The meeting was difficult, and there was aparently little real communication between the young President and the old Chancellor, who could have been his grandfather. Adenauer had enjoyed close ties and a superb rapport with former Secretary of State John Foster Dulles and, with his old friend gone, feared a weakening of the American commitment to Germany and to Europe.

The question of a meeting with Khrushchev had been considered dead-letter after the Bay of Pigs, but in mid-May Khrushchev answered Kennedy's earlier letter and proposed a meeting in Vienna in early June. The President had by this time come to feel that, in light of deteriorating U.S.–Soviet relations, a meeting with Khrushchev was urgent and he quickly agreed. An agenda covering Laos, the test-ban negotiations, and Berlin was agreed upon, but it was also agreed that the meeting would not be the occasion for actual negotiations but rather an opportunity for the two leaders to become acquainted personally and to exchange views. Kennedy's meeting with De Gaulle, previously the highlight of the trip, was reduced to the status of a prelude—a point surely not lost on the sensitive French President.

The coming summit was regarded with mixed feelings by White House and State Department officials. Some feared that Vienna might prove a stand-off and thus heighten cold-war tensions. Others felt that confrontation was the only chance for opening areas of negotiation, that Khrushchev would back away if he felt that he was close to war. Kennedy, therefore, would have to convince him that the danger was real. To what extent President Kennedy personally shared this hard-line view is not certain, but his speeches just prior to departure cannot be called conciliatory.[13]

In his address to the Canadian Parliament on May 17—on his first foreign trip as President—and again in the second State of the Union Message to Congress on May 25, President Kennedy set out his view of the world struggle between communism and freedom. His words suggested the messianic nature of American foreign policy that was to characterize his administration—a prescription for a new kind of American ideological imperialism:

> . . . our historic task in this embattled age is not merely to defend freedom. It is to extend its writ and strengthen its covenant. . . . We should not misjudge the force of the challenge that we face—a force that is powerful as well as insidious, that inspires dedication as well as fear, that uses means we cannot adopt to achieve ends we cannot permit.
>
> Nor can we mistake the nature of the struggle . . . It is an age-old battle for the survival of liberty itself. And our great advantage—and we must never forget it—is that the irresistible tide that began five hundred years before the birth of Christ in ancient Greece is *for* freedom, and *against* tyranny. And that is the wave of the future—and the iron hand of totalitarianism can ultimately neither seize it nor turn it back.

In his message to the Congress—its importance underlined by the personal appearance of the President—he called for additional appropriations for foreign aid, for a reorganization of the armed forces, for a massive fallout-shelter program, and for putting a man on the moon in the 1960's. But perhaps even more important than the specific programs was the extravagant rhetorical tone at a point so close to his departure for Vienna.

> These are extraordinary times. And we face an extraordinary challenge. Our strength as well as our convictions have imposed upon this nation the role of leader in freedom's cause.
> No role in history could be more difficult or more important.
> The great battleground for the defense and expansion of freedom today is the whole southern half of the globe. . . . It is a contest of will and purpose as well as force and violence—a battle for minds and souls as well as lives and territory. And in that contest, we cannot stand aside. . . . And we do not intend to leave an open road for despotism.

President Kennedy's emphasis on the long-term struggle between communism and freedom in his major addresses just prior to his departure disappointed those who looked for a new effort toward a relaxation of cold-war tensions. Instead of new approaches, and in spite of high hopes, they found an echo, perhaps unconscious, of the views of militant cold-war ideologue Robert Strausz-Hupé, promoter of the "forward strategy" policy of "active pressures against the communist bloc." The "forward strategy" theory stops short of advocacy of preventive war, but maintains that "we should use force when we must, to limit communist aggression and keep irresponsible elements from plunging the Free World into anarchy."[14]

While there is no evidence that the ideas of Strausz-Hupé were being advocated or even listened to in the

White House, there is a parallel in both tone and substance in the world view presented by President Kennedy in these speeches and Strausz-Hupé's presentation which stressed the "permanent struggle against a force unparalleled in history."[15]

In the light of his views at the time, it appears that President Kennedy's reasons for going to the summit were negative rather than positive—that is, he sought to ward off further deterioration in relations with the Soviet Union by taking a hard-line position rather than by moving in new directions away from the cold war.

Other approaches were suggested but apparently were not seriously considered in the White House. The new administration might, for example, have made of the summit meeting an opportunity to begin to brush aside some of the cobwebs of the cold war as a first step toward restoring flexibility in East-West relations. U.S. military bases ringing the Soviet Union and China had long been a cardinal feature of the forward strategy and one of the hardiest cold-war shibboleths. But even if the aim of American policy—defeat and containment of communism—remained the same (and particularly if Kennedy wished to change it), the marked change in the military situation as a result of new technology opened new possibilities.

Were all the bases really necessary in an age of intercontinental ballistic missiles and nuclear submarines? The United States had been heavily committed over the years to a series of client states with governments of dubious character on the grounds that massive military assistance to such governments was required to assure continuation of American base rights and to strengthen "forward defense countries," a State Department euphemism for nations on the borders of the Soviet Union and China. Thus, over the years, America's best friends, at least in terms of the extent to which the United States supported their military forces, became such nations as Spain (submarine bases), Libya (Wheelus Air Force Base), Ethiopia (secret Army communications base), Pakistan (intelligence installations from which U-2 pilots flew), as well as Iran, Turkey, Greece, Nationalist China, and South Korea.

In Laos the Eisenhower administration had spent $350 million in a futile effort to build an anti-Communist bastion out of a country of some two million people—they can hardly be called a nation, for many of them are not aware even in 1971 that they are part of what the rest of the world calls Laos. Despite this effort, by 1961 the prospects for preventing the collapse of the fragile Laotian government and the eventual absorption or tacit control of the area by one of its more powerful neighbors—Thailand or North Vietnam—were dimmer than ever.

Could the United States agree to accept the neutrality of such peripheral areas, or even write them off? Could it reject in practice, as John Kennedy rejected in theory, John Foster Dulles's view of the immorality of neutralism?

It could be argued that by 1961 Jupiter missiles in Turkey, and even bomber bases in Britain, were no longer vital to U.S. national security. America was adequately protected by more advanced instruments of destruction. Would it not be better to negotiate the bases while they still had some value? Khrushchev was, to a large extent, a prisoner of his own propaganda on the base issue. While the Soviet military was certainly as aware as was the United States government of the diminishing importance of American bases, Soviet propaganda constantly denounced them as a major threat to the Soviet Union. If the United States should even hint at negotiating this issue, Khrushchev would be forced to respond in order to make good on his promise to free the Soviet people from this dreadful menace. The question, so this argument runs, was: Could we trade, for example, obsolescent missile bases in Turkey or Italy for firm, long-term guarantees on West Berlin?

The U.S. military, of course, opposed any suggestion that the bases were negotiable. Further, it could be argued that President Kennedy went to Vienna with few cards in his hand—weakened by his mishandling of the Bay of

Pigs and by the necessity to retrench on the American investment in Laos.

From the meeting with Khrushchev, President Kennedy sought insight rather than solutions to the outstanding questions. He appears to have felt that fruitful negotiations would be possible in the future only if Khrushchev was convinced that the West had the strength, the determination, and the resourcefulness to check the spread of communism. He frequently noted that in his relatively short lifetime—he turned forty-four on May 29, 1961—there had been three wars: World War I, World War II, and Korea. "It is impossible," he said, "to study the origins of each of these struggles without realizing the serious miscalculations which were made by leaders on both sides." A meeting with Khrushchev, he felt, would contribute to avoiding Soviet miscalculation. He hoped to warn Khrushchev against a catastrophic misjudgment of our determination to resist Soviet pressures, to discuss the danger of a breakdown in test-ban negotiations and of Soviet insistence on a veto in all international dealings. He apparently felt that he would have to convince Khrushchev that he was not an inexperienced blunderer, that he could be just as tough as the Communists.

President Kennedy arrived in Paris on May 31, 1961, on the first leg of his journey to the summit. Over the next three days he conferred at length—and frequently alone, except for interpreters—with the French President, General Charles de Gaulle.

Kennedy was surely mindful of the dramatic quality of the encounter of America's youngest President with the great captain of the West, the only World War II leader who still held power.

To the world, the two leaders appeared to be of one mind on the major subject of their meeting—the issue of Berlin. Yet their accord on Berlin was a foregone conclusion and discussions on this matter took less than a quarter of an hour. De Gaulle reminded Kennedy that Khrushchev had given six-month deadlines on Berlin in the past, and he expressed the view that if Khrushchev meant war over Berlin, war would already have come. But the West could not retreat. He told Kennedy to emphasize to Khrushchev that it was the Soviet Union that sought change, and he must make Khrushchev understand that an attempt against Berlin would not be met locally but would mean general war. De Gaulle was certain Khrushchev would not risk that. In spite of De Gaulle's strong stand, the question remained: Would the French fight to save a German city?[16]

The two Presidents seemed admirably suited to one another; both were students and writers of history as well as its protagonists. What divided them was more subtle. One might call it their philosophical approach to power—individual power as well as national power. On this level there could hardly have been a greater contrast: the pragmatic American, fascinated by the challenge of the job to be done, impressed by leaders of concrete accomplishment rather than by those who educated the people or embodied their will; the towering Frenchman, already a historical figure in his own lifetime, always conscious of destiny—his own and that of France—twice the savior of his country's honor, first in rallying the Free French in World War II and then in saving France from civil war in 1958, convinced (as he wrote in *The Edge of the Sword* in 1932) that "Leaders of men are remembered less for the usefulness of what they have achieved than for the sweep of their endeavors . . ."

A classical nationalist, De Gaulle believed, as he expressed it in his stirring evocation of the nation's spirit in the opening of his memoirs, that France was

dedicated to an exalted and exceptional destiny. . . . If mediocrity shows in her acts and deeds, it strikes me as an absurd anomaly, to be imputed to the faults of Frenchmen, not to the genius of the land. . . . France cannot be France without greatness [*la grandeur*].

"I was convinced," he wrote, "that France would have to go through gigantic trials, that the interest of life consisted in one day rendering her some signal service, and that I would have the occasion to do so."[17]

His view of the world also differed markedly from the American President's. De Gaulle saw not a contest between freedom and communism, between two hostile alliance systems trying to tear each other down, but an ensemble of nations in which Europe, led by France, would have its hands free to play its own role as a third force between the superpowers.

The main point at issue between the United States and France derived from De Gaulle's vision of Europe's role and France's role. The general had his own view of the future of NATO. At issue also was the question of U.S. assistance to the French nuclear-weapons program, the program which De Gaulle saw as the vital symbol of French sovereignty and prestige.

De Gaulle was challenging America's nineteen-year-old leadership of the Western alliance on both political and military grounds. After World War II the United States was the only Western power to have survived relatively unscathed militarily, politically, and economically. But by the end of the 1950's, America's exclusive control of nuclear weapons and delivery systems was gone. Further, Europe had recovered economically and politically and was imbued with new confidence on the international scene. In the view of De Gaulle and many other Europeans, the United States had peripheral foreign policy interests and commitments (and failures) that might involve Europe in wars that were not in its interest. (The Cuban missile crisis in 1962 and the Vietnam war in the late 1960's became particular examples.) De Gaulle also questioned the credibility of the U.S. nuclear deterrent in defense of Europe. Before the development of long-range missiles by the Soviet Union, the United States could credibly state its determination to launch a retaliatory attack on the Soviet Union if, for example, the Russians should attack Paris. But would the United States risk New York or Washington for Paris or Berlin?

In the view of the French President, Europe must have an equal voice in the employment of the NATO nuclear arsenal as well as an independent nuclear capability. U.S. policy, as President Kennedy was developing it by the time of his meeting with De Gaulle, was to raise the threshold for the employment of nuclear weapons by increasing NATO's conventional war capability. In De Gaulle's view, because Europe would suffer the consequences of any decision to employ nuclear weapons, she must have a role in such a decision. Thus he had insisted on a three-power accord (read French veto) on any NATO decision to use nuclear weapons.

The two Presidents began their discussion with the problem of Laos, and De Gaulle offered Kennedy the benefit of France's unhappy experience with the slippery terrain of Southeast Asia. The French President favored neutralization as a solution not only for Laos but for the whole of Southeast Asia—a position he maintained consistently in the later 1960's as the United States sank deeper into the mire of Vietnam. Kennedy felt that to bring about a neutralist solution in Laos, the West might have to threaten military intervention. De Gaulle thought that military action was a losing game, but said he would not publicly oppose the U.S. position.[18]

The communiqué issued at the end of President Kennedy's visit to Paris was short. It mentioned only that the two Presidents had "confirmed the identity of their views on their commitments and responsibilities towards Berlin." The two leaders were perhaps farther apart on the crucial issues of the alliance than Kennedy realized at the time.

On June 3, John F. Kennedy flew to Vienna to meet Soviet Premier Khrushchev. Again the contrast between the two leaders was spectacular. Khrushchev, a tough, shrewd, resourceful peasant, illiterate until adulthood, had worked his way up through the Communist Party apparatus, and had outlasted and outfoxed his rivals for power; Kennedy was an American aristocrat, cultivated, literate, his way to power smoothed by wealth and influence. No doubt Khrushchev, too, wished to take the measure of his capitalist adversary. He was reputed to rely heavily on his intuitive personal judgments.

It seems likely that the Soviet Premier regarded Kennedy as a lightweight and an inexperienced fumbler. The new American President had made a clumsy attempt to overthrow Castro. This Khrushchev could understand; states move in such ways to protect their interests—after all, he had his Budapest. But Kennedy had failed to follow through to the success that certainly was within his power. This Khrushchev could not understand. To incur the odium of the international community without at least the solace of having accomplished his purpose—a contemptible situation for a great power. Surely this was a weak, indecisive man who could be bullied. Khrushchev clearly expected to impress Kennedy with his toughness, and thought he had a good chance of persuading the American that the balance of power had swung to the Soviet Union. The Soviet position was greatly strengthened since the ill-fated summit conference of 1960. Khrushchev no doubt anticipated a propaganda value from the summit; it would enhance his public image as a friend of peace.

The limits of Soviet policy were well established. On Berlin, the Soviet leader could be expected to settle for nothing less than the "free city" solution he had first called for in 1958 and a new ultimatum on Berlin was a distinct possibility. Khrushchev could also be expected to insist on unanimity, i.e., a Soviet veto, in any mechanism for inspection and enforcement of the test ban. The idea of unanimity was referred to as the troika formula, as the Soviet Union was insisting that all international decision-making be carried out by a triumvirate consisting of representatives from the West, the socialist countries, and the neutrals, and which could act only when the three were in accord. The United States, of course, viewed the troika formula as a prescription for paralysis.

On Laos, Khrushchev was expected to insist that the United States accept the consequences of its apparent decision to refrain from military intervention—i.e., neutralism as a prelude to a peaceful Communist takeover.

Almost from their first minutes together, Khrushchev and Kennedy became enmeshed in an ideological dispute. Khrushchev pressed hard on his view of the inevitability of the success of communism in the third world and the unacceptability of any attempt by the United States to arrest the forces of history. Communist ideas would never be imposed by war, he said. War would come only if the United States was determined to prevent the natural development of communism.

Khrushchev emphasized that the USSR would support wars of national liberation, but maintained that such wars could not be instigated from the outside without the support of the people concerned.

Though Kennedy had read widely on Soviet affairs, he may not have felt confident enough of his own knowledge to challenge Khrushchev's arguments.

Ambassador Llewellyn Thompson, who accompanied the President to Vienna, felt it was unfortunate that the discussion got off on ideological matters.[19]

Another veteran American expert on Soviet affairs, George Kennan, then ambassador to Yugoslavia, was not present in Vienna but was later sent to Paris to review the transcript of the discussions. He says:

> I was very disappointed when I read the account. . . . I felt that he [Kennedy] had not acquitted himself well on this occasion and that he had permitted Khrushchev to say many things that should have been challenged right there on the spot. But he, feeling his way, preferred to let Khrushchev talk and not to rebut any

of this. I think this was a mistake. I think it definitely misled Khrushchev. I think Khrushchev failed to realize on that occasion what a man he was up against and also thought that he'd gotten away with many of these talking points, that he had placed President Kennedy in a state of confusion where he had nothing to say in return. . . .

I think they [the Soviets] thought that this is a tongue-tied young man who's not forceful and who doesn't have ideas of his own. They thought they could get away with something.

He was, I thought, strangely tongue-tied in this interview with Khrushchev and numbers of these typical, characteristic Communist exaggerations and false accusations were simply let pass . . . instead of being replied to, being rebutted.[20]

The ideological diatribe finally cooled and the leaders took up the question of Laos. American misadventures in that insignificant Asian backwater have consumed the attention of four administrations and are perhaps the classic demonstration of the tendency of American foreign policy to become impaled on spears in the wings.

A landlocked, backward country of between two and three million, Laos has been called "neither a geographical nor ethnic or social entity, but merely a political convenience, a geographer's nightmare of small deep valleys surrounded by saw-toothed mountains covered with jungle almost to the tips."[21] Laos was granted its independence when the French liquidated their commitments in Indochina. Since that time it has been ruled, at least in theory, by a royal family resident in either Vientiane or Luang Prabang (the existence of two capitals is the least of the muddles of Laos).

During the Eisenhower administration there were those who considered that because of its "strategic position," Laos was the "gateway to all of Southeast Asia."

Roger Hilsman, director of intelligence and reseach in the State Department and later Assistant Secretary of State for Far Eastern Affairs in the Kennedy administration, constructed an elaborate rationale for the importance of Laos "astride [the] land-locked fourth route" through which "Chinese power could be most easily projected southward to dominate Southeast Asia."[22] At the time of the Vienna meeting (June 4, 1961) *The New York Times* called Laos the "very heart of Southeast Asia" and a possible base for subversion. It spoke of "vast human and material resources" somewhat mystifyingly since, in an area the size of Italy, the total population numbers between two and three million and the principal cash crop is opium.

Geography has assured that the majority of the people remain out of touch with their supposed government. Many of the inhabitants of Laos are not ethnic Lao but mountain aborigines, who eke out a meager existence through a nomadic slash-and-burn agriculture.

In an age of intercontinental missiles it is difficult to conceive of Laos as having any real strategic significance. On the contrary, it has become a tragic example of an innocent and essentially peaceful population in a peripheral area caught up and decimated in an ideological power struggle that most of the victims can barely understand.

The Eisenhower administration had lavished some $350 million in foreign-aid funds on the passive peoples of Laos. The chief effect of American largesse, 85 percent of which went to the Royal Lao Army, seems to have been the appearance of Mercedes limousines and comfortable villas for the generals and their wives.

At the time President Kennedy met with Khrushchev in Vienna the jungles of Laos were the scene of sporadic fighting, while in Geneva representatives of fourteen nations sought a formula that would assure the neutrality and independence of the kingdom. The ins and outs of Laotian politics—literally, for the factions overturned each other regularly—are unbelievably intricate. Very briefly, in

June of 1961 there were these groups: the incumbent pro-West Premier Prince Boun Oum; the neutralists of former Premier Prince Souvanna Phouma; and the Communist-led Pathet Lao rebels headed by Prince Souphanouvong, half-brother of Souvanna Phouma. The CIA was backing Boun Oum, and the Soviets were backing the Pathet Lao, who controlled more than half of the country.

From the Soviet point of view, things were going fairly well in Laos. They were not anxious to push for a cease-fire or to permit supervision of a cease-fire by the International Control Commission (ICC) that had been set up at the time of the Geneva accords of 1954. Thus, they argued that a cease-fire was already in effect and that it was not necessary to give the ICC any further powers.

The United States had accepted the idea of a cease-fire and a conference, thus backing away from its previous contention that these were mere covers for a Communist takeover. The United States refused to discuss other matters at Geneva until the fighting ended. Having abandoned hope of a pro-West Laos, the Kennedy administration sought guarantees that would—at least—keep Laos out of Communist control.

President Kennedy's decision both to seek a neutralist solution and to try to protect his flank by taking a tough line were apparently a direct result of the Bay of Pigs fiasco. Arthur Schlesinger reports that on April 20, the day when the magnitude of the Cuban disaster became clear, Kennedy, lest he be thought irresolute for not following through and using American forces in Cuba, authorized the American military advisers in Laos, who had previously worn only civilian clothes, to don their uniforms and to assist the Royal Lao Army openly.[23]

President Kennedy appears to have decided against direct military intervention in Laos at least partially because if he would not intervene in Cuba ninety miles away he could hardly justify intervening in Laos. Yet he is pictured by Schlesinger as being confident that the American people would have supported intervention.[24]

Before the Bay of Pigs, Schlesinger was convinced that President Kennedy intended to authorize limited military intervention in Laos. Referring to the French loss of Indochina, Kennedy told Walt Rostow, "I can't take a 1954 defeat today."[25]

Thus Kennedy went to Vienna with few cards in his hand on Laos, unwilling to intervene openly, but equally unwilling to offer any concessions lest Khrushchev think him weak.

The discussion on Laos was inconclusive and the matter remained at a standstill.[26]

Over the next two and a half years of his term, President Kennedy secretly deepened American involvement in the war in Laos. That secret involvement was continued and expanded by his successor. The story of the secret American war in Laos began to leak out in the press only in the late 1960's. Investigations by the Senate Foreign Relations Committee in the early 1970's and the publication of the Pentagon Papers filled out many of the details. But even today, much of the story has never been told.

Kennedy and Khrushchev next moved to the subject of a nuclear test-ban treaty. Three-power talks (U.S., U.K., USSR) had begun in Geneva in 1958, and while some understandings had been reached, the key to final agreement was missing. That key was the system of inspection and control by which a test ban could be policed to assure that neither side violated it in secret. The United States, putting a high value on the possibility of cheating, insisted that it would not be possible to determine the nature of "suspicious events"—whether they were earthquakes or underground tests—without on-site inspection. The Soviet Union, fearful of espionage, would agree to no more than three on-site inspections a year; this the United States considered insufficient.

Khrushchev also insisted on a troika system in the control machinery; no inspection could be authorized unless the three parties (Western, Socialist, and neutralist) were in agreement. The United States refused to accept what it said would amount to a Soviet veto over inspection.

The Soviet Union also wished to link the test ban with negotiations on general disarmament. Kennedy claimed that general disarmament was a very complex matter on which it might take years to agree, while agreement on a test-ban treaty would at least be a step in the right direction. The United States, he insisted, could not enter into negotiations on general disarmament without the assurance that speedy agreement could be reached.

Failure to make progress at Vienna on a test ban was perhaps inevitable in light of President Kennedy's already evident efforts to increase substantially America's strategic arsenal. These efforts, foreshadowed in his State of the Union Message on January 30, were confirmed in his defense-budget message to the Congress on March 28 and his second State of the Union Message just before his departure for Europe. Khrushchev referred to those messages during the Vienna talks;[27] he obviously considered them an American escalation of the arms race. Had Khrushchev read only the paragraph headings on the March defense-budget message, he could not have failed to notice that the direction was clearly upward:

> Improving our missile deterrent—
> Protecting our bomber deterrent—
> Increased ground alert force and bomb alarms—
> Improving our continental defense and warning systems—
> Improving the command and control of our strategic deterrent—

As Khrushchev must have seen it, the new President was not seeking restraint in military expenditures. He was, to all intents and purposes, pulling out the stops that President Eisenhower had insisted upon.

Khrushchev—already at a disadvantage in the strategic arms race, and facing a new American build-up—must have known the real missile gap was against *him*, not, as Kennedy had claimed, against the United States. He was not prepared to agree to a test ban, which would preclude the Soviet Union's catching up. He would only agree to a ban in the context of a general agreement in which he could hope to limit the American build-up against him.

Dr. Jerome Wiesner, now head of the Massachusetts Institute of Technology and former science adviser to President Kennedy, believes that Kennedy's decision in favor of an arms build-up in 1961 was responsible for the failure to reach agreement on a test ban and for the Soviet resumption of testing in the atmosphere in the fall of 1961.[28]

It is difficult to reconcile President Kennedy's arms-build-up decisions with any serious attempt at an arms-control agreement or test-ban treaty. Had it not been for the build-up, which clearly affected Khrushchev's attitude, agreement might have been possible in 1961. The troika was not really the stumbling block it seemed; rather, it was something the United States could tolerate. After all, the United States had tolerated a Soviet veto in the United Nations Security Council. Moreover, extensive American testing had shown that instrumentation was capable of detecting all but the most inconsequential—and therefore militarily insignificant—underground tests. Inspection was not that vital a factor.

Since the United States had at that time conducted many more tests than had the Soviet Union and was relatively far ahead of the Soviets in the critical technology, it was in the American interest in 1961 to prevent test resumption by the Soviet Union, even at the price of the troika.

The grimmest and most sobering discussions in Vienna were those concerned with Germany and Berlin.

For fifteen years the former German capital had been

the most sensitive flash point of East-West tension. Berlin was the key to Germany, and therefore to Europe and to America's relations with the continent. The situation was a legacy of war, both a cause and the result of cold-war tensions. As Ronald Steel has put it:

> Germany's status remains unsolved because the Western powers . . . secured a foothold in Berlin. . . . Were it not for that foothold, and the decision to continue the Western allies' presence in West Berlin the territorial changes resulting from the Second World War would not still legally be in doubt. . . . [Berlin] would have been absorbed into East Germany, and we would have ceased to think about Berlin just as we have ceased to think about Dresden. It is Berlin which has kept open the wound of Germany's partition, and it is the unwillingness of the Germans to accept the consequences of that partition that keeps America and Russia at odds in Central Europe.[29]

Two million people in the enclave of West Berlin, a little over a hundred miles inside East Germany, were dependent upon the West for their survival. American, British, and French troops maintained the Western presence in the divided city, but the ultimate guarantee of the freedom of the city was the will of the Western powers to defend it.

For the Soviets, the exposed geographical position of Berlin made it an ideal subject for the exertion of pressure on the West—the means of access could be so easily controlled. Berlin may have been a bone in Khrushchev's throat, but as Coral Bell has suggested, for the West it was "an extended arm, eminently twistable."[30]

Twice before, the Soviets had attempted to force the Western powers out of Berlin. In 1948 Stalin had cut off land access, and for nearly a year the city had to be supplied by an airlift. Ten years later, on November 27, 1958, Khrushchev had issued a six-month ultimatum threatening that if the Western powers would not agree to a German peace treaty in that time, he would sign a treaty with East Germany, and with that signature American, British, and French occupation rights in West Berlin would cease. Khrushchev had talked of a "free city," possibly under some kind of United Nations arrangement. Western troops might remain in West Berlin, he had said, but, of course, Soviet troops would join them.

But the six months passed and Khrushchev rescinded the ultimatum. The situation continued as before. Yet, for the Soviet Union, Berlin was a problem that could not be ignored for long. Some two hundred thousand East Germans were escaping through Berlin to the West each year. Apart from the propaganda problem created by this mass exodus from a nation supposedly enjoying the benefits of communism, the manpower drain threatened East Germany's economic viability. Many of those who escaped to the West were skilled workers or professionals.

President Kennedy was no more prepared to negotiate on Berlin than was Khrushchev. In this respect, Kennedy's position was a hardening of the American attitude as presented by President Eisenhower. The Foreign Ministers' Conference in the summer of 1959 had discussed an interim agreement with the possibility of reduction of garrisons and other concessions. Eisenhower had planned to offer some concessions at the 1960 Paris summit. Those plans were never carried out because the meeting collapsed over the U-2 affair, but the incoming administration had been informed of the plans. Now Kennedy moved to "disengage" himself from Eisenhower's more flexible position.[31] Arthur Schlesinger brushes aside Kennedy's move, but concedes that Moscow had undoubtedly considered it a hardening of American policy. Indeed, it is difficult to construe it in any other way. Why President Kennedy felt he had to be more recalcitrant than Eisenhower is unclear, but it may be, as in the case of Laos, a legacy of the Bay of Pigs.

President Kennedy had assumed in preparing for the

summit that to fail to adhere firmly to the Western powers' occupation rights in Berlin would be to show weakness. Crisis planning in Washington was already under way and a series of military steps were under consideration to demonstrate the American will to risk war over Berlin. The President seemed to be expecting the worst.

When the discussions in Vienna turned to Berlin, the Soviet Premier moved immediately to the offensive. The situation was intolerable, said Khrushchev, and must be settled. He repeated the threat the Soviets had made in 1958: if the West would not agree to a German treaty in six months, he would sign one with East Germany. But this time he added that if the Western powers tried to exercise their occupation rights after a treaty was signed, it would be a violation of East German sovereignty and would mean war. Kennedy replied that it was not the West but the Soviet Union that wished change. War might indeed come, but it would be Khrushchev who would be responsible for it.

The two leaders parted on this somber note. The clash had been deep and bitter. Kennedy was reported to be convinced by the Soviet leader's intransigence that the need for strengthening defenses was greater than ever.[32]

In retrospect, Vienna has the air of a self-fulfilling phophecy. President Kennedy apparently sensed the possibility that his defense build-up precluded an agreement on a test-ban treaty, although it was not necessarily responsible for the Berlin ultimatum. That may be explained in terms of Soviet policy rather than American. Schlesinger reports that President Kennedy himself often wondered what had gone wrong in Vienna. The President speculated that his calls in March and May for increased defense spending may have been "too threatening." Possibly, the step-up in the Polaris and Minuteman programs had been misunderstood by the Soviets and perhaps they now felt required to match the American build-up.[33] This, as noted above, is also Dr. Wiesner's interpretation. One might ask what effect President Kennedy expected the build-up to have and what overriding reason he might have had for ordering it—a reason that presumably, in his eyes, outweighed the obvious escalating effect on the arms race.

Schlesinger seeks to ease the weight of responsibility on President Kennedy by stressing that Khrushchev's belligerent January speech preceded Kennedy's defense messages. But Khrushchev's message was words, Kennedy's was action; Khrushchev's message related largely to wars of national liberation in the third world—a problem of conventional warfare; Kennedy's messages dealt with the nuclear strategic balance. He was moving the arms race to a higher level, and the Berlin crisis which broke out at Vienna provided the occasion for further steps.

Evaluations of President Kennedy's performance at Vienna differ—as do judgments as to the effect of the meeting on future developments in U.S.–Soviet relations. Ambassador Llewellyn Thompson felt that the President handled himself well and that he impressed Khrushchev with his knowledge of Soviet affairs. Thompson recalls that the President later occasionally teased him for having recommended the meeting that turned out badly, but the President always ended up admitting that it had been useful to meet Khrushchev in person.[34]

Ambassador George Kennan, on the other hand, felt that the impression Kennedy made on Khrushchev at Vienna may have influenced the Soviet attitude toward putting missiles in Cuba. It might have encouraged an aggressive attitude in Soviet military circles, which would have been aware of Khrushchev's impression of Kennedy and which might have tried to take advantage of it.[35]

The reaction of Sir Alec Douglas-Home, then British Foreign Secretary, appears typical of the European attitude.

I confess I was disquieted when, instead of giving himself time to play himself into international affairs, he [Kennedy] launched into a meeting with Mr. Khrushchev. I did not think he would have over-estimated himself or underestimated his opponent. He never did either again, but on that occasion he made, in my opinion, a very bad mistake from which it took a lot of time to recover. Khrushchev, being a very shrewd man, probably summed up the situation fairly well but his advisers almost certainly concluded that here was a young man round whom Khrushchev could make rings. They found out that they were wrong, but only after the most anxious moments of trial and error and brinkmanship.[36]

President Kennedy's radio-TV report to the American people, delivered on June 6, 1961, reflects his own somewhat ambivalent feelings about the meeting. It also lays down patterns for the coming U.S.–Soviet confrontations on the strategic level over Berlin and Cuba and in the tactical sphere over the roles of the superpowers in the revolutions boiling up in the third world.

The President set forth two major reasons for the trip to Vienna: "the unity of the free world . . . and the eventual achievement of a lasting peace." Like most Americans, he failed to recognize that "the unity of the free world" is a euphemism for a world compatible with American interests and American principles, although nothing so crude perhaps as an American hegemony or Pax Americana. This concept, insofar as it fails to allow for the interests and principles of the adversary, is incompatible with the second aim, the achievement of a lasting peace.

Kennedy's comment that in his meeting with General De Gaulle "Certain differences in our attitudes on one or another problem become insignificant in view of our common commitment to defend freedom" was a considerable understatement of the very fundamental differences with the French President over issues of the greatest importance to him—France's role in NATO and particularly the question of nuclear sharing. That problem, however, was to remain out of the headlines for some time while De Gaulle, who felt that Khrushchev was bluffing, supported a policy of firmness on Berlin.

With respect to his conversations with the Soviet leader, Kennedy reported, "I will tell you now that it was a very sober two days. There was no discourtesy, no loss of tempers, no threats or ultimatums by either side . . ." (This last was a bit of dissimulation; it was technically true because Khrushchev's formal ultimatum on Berlin was presented as an *aide-mémoire* at the end of the meeting.) Kennedy failed to mention that Khrushchev had presented a six-month deadline for settlement of the Berlin question, but he did reiterate that we were determined to maintain our "rights" in Berlin "at any risk. . . We and our allies cannot abandon our obligations to the people of West Berlin."

Most of the President's report dealt with the ideological conflict with the Soviet Union, with the differing views of history of the superpowers, and it expressed Kennedy's confidence that American know-how could prevent the newly independent nations from slipping into the Communist grasp.

President Kennedy noted Khrushchev's certainty that "the world will move his way without resort to force. . . . This is the Communist theory."

> But I believe just as strongly that time will prove it wrong, that liberty and independence and self-determination—not communism—is the future of man, and that free men have the will and the resources to win the struggle for freedom.

He noted that the Communists ought not to be blamed for all antigovernment and anti-American uprisings throughout the world. The Communists may exploit misery in the underdeveloped areas, but "the Communists did not create the conditions . . ." He concluded with a statement that if only the nation will meet its responsibilities through increased foreign military and economic aid the Communist advance can be stopped.

This is a restatement of one of the basic assumptions of the Kennedy doctrine: the idea that if only American know-how, American efficiency, and American determination could be brought to bear, our problems could be solved and peace could be assured. In fact, what was needed was not a more efficient application of America's skill in problem-solving within the cold-war framework but a reassessment of the role America has played in the world since World War II, a reevaluation of the tendency to seek military solutions to problems that were essentially political; an understanding of the limits of American power; and, finally, a new definition of the true American national interest.

At President Kennedy's direction, the problems of counterinsurgency and political warfare were under intensive study within the administration. The decision was being reached to meet the Communists on their own grounds, with their own techniques.

But that was for the long term. For the immediate future there was the problem of Khrushchev's ultimatum. What was to be the American response to the crisis over Berlin?

Four | *"Ich Bin Ein Berliner"*

The Berlin crisis of the summer of 1961 arose partly from Khrushchev's feeling, as a result of President Kennedy's performance in the Bay of Pigs incident and at Vienna, that the American President was weak and clumsy. Such a man, the Soviet leader must have thought, could be bullied, But Khrushchev had other motives. The situation in Eastern Europe was unstable. Eastern Germany had made a remarkable economic recovery after having been stripped of its industrial plant by the Russians as World War II reparations. Now its economic recovery was threatened as skilled workers and technicians fled through the Berlin escape hatch. Added to this was the Soviet fear, which the West has always tended to dismiss too lightly, of a revived German militarism. During the Eisenhower-Dulles years, when American policy was tied so closely to Bonn, there was a tendency to forget that Europe, with our help, had had to fight the Germans twice in little more than a generation.

Some State Department experts on the Soviet Union felt that the new Soviet *aide-mémoire* on Berlin reflected in large measure Khrushchev's desire to achieve security in Eastern Europe. They favored negotiation on Berlin and other European issues.

Others in the department, particularly those whose views were influenced by the German position, felt that Khrushchev's main purpose was to destroy NATO. This faction opposed negotiation, claiming that for the United States to put forward new proposals would be to demonstrate weakness.

The American response to the Berlin crisis preceded the crisis itself. John Kennedy had long been determined to substantially increase American conventional military forces so that, as he saw it, the Commander in Chief would have an alternative to massive retaliation as a response to a limited hostile action in an area of American interest. Kennedy believed that an attack by conventional forces could best be deterred by an ability to respond in kind.

President Eisenhower had ruled out mobilization in the earlier Berlin crisis because he felt that limited war or conventional war in Europe was impossible. President Kennedy believed that it was possible, that if we were prepared there could be a "pause" of conventional fighting before the nuclear threshold was reached.

Once the Soviet Union had developed the capacity to strike the United States with nuclear missiles, our nuclear deterrent was no longer credible in a conventional war situation. Khrushchev would be well aware that we would not be willing to initiate a nuclear war—and risk the nuclear devastation of the United States—in response, for example, to a Soviet move against Turkey, or even against Berlin.

A build-up of non-nuclear strength began as soon as

the Kennedy administration took office. President Kennedy's State of the Union Message, his March defense message, and his second State of the Union Message in May, just prior to his European trip, all emphasized new defense measures. His experience in Vienna strengthened his determination to push ahead in both strategic weapons and conventional forces, as well as in the new counter-insurgency techniques. On June 7, 1961, the day after the President's radio-television report on the Vienna meeting, the *Christian Science Monitor* commented:

> He plainly counts on continued Soviet intransigence as displayed at Vienna to convince a somewhat reluctant Congress and the public doubters of the urgency of bolstering new nations against Communist subversion.

Noting that the President had "already established something of a record for warnings to the American public on the perils of the future," the *Monitor*, with amazing prescience, saw foreshadowed in his remarks trends toward higher federal budgets, increased defense spending, a realignment of defense to include more paramilitary capability, probably a resumption of nuclear testing, increased economic and technical assistance to the new nations, long-range foreign economic aid, tightened free-world alliances, continued work for limited arms control with little expectation of success, and increased nuclear offensive and deterrent power.

But the problem of Berlin was far from a pretext for rearming. Its complexities consumed most of the President's time and attention throughout the summer of 1961. The American commitment to Berlin was the symbol, in the eyes of the Germans, of the American commitment to the defense of Europe.

The division of Germany was sealed shortly after the outbreak of the Korean War when Washington, fearful of a Soviet move in Central Europe, determined that a massive military build-up was necessary. The West could hope to match the numbers of Russian divisions in Europe only if Germany's effort were included, and, therefore, in the fall of 1950 Secretary of State Dean Acheson called for the rearmament of Western Germany and for the incorporation of German divisions into NATO. German rearmament was to be made palatable to Germany's World War II victims in Western Europe by putting the West German units under an Allied Command.

The new Federal Republic of Germany, formed out of the three Western occupation zones, grew in political, economic, and military strength in the late 1950's. As it grew, the unspoken threat of the development of an independent West German nuclear force became a lever that Bonn was able to use on American policy in Europe. Some went so far as to suggest that Konrad Adenauer exercised a veto over American policy. While this claim surely overstates the close relationship between Adenauer and John Foster Dulles, a strong "old German hand" faction in the State Department persisted into the Kennedy administration.

As Coral Bell has noted, the most obviously negotiable element in the Western position in Europe is Germany's military contribution to NATO. But from September of 1950 on, Western policy made it clear that this was not to be regarded as a negotiable issue. Since the West was always unwilling to give any ground on this aspect of the issue, proposals for German reunification—the espoused aim of our policy—had a rather tongue-in-cheek quality. It was clear that the precondition, Germany's adherence to the West, was unacceptable to the Soviet Union. As the years passed, the possibility for movement appeared even less real. "The governing concept of what is a legitimate bargain in this field has more and more, since 1955, come to be the German one."[1]

Under President Kennedy, the views of the German Chancellor enjoyed somewhat less weight than they had under the previous administration, but the force of bureaucratic inertia was strong, as the new President was to learn when he came to grips with the Berlin problem.

Khrushchev's *aide-mémoire* of June 4 had repeated in only slightly altered form the Soviet proposals advanced on many occasions over the years for a German peace treaty to be signed with a confederation of the two German states and for a free city status for West Berlin. Khrushchev was, in essence, proposing to pass to East Germany what he said was his legal right to control access to West Berlin. The threat, however, was potential rather than actual. A real crisis would develop only if Khrushchev or East German Communist Party leader Walter Ulbricht actually took physical action to interfere with Allied access.

At that time the proposals offered by each side were as follows:

The Soviets felt that the four powers should persuade the two parts of Germany to form a voluntary confederation on equal terms and that a peace conference should be convened to agree on a treaty with the confederation; this process should take not more than six months. The treaty need not entail, the Soviets claimed, diplomatic recognition of either state; for a certain period both German states could retain NATO and Warsaw Pact forces respectively.

As to Berlin, the Soviets were proposing that West Berlin be converted into a demilitarized free city, guaranteed by the stationing of token contingents of American, British, French, and Soviet troops. The occupation regime would have to be liquidated and the question of access settled with East Germany.

Countering, the West proposed that German reunification should take place on the basis of self-determination of all Germans through free elections. An all-German government should negotiate the final peace treaty, and a reunited Germany should be free to choose its own foreign policy.

As far as Berlin was concerned, the West wanted the whole city reunited within the context of a reunited Germany. During an interim "stand-still" period, minor adjustments could be made in the status quo to meet Soviet grievances about Western propaganda and the size of Western garrisons.

A few months before, in March, President Kennedy had charged Dean Acheson with the task of studying the problems of NATO and Germany and of beginning preparations for meeting a new crisis over Berlin should one arise. Putting the former Secretary of State in charge at such an early stage was probably a mistake. To Acheson, the problem was not Berlin or even Germany or Europe. He saw it as a test of wills with Khrushchev, where the slightest interest in negotiation would be interpreted as a sign of weakness. He therefore counseled a swift, decisive military response. Thus the reliance on Acheson to prepare the groundwork tended to set the whole range of possible actions well toward the side of a hard-line military response rather than toward negotiation.

Arthur Schlesinger defends the choice of Acheson for the job on the grounds that, as the President respected the former Secretary's experience, he was right to avail himself of it before making up his own mind. Yet Theodore Sorensen relates that Kennedy had to wage an uphill struggle all summer against the advocates of the hard line who had gained the upper hand at the outset.[2]

At the time of Harold Macmillan's visit to Washington in April, the British had been disturbed by Acheson's crisp and confident formulation of military countermeasures to any Soviet threat to Berlin. Acheson's plans were at that stage only preliminary; they had not been accepted by the President. But Kennedy remained relatively silent during the meeting with the British, and

Acheson was permitted to dominate the discussion.[3] The
State Department position was that negotiations should be
avoided, since any agreement that might be reached was
bound to be less favorable to American interests than
was the status quo.

Acheson's paper, presented to the President three
weeks after the Vienna conference in early June, contained
an analysis of Khrushchev's motives in laying down the
ultimatum and proposals for an American response to the
Soviet thrust. Acheson felt that behind the façade of formal proposals, behind the threat of the ultimatum,
Khrushchev had five objectives in mind: stabilizing East
Germany and preparing for its eventual recognition and
acceptance by all nations; legitimization of the eastern
frontier of Germany, i.e., the Oder-Neisse line; neutralization of Berlin, which Khrushchev would consider a
first step toward its eventual takeover by East Germany;
weakening of NATO; and discrediting or at least seriously
injuring American prestige.

American real objectives, as Acheson saw them, were:
to detach East Germany from Soviet influence; to help
the nations of Eastern Europe regain some degree of
national identity; and to limit armaments so as to reduce
the chance of successful offensive action by either side in
Europe. Our principal objective in the summer of 1961,
he felt, should be to maintain the status quo in Berlin,
for neither we nor the Soviets could be expected to accept
less.

Acheson next discussed the methods by which the
United States might achieve its objectives in light of the
ultimatum. First, the United States might threaten nuclear action. Acheson felt this would be unwise because
the threat would not be believed. It would be clear to the
Soviets that we would not be prepared to sacrifice New
York or Washington for the maintenance of our rights of
access to Berlin. Another step, one advocated by some
American military leaders, would be a more limited use
of nuclear weapons—that is, the United States might

drop one bomb as a kind of demonstration. Acheson felt that this, too, would be unwise because dropping one bomb would not make the threat more credible, but would remove it altogether.

Rather, Acheson thought, we could convince the Soviets of our determination by making a substantial increase in our forces in Germany. They would then realize that we had made too vast a commitment to back down and would realize that *they* would have to do the backing down. Acheson felt that two or three more American divisions should be sent to Germany and that the reserve should be built up by three to six divisions or more. He also favored a substantial increase in transport capability at short notice.[4]

Acheson's basic thesis disturbed some in the administration, including Adlai Stevenson, who remarked,

> Maybe Dean is right, but his position should be the conclusion of a process of investigation, not the beginning. He starts at a point which we should not reach until we have explored and exhausted all the alternatives.[5]

Even some members of the Berlin task force, the group in the State Department working on the problem, questioned the President's judgment that something dramatically different had happened which upset the balance of forces in the world.[6]

The reaction in the West to the Soviet threat on Berlin fell across a broad spectrum. At one extreme was the feeling that, since Berlin was difficult to defend and since German reunification was unattainable for the time being, the West should by negotiation seek an honorable way out of an untenable position. The British official view leaned in this direction. At the opposite pole was the view, closer to the Acheson view, that the West had an undeniable legal right to be in West Berlin and to waver before the Communist threat to the free world in Berlin would encourage a repetition of it in other places and other circumstances.

On June 15 Khrushchev gave his own report on the Vienna meeting, noting that "a peaceful settlement in Europe must be attained this year."[7] At the same time, Walter Ulbricht stated that after a separate peace had been signed with the Soviet Union, one of the first acts of his government would be to move against the refugee camps in West Berlin. He also threatened to close Templehof Airport in West Berlin. (Eighty percent of East German refugees were flown to the West from Templehof.) Ulbricht also indicated, however, that East Germany was ready to give "realistic guarantees" of continued Allied access by land, air, and water to West Berlin.[8]

President Kennedy, apparently largely on Acheson's advice, appeared to be moving toward a hard-line response, but other voices in Washington called for a new approach. One of these voices was that of Senate Majority Leader Mike Mansfield, an authority on foreign affairs whose views are remarkably free of cold-war strictures. In a speech in the Senate on June 14 Senator Mansfield asked whether there was not some "third way" between the Soviet and Western positions. He noted that the position of the Soviet Union on the Berlin issue, like our own, was essentially unchanged, except with respect to its time schedule, since 1958. Summarizing the difficulties of both sides, Mansfield said,

> We insist, in effect, on the continuance of the status quo in Berlin for the present and presumably until such time as Germany is unified. The Russians are intent upon changing the status quo in a particular fashion in the near future, regardless of the eventual solution of the question of German unification . . .
> I do not think we can safeguard most effectively

our own interests or advance the interests of peace when we insist upon remaining directly under a Communist sword of Damocles, as is now the case in Berlin, if a rational alternative may be found to that position through diplomacy. Further, I have long questioned and I will continue to question a position on Berlin which was assumed immediately after World War II and has been maintained unchanged despite the enormous changes which have occurred in both parts of Germany and in Europe since that time. . . . a position which, through subordinate irresponsibility, error or provocation on either side invites the precipitation of a nuclear conflict.

Mansfield suggested that even if Western rights in the half city were fully guaranteed, this would not be satisfactory, for Berlin as a symbol for unification would still persist. "A third way may lie in the creation of a free city" in all Berlin, to be "held in trust and in peace by some international authority until such time as it is again the capital of Germany." Under this proposal, routes of access would be guaranteed by international peace teams and the interim status of the city would be guaranteed by both NATO and the Warsaw Pact powers. Senator Mansfield concluded that this would be difficult to achieve but he felt that the difficulties arising from pressure for a military solution would be infinitely greater.[9]

Pressure for negotiation came from abroad as well, particularly, to President Kennedy's annoyance, from London. In the wake of the Khrushchev speech, London felt that it was important to reinforce Western solidarity to avoid an error of calculation on the part of the Russians. At the same time, the British felt that the West ought to be ready to negotiate, and that negotiation ought not to be limited to Berlin; rather, it should encompass the whole German problem. Obviously, for tactical reasons and to avoid the appearance of division in the West, the British refused to discuss publicly a negotiating position that suggested any change in the Western attitude. It was not a question of compromising Western rights and rights of access, the Foreign Office indicated, but rather of reaffirming those rights under a new negotiated statute which might be accompanied by Western concessions that could ease Khrushchev's internal position (the British felt the Soviet leader was under serious pressure from hard-line elements in the Kremlin).

Elements of the British Conservative press spoke of the possibility of recognition of the Oder-Neisse line—a position which De Gaulle was also thought to favor. Even the Conservative-minded London *Daily Telegraph* spoke of eventual recognition of East Germany.[10] It was suggested, in addition, that the West might agree not to try to unify Germany by force in return for a Soviet pledge on a new status for Berlin. British sources took care to note, however, that all of these suggestions were speculative and any proposals must be put in accord with French and American policy.

Khrushchev could hardly have been unaware of the state of British public opinion. His main trump card was his conviction that the West would not fight for Berlin. The French newspaper *Le Monde* remarked that lack of British interest was a serious handicap in the Berlin poker game, but that, short of a unilateral Soviet gambit, nothing was likely to stir it.[11]

There was some impatience in the White House too, at what was considered to be British foot-dragging. The British were not sufficiently militant, it was felt; they were too interested in negotiation, not willing enough to consider the use of force. Sorensen notes that from time to time "The President had to discourage the Prime Minister's temptation to play the role of peacemaker between East and West."[12]

(The French were opposed to any negotiations. De

Gaulle thought that Khrushchev was bluffing, that if the Russians had wanted war over Berlin it would have already come. The Germans were somewhat fearful as they sensed that their influence in Washington had diminished.)

While the debate continued, the State Department laboriously ground out a reply to the Khrushchev *aide-mémoire* of June 4. This project, which to the disgust of the White House consumed over six weeks, resulted in a lengthy, tedious, and uninspired document filled with cold-war clichés. In such cases, the most important criterion in the bureaucracy is to ensure that the new document is in perfect compatibility with all that has been said on the subject in the past; thus any new or fresh ideas are inevitably edited out in the process of clearance within the government. The President, discouraged, was tempted to throw it out and have them start over, but, when advised that this would require repeating the whole tortuous process of inter-agency and Allied clearance, he decided to issue the document anyway. At the same time, on July 19, he issued a White House summary which stated the American position more succinctly.

It presented what the President felt was the "irrefutable legal, moral and political position" of the United States:

> Today there is peace in Berlin, in Germany and in Europe. If peace is destroyed by the unilateral actions of the Soviet Union, its leaders will bear a heavy responsibility before world opinion and history.
>
> Today the people of West Berlin are free. . . .
>
> Today the continued presence in West Berlin of the United States, the United Kingdom and France is by clear legal right, arising from war, acknowledged in many agreements signed by the Soviet Union, and strongly supported by the overwhelming majority of

the people of that city. Their freedom is dependent upon our exercise of these rights—an exercise which is thus a political and moral obligation as well as a legal right. Inasmuch as these rights, including the right of access to Berlin, are not held from the Soviet Government, they cannot be ended by any unilateral action of the Soviet Union. . . .

While the United States has consistently sought a "just and comprehensive peace treaty for all of Germany," the President continued, the Soviet Union has blocked progress toward that goal and "has instead repeatedly heightened world tensions over this issue."

In his press conference of June 28, President Kennedy called the Berlin crisis "Soviet-manufactured." Yet he hardly attempted to downgrade its importance:

It is of the greatest importance that the American people understand the basic issues involved and the threats to the peace and security of Europe and of ourselves posed by the Soviet announcement that they intend to change unilaterally the existing arrangements for Berlin.

On July 8, Khrushchev announced that he had ordered a suspension of proposed reductions in the Soviet armed forces and gave notice of a three-billion-ruble increase in the current defense ceiling. He cited the Western military build-up, especially the increases in the American defense budget. He noted particularly the increase in the number of strategic nuclear bombers constantly kept in the air ready for action. He cited President Kennedy's "so-called 'new course'" in recent defense messages:

It provides for stepping up the program of developing rocket-missile strategic weapons, and the raising of military readiness of all services.

For this purpose President Kennedy has proposed to increase military allocations as compared with the

draft budget submitted by the previous President by
more than $3,500,000,000. . . . This is how the Western
powers are replying to the Soviet Union's unilateral
reduction of armed forces and military spending conducted for several past years.[13]

Discussion continued within the administration, It
was argued that the President ought to order calling up the
reserves and declare a state of national emergency. This
would mean an increase in the defense budget of some $5
billion and probably a tax increase. Those, including Acheson, who supported the proclamation of a national emergency argued that only such drastic measures would have
enough psychological effect on Khrushchev to cause him
to back down. The State Department, where the "old German hands" prevailed, continued to oppose negotiation.
The President initially favored the idea of a tax increase,
but the projected increase in defense spending for the
build-up turned out to be smaller than had been anticipated and it was finally decided that no tax increase would
be needed. The proposed national-emergency proclamation
was abandoned as being too alarmist.

By July 23 the general tenor of the American response
had become clear. James Reston of *The New York Times*
reported on that day that the President had decided on a
step-by-step plan to increase the political, economic, and
military strength of the Western alliance. Although inspired by the Soviet threat to Berlin, Reston wrote,

> it is understood that the new plan is not directed
> primarily at the defense of the former German capital
> but at improving the ability of the Western Allies to
> wage all kinds of war in any part of the world. . . .
> What is envisaged now is the strengthening of the
> Western forces so that they could make an effective
> stand in a limited area and test the intentions of the
> Communist troops with conventional weapons before
> it was decided whether it was absolutely essential to
> use nuclear weapons.

The President had made the decision to proceed with partial mobilization and a considerable defense build-up, but he stopped short of the most extreme proposals of his advisers. The build-up fitted in with his general plans to increase conventional as well as strategic capability. In addition, the state of the American economy at the time made some pump-priming desirable, yet, for political reasons, a tax cut and increased public welfare spending had been ruled out. As one writer has put it:

> Congress has frequently refused to enact presidential proposals for pump-priming expenditures designed to invigorate a slumping economy, but since World War II it has seldom seriously challenged requests for additional funds to bolster national security. Thus in 1961 Kennedy used the Berlin crisis to justify a sizeable increase in military spending. His action had a double purpose: to strengthen America's position in its cold war confrontation with the Soviet Union, and, he hoped, to stimulate business and relieve unemployment.[14]

While it did not close the door on the possibility of negotiations, the President's address to the nation on July 25 outlining his response to the Berlin crisis was generally regarded as belligerent. From its tone, it seems clear that Kennedy accepted the Acheson thesis of the test of wills while rejecting some aspects of the Acheson program. The President is reported to have told James Wechsler of the *New York Post,* "If Khrushchev wants to rub my nose in the dirt, it's all over."[15] He may have felt, in addition, that, having had to scale down earlier American objectives in Laos, he needed all the more to make a strong stand.

West Berlin, he told the American people, had become "The great testing place of Western courage and will. . . ." To waver would bring our resolution into question.

> We must meet our oft-stated pledge to the free peoples of West Berlin—and maintain our rights and their safety, even in the face of force—in order to maintain the confidence of other free peoples in our word and our resolve.

He acknowledged that the new measures he was proposing were a response to a wider threat, not just to the pressure against Berlin.

> The new preparations that we shall make to defend the peace are part of the long-term build-up in our strength which has been underway since January. They are based on our needs to meet a world-wide threat, on a basis which stretches far beyond the present Berlin crisis. . . . We need the capability of placing in any critical area at the appropriate time a force which, combined with those of our allies, is large enough to make clear our determination and our ability to defend our rights at all costs—and to meet all levels of aggressor pressure with whatever levels of force are required. We intend to have a wider choice than humiliation or all-out nuclear confrontation.

He requested a $3.2 billion increase in appropriations for the armed forces; an increase in the Army's total strength from 875,000 to one million; increases of 29,000 and 63,000 in the active-duty strengths of the Navy and Air Force; the doubling and tripling of draft calls; and authority to activate certain ready reserve units and to extend tours of duty.

Perhaps most sobering of all, he called for a massive fallout-shelter program—in essence, preparing the people for nuclear war while attempting to give the impression that victory somehow was possible. "In the event of an attack, the lives of those families which are not hit in a nuclear blast and fire can still be saved—*if* they can be warned to take shelter and *if* that shelter is available," he claimed, passing over the massive problems other than blast and fire which would arise in the wake of a nuclear attack and which make any real survival problematic.

These ill-advised remarks marked the beginning of the idea of "thinking the unthinkable," toward which American strategy later moved. No longer would we be concerned primarily—if we ever were—to deter nuclear war; instead, we would begin to think in terms of "damage limitation" and of techniques for survival in the nuclear environment, techniques whose development would permit us to take greater risks in diplomacy.

As a result of President Kennedy's remarks, many Americans began frantically building and stocking fallout shelters in their backyards, and the fallout-shelter industry boomed overnight. The British press noted that American war hysteria over Berlin had brought "a rush of business to the vast network of salt mines beneath Hutchinson, Kansas, with banks, insurance companies, etc., storing their records against nuclear attack."[16]

Reactions within the United States to President Kennedy's proposals for a build-up were favorable and, in some cases, enthusiastic. Congress promptly voted the necessary increase in funds and authority for the reserve call-up. There was some expression of relief that the proposals were in a relatively low key, mainly because it was known that some of the President's advisers had wanted to go much further.

Abroad, response was mixed. France was preoccupied with problems in Tunisia. But, in general, the British were prepared to go along. Macmillan had issued a strong statement on July 1:

> We in the West have always been willing to talk about the future of Germany. . . . But the fact of our right to be in Berlin cannot be in question.
> We have not forgotten the lessons learned so

painfully in the 1930s and we are not prepared to accept acts of force. Let there be no mistake. This is an issue on which the people of the Western world are resolute. It is a principle which we will defend.[17]

While treading softly, the British were prepared to be as firm as anyone else over Western rights in Berlin. They believed, however, that it would not be helpful to make an excessive public fuss about the military aspects of a possible crisis. The British felt strongly that progress on the political front was a far more urgent matter than military contingency planning; theirs was the opposite of the American view of priorities. But British military planning went forward anyway. The British Army of the Rhine would be brought up to full strength by canceling leaves, and, as a second step, warning notices would be sent to men of the first reserve. A third step would be to call up the territorial reserve in the late summer, when in any case many of them would be doing their annual training.

But the British had some reservations about American policy. They noted the President's assumption that while Berlin was the immediate target, the threat was world-wide. They were more inclined to view the situation in terms of the problems of East Germany. While there was general approval of some choice between "thermo-nuclear cataclysm and spineless surrender," as *The Sunday Times* put it:

It is pointless to pretend . . . that this thesis, which has for years been at the heart of NATO's strategy, can be applied to Berlin at this moment. To begin with, there is no certainty—indeed, it is exceedingly unlikely—that when and if Mr. Khrushchev signs a separate treaty with the Ulbricht regime, either the Russians or the East Germans will act in such a way in Berlin as to constitute a clearly identifiable *casus belli*.[18]

The British Foreign Office also was anxious to get negotiations under way for fear that the manpower drain from East Germany through Berlin might become so great that East Germany would be obliged to halt it, possibly precipitating another uprising which might lead to Soviet intervention.

This possibility does not appear to have occurred to the White House, the State Department, or the Pentagon, for, by all accounts, American policy-makers were caught completely off guard by the erection of the Berlin Wall beginning on August 13.

But there were voices in Washington that lamented the failure of the Kennedy administration to move into negotiations simultaneously with the military build-up. Senator J. W. Fulbright told a national television audience on July 30, "I think we have been remiss in not making proposals that would give some opportunity for negotiation. I think there are alternatives and I don't think we have been as aggressive in suggesting them as we should be." Fulbright saw as the alternative a different status for Central Europe and possibly disengagement; he thought Senator Mansfield's proposal was a step in the right direction. Fulbright decried the tendency to suggest that any willingness to negotiate would be interpreted as weakness. "I do not so interpret it," he said.

> I believe in negotiation and discussion as opposed to ultimatums and showdowns as a general approach. One thing that bothers me is the idea that we cannot afford to talk and negotiate. . . . This seems inconsistent with our whole philosophy of life, of politics, both national and international. . . . I think it is too bad that anyone who suggests we discuss these problems is immediately said to be an appeaser, that you are getting ready to give up something or that you are going to compromise—it is going to be a Munich.

Senator Fulbright also wondered why the East Germans did not stop the crossings into the West, since it was clearly within their power to do so. "I confess it is a mystery that the East Germans don't stop the emigration of these people. I don't know why they don't."[19]

Once his military build-up was launched, President Kennedy did begin to move to get negotiations started. Dean Rusk was sent to Paris early in August to work out an agreed Allied negotiating position. It was hoped that there would be sufficient agreement so that the Soviet Union could be invited to a four-power conference, but there was no definite American proposal for a conference. The British favored the idea and the Germans were receptive, but the French opposed it.

There the situation rested and Rusk returned from Europe without agreement. Then on August 13 the Soviets made the move to which the West was least able to respond; they began closing off East Berlin from the West. Within a few days a concrete wall had been built and traffic between the two halves of the city ceased.

Washington was stunned. Despite months of planning for—they thought—every possible move that Khrushchev might make and working out every possible response, none of the contingency plans were prepared to deal with the dropping of the Iron Curtain down in the heart of Berlin.

The people of West Berlin pleaded for action to tear down the Wall as it was being erected. Arthur Schlesinger notes that "Kennedy, remarking that there was one chance out of five for a nuclear exchange, instantly mobilized the resources of government."[20] But since the action had taken place within East Berlin, and since it did not interfere with Western rights in West Berlin or with access to the city, it was clearly not a *casus belli*. Four days later the United States, Britain, and France sent identical notes of protest, which were promptly rejected.

Finally, after frantic, round-the-clock meetings in Washington, a symbolic action was decided upon. Fifteen hundred American troops were to be sent across East Germany along the Helmstedt-Berlin autobahn in armored vehicles. And Vice President Lyndon Johnson was to go to Berlin to bolster morale. With him would go retired General Lucius Clay, who had commanded U.S. forces during the Berlin airlift in 1948–49 and who was a symbol to Berliners of American steadfastness.

The sealing of East Berlin and the inability of the West to respond aroused disgruntled and resentful feelings among West Berliners. In London, *The Sunday Times* remarked that the Wall had "produced the worst drop in Western prestige since the war. . . . There is an outspoken contempt for the West which has shocked and alarmed officials" in Berlin.[21] Twenty Bonn undergraduates, incensed at the lack of pugnacity in the Western response, sent President Kennedy an umbrella.[22]

Some felt that President Kennedy should have ordered American troops to move into East Berlin and tear down the Wall as soon as it was built. But then it would have been rebuilt fifty yards farther back and, if necessary, another fifty yards, and another. The question then becomes: Are we prepared to go to war with the Soviet Union, not over the freedom of West Berlin, where we have long-standing obligations, but over the right of the Soviet and East German governments to control the flight of East Germans from East Berlin? However morally offensive and reprehensible the Wall might be, no vital American or Western interest was threatened, and thus it was clearly not a matter which could justify war with Russia.

Mansfield and others continued to press for negotiations and urged Khrushchev to be more specific about how our rights in the city would be protected if the situation in West Berlin were to change.

But, still bound by the outlook and tactics of the cold war, President Kennedy failed to seek a new accomodation, a new modus vivendi appropriate to the changed situation in Central Europe sixteen years after the end of the war. The real question was: How far was the West prepared to go toward recognition of the political realities in Central Europe? Would we, in exchange for some kind of guarantee of Berlin, acknowledge the existence of East Germany and recognize the Oder-Neisse line, thereby abandoning what was essentially the lip service we had been paying to the idea of reunification? American policy was no more prepared under Kennedy than it had been under Eisenhower and Dulles to seize the opportunity or really even to explore it. Hope of progress was sacrificed to the myth of reunification, as had been the case so often in the past.

Finally, the crisis abated as the flow of East German refugees was cut off and the immediate threat to the viability of the East German regime was ended. For Khrushchev the most pressing problem was solved with the erection of the Wall. And the United States, after some saber rattling, was left no course but confused retreat.

Because President Kennedy chose confrontation instead of negotiation, he risked much and gained little; and he lost greatly in terms of prestige. The Wall would not yield to military threats; it could be removed only by negotiation.

Khrushchev finally withdrew the Berlin ultimatum, as he had his previous threats over Berlin. The Soviet leader did not need to heed public opinion and could pull back from a position as he had done on several previous occasions. An American President, on the other hand, must not only pay attention to public opinion in his own country; he must also, if he is to act within our national tradition, have some respect for "the decent opinion of mankind." Thus, as *Le Monde* noted, Kennedy could not permit himself to draw back or seem to shy away once having gone to the brink "without his prestige, already greatly shaken by Cuba and Laos, suffering a decisive blow."[23] Protection of the personal prestige of the President, an enduring theme of the Kennedy administration, severely circumscribed the government's response to challenges, and this lack of flexibility was to bring the world to the brink of nuclear war a year later.

Five | Was the Cuban Missile Crisis Necessary?

In October of 1962, in order to force Soviet missiles off the island of Cuba, John F. Kennedy risked a nuclear war that might have meant the destruction of all life on earth.

President Kennedy's handling of the Cuban missile crisis is generally considered to be the greatest triumph of his Presidency. It is often described as courageous in its firmness and brilliant in its measured application of force. The crisis has frequently been called a psychological watershed in Soviet-American relations. It has been said that a new era of détente dawned because both sides went to the brink and looked into the abyss.

The world survived the "thirteen days." Only later did it begin to ask: Was it worth it? Did it have to be?

On October 22, 1962, President Kennedy delivered a public ultimatum to the Soviet Union. During the next few days, as the world seemed to teeter on the edge of nuclear destruction, he kept careful control of all of the characters and elements on the American side of the drama. His restraint in not invading or bombing Cuba has been praised, but many have forgotten, in the flush of success and relief from danger, that Kennedy was determined to force Khrushchev's total capitulation—no matter the cost.

The Russians, who probably never intended or expected war, backed down. But the basic question remains: Was President Kennedy justified in risking a nuclear holocaust?

In his note to Robert F. Kennedy's account of the crisis, Theodore Sorensen has written:

> It was Senator Kennedy's intention to add a discussion [to his book] of the basic ethical question involved: what, if any, circumstance or justification gives this government or any government the moral right to bring its people and possibly all people under the shadow of nuclear destruction?[1]

The loss to history of Robert Kennedy's reflections on the fundamental ethical issue, the issue that was apparently not considered by anyone at the time, deepens the tragedy of his death.

By all accounts, President Kennedy never considered any course other than military confrontation. When he learned of the missiles on the morning of October 16, his immediate reaction was that they must be removed.[2] From the first, he sought unconditional surrender and he never deviated from that objective. The deliberations of the National Security Council's Executive Committee (Ex Comm), the group of officials who met almost continuously during the thirteen days of the crisis, have been described by several participants. But the Ex Comm did not make or recommend the basic decision; they were concerned only with carrying out the President's decision. They debated whether a blockade or an air strike or an invasion would achieve the President's objective most efficiently and at the least cost. The objective itself was never seriously questioned.

According to Robert Kennedy, during the first five days after the discovery of the missiles, more time was spent discussing the "moral question" of whether the United States should launch a surprise attack against Cuba than any other matter.[3] Some of the Ex Comm members felt that the missiles in Cuba did not increase the strategic threat to the United States. Yet, with one exception, they all thought and planned exclusively in terms of a military confrontation to force them out.

Only one official, Adlai Stevenson—and he was not even a regular member of the Ex Comm—appears to have viewed the situation with something resembling historical perspective. Instead of an ultimatum and a military confrontation, Stevenson suggested a political solution. His proposal was instantly rejected by Kennedy, although Kennedy had assumed office with the words "Let us never fear to negotiate."

Although the Cuban missile crisis has been described at length by participants and by close observers, and analyzed by scholars, most accounts concentrate on the thirteen days following the discovery of the missiles. Less attention has been paid to the events leading up to the crisis, to the factors that led President Kennedy to his fateful decision to bring about a military confrontation.

Since midsummer of 1962, reports had been coming into Washington that Soviet arms and troops were landing in Cuba. Many of these reports originated with Cuban exile groups and were treated with suspicion by American intelligence. As one State Department official put it:

> Most of the Cuban exiles, in my judgment, spent a great deal of their waking hours trying to figure out ways to create incidents that would make it difficult for the United States not to become involved in some kind of military action against Cuba.[4]

Badly burned once by faulty intelligence on Cuba, the Kennedy administration was understandably cautious. It relied on two principal sources of information. The first, reports of agents in Cuba and of Cuban refugees, suffered a time lag in reaching Washington, and in the case of the refugee reports, were difficult to evaluate. The second, more reliable source of information was U-2 photographs, photographs of such high resolution that from a height of nearly fourteen miles one could make out the painted lines on a parking lot.

On August 24, 1962, in a background briefing for the press, Roger Hilsman, State Department chief of intelligence, confirmed that Soviet shipments of military equipment and technical personnel to Cuba had increased. The Soviet personnel, apparently military technicians although not in uniform, numbered between three and five thousand. Hilsman said he doubted that the Soviet arms supplied were sufficient for an offensive capacity against the United States.[5]

The next day, August 25, a Cuban exile student group based in Miami raided the Cuban coast and, according to Castro's claims, damaged a hotel in which Soviet technicians were housed. The U.S. Justice Department warned the exiles against further violations of the neutrality laws, but no arrests were made.

On August 28 Republican Senator Homer Capehart of Indiana, locked in a tough reelection battle,[6] charged that Soviet combat troops were in Cuba and he demanded that President Kennedy order an immediate invasion of the island. Responding the following day in a press conference, the President denied Capehart's charges and defended his policy of isolating Cuba. He opposed an invasion "now," he said, because he doubted that the Soviet personnel in Cuba were combat troops.

Then, on August 31, an American attack bomber, on what the White House described as a training mission fifteen miles off the Cuban coast, was fired upon by what appeared to be Cuban vessels. Washington sent a strong protest to Havana and the White House announced that henceforth, if attacked, American planes would return the fire.

On the same day, Republican Senator Kenneth Keating of New York took the floor of the Senate to claim that, in addition to military equipment, twelve hundred Soviet troops in uniform had been sent to Cuba. "More ominous reports suggest," Keating continued, "that the Soviets are constructing missile bases and sending over technicians and experts to man them." But Keating's speech did not emphasize a possible threat to the national security from these missile bases. What he claimed was that the Soviets probably intended to interfere electronically with American space activities at Cape Canaveral, thereby sabotaging the American effort to be first on the moon. Keating said,

> On July 27 the unholy alliance between Castro's Cuba and the Soviet Union took its most serious turn. Between July 27 and August 15 their joint activities have been coordinated in an alarming way, which poses a serious threat to the security of the Western Hemisphere.
>
> So far no action has been taken by our Government. The President has said that he has no evidence of Soviet troops in Cuba. If he has no evidence, I am giving him evidence this afternoon.[7]

But Keating presented no evidence other than his own statement.

From the end of August on, the situation in Cuba was daily front-page news in most major American newspapers. Intense Congressional pressure mounted against the possibility of a Soviet offensive military build-up, and President Kennedy, forced to defend his policy of "inaction" against Republican criticism, became more and more precise in his public statements as to what the United States would and would not tolerate.

On September 2, during Che Guevara's visit to Moscow, the Soviets announced that they had agreed to supply arms and technicians to train Cuban forces to meet aggressive imperialism. American officials denied that the agreement contained anything new and they viewed it as a modernization of Cuban forces. But Senator Keating attacked the administration's "do-nothing policy" and Senator Strom Thurmond of South Carolina called for an invasion of Cuba. On September 4, Keating claimed that Soviet troops in Cuba numbered five thousand. While "they are sometimes spoken of as technicians," he said, "they are what are used as armed forces in the U.S. Army."[8] (An ironic parallel with American "advisers" in Southeast Asia.)

President Kennedy found himself caught between Cuban charges that he was planning an invasion of Cuba and rising Congressional demands that he do just that. In an attempt to head off further Congressional criticism, he conferred with Congressional leaders on September 4 and afterward issued a statement confirming the introduction of anti-aircraft defense missiles, radar, and other electronic equipment as well as technicians. Then he added,

> There is no evidence of any organized combat force in Cuba from any Soviet bloc country; of military bases provided to Russia; of a violation of the 1934 treaty relating to Guantanamo; of the presence of offensive ground-to-ground missiles; or of other significant offensive capability either in Cuban hands or under Soviet direction and guidance. Were it to be otherwise, the gravest issues would arise.[9]

Although Senate Minority Leader Everett Dirksen denied that the Republicans were making the Soviet build-up in Cuba a campaign issue and former President Eisenhower said that neither Cuba or any other foreign policy question should be a partisan issue during the campaign, the Republican attack continued. Senator Alexander Wiley of Wisconsin, the ranking Republican on the Senate Foreign Relations Committee, joined in. "Militarily," said Wiley in the Senate on September 5,

> Cuba represents no serious threat to the United States, for it could be snuffed out in a matter of minutes. The real danger, however, lies in the attempted re-export of armaments to other countries in Latin America; provocations—such as the firing on the U.S. naval training plane—disturbing the peace; and a general uneasiness with the existence of an alien, armed, wishfully aggressive Cuba in the Western Hemisphere.[10]

Later that day, Democratic Senator Clair Engle of California provided a detailed defense of Kennedy's policy, asserting that the administration had been telling the American people the whole truth, in spite of Senator Keating's claims to the contrary. Engle maintained that as long as the Soviet equipment in Cuba was defensive, it posed no threat. He continued:

> On the other hand, if ground-to-ground missiles are put in place in Cuba they could deliver a nuclear warhead against targets in the United States. I think it is clear that in that event we must take action immediately. I believe that the Cuban Government, and the Soviets, too, ought to be put on notice that if ground-to-ground missiles capable of carrying nuclear warheads are put in place in Cuba, we intend to move to take them out.[11]

In the House, a blockade of Communist munitions and manpower was proposed. Democratic Representative Dante Fascell of Florida claimed that a Soviet missile base existed in Cuba and called for military action against Castro. President Kennedy's statement after the Bay of Pigs that the inter-American policy of nonintervention must not be permitted to conceal or excuse a policy of inaction was thrown back at him.[12] In these Congressional calls for action, the treaty commitment of the United States under the OAS Charter not to interfere, militarily or otherwise, in the affairs of any other American state was ignored or it was declared that the national interest demanded action in spite of the treaty.

The influential Knight newspaper chain took up the cry in a *Miami Herald* editorial asking how long the United States was to stand by and watch Cuba becoming a base for communism in Latin America. It asked whether Kennedy intended to permit Soviet rocket and missile bases ninety miles from our shores.

> For people will not long understand why U.S. troops are sent to root out Communist guerrillas in South Vietnam when we do nothing to prevent the Russians from taking over Cuba.[13]

Secretary of State Dean Rusk told the press on September 5 that the United States was determined to block the spread of communism from Cuba to the rest of the Americas. Rusk, McNamara, and General Charles P. Cabell, deputy director of the CIA, briefed Congressional committees on the situation in Cuba, and Senate Majority Leader Mansfield expressed the hope that the Republicans would keep the Cuba issue out of politics.

But Republican Senator James Pearson of Kansas condemned the administration's failure to challenge Soviet military aid to Cuba.

> It is a painful paradox to recall American military intervention in South Korea, Lebanon, and the Dominican Republic, and to observe current action in South Vietnam, Laos and Thailand, while we verbally sidestep the Soviet takeover of Cuba at our very doorstep.[14]

On September 7, the dean of the Senate Republicans, Senator Alexander Wiley of Wisconsin, made a reasoned appeal for calm. Wiley told the Senate that he had that morning received a letter asking why we did not "go in and knock the blazes out of Cuba?" He continued,

> There is even condemnation of the President. I do not agree with that condemnation. I feel we must use common sense and use reason and judgment. If we got into a war, we do not know whether it would start a universal blaze or whether it could be kept local. In my opinion, in view of the fact that Cuba is more or less a satellite of the Soviet Government, it would probably precipitate a third world war. That we must not have.[15]

Partisan criticism then subsided briefly when Senator Dirksen and Representative Charles Halleck, Republican Senate and House leaders, urged calm, although they tempered their remarks with warnings against inaction. Dirksen and Halleck also urged passage of a Congressional resolution authorizing the President to use American troops if needed.

The Republican proposal for a resolution posed a problem for President Kennedy. There was little he could do about Cuba, yet passage of such a resolution would virtually force him to act. In addition, and perhaps most important in this political year, its adoption would appear to give the Republicans the initiative on the issue. Therefore, on September 7, he took his own step, asking Congress for stand-by authority to call up 150,000 members of the ready reserve to active duty for not more than twelve months.

The press continued to carry reports, largely from exile sources, of the deployment of Soviet troops in Cuba and of missile bases. But, as Tad Szulc of *The New York Times* noted on September 9, the problem of the Cuban build-up was "more political than military." Szulc wrote that the embarrassment lay in the fact that the Soviet Union had established a military presence in Cuba, "with all the unfavorable implications for United States prestige reflected in this act of defiance."

The attacks continued. Republican Senator Karl Mundt, a member of the Foreign Relations Committee, urged an immediate air and naval blockade of Cuba; the National Maritime Union threatened a world-wide shipping boycott against Cuba. Alpha 66, a Cuban exile organization apparently based in Miami, raided the Cuban coast and machine-gunned ships loading sugar. On September 11 the Soviet government announced that an attack on Cuba, or upon Soviet ships bound for Cuba, would mean a nuclear war.

President Kennedy replied to this Soviet threat in his news conference of September 13. He reiterated that the build-up in Cuba was under "our most careful surveillance," but that the new shipments were not a serious threat. He warned,

> If at any time the Communist build-up in Cuba were to endanger or interfere with our security in any way, including our base at Guantanamo, our passage to the Panama Canal, our missile and space activities at Cape Canaveral, or the lives of American citizens in this country, or if Cuba should ever attempt to export its aggressive purposes by force or threat of force against any nation in this hemisphere, or become an offensive military base of significant capacity for the Soviet Union, then this country will do whatever must be done to protect its own security and that of its allies. . . . As President and Commander in Chief I have full authority now to take such action. . . .

This was the President's most detailed elaboration of the conditions the United States would find intolerable.

The political hue and cry continued. Senator Barry Goldwater assailed the Kennedy "do-nothing policy," and Senate Republicans tried to add a military warning to Cuba to the bill authorizing the reserve call-up.

In his *New York Times* column of September 16, James Reston took note of the increasing calls for a blockade of Cuba, pointing out that since a blockade was an act of war, it could be established formally only by declaring war on Cuba. Reston asked whether the senators who were calling for a blockade would be willing to blow up the ships of our allies if they resisted. Reston also brought up the American missile bases in Turkey which were aimed at the Soviet Union, and asked what the United States would do if, in retaliation, the Russians should blockade our arms shipments to Turkey. The purpose of a blockade, said Reston, "is to make the enemy surrender."

The matter of the bases in Turkey was also raised in the Senate during the debate on the Cuba resolution. Senator Dennis Chavez of New Mexico asked how we could justify saying that we objected to the Soviets' having a base in Cuba ninety miles from our shores when we had a base in Turkey only sixty miles from their frontier. In an outstanding example of the double standard of judgment that characterized American policy—and which persists to this day—Senator John Sparkman, who reported the resolution from the Foreign Relations and Armed Services committees, replied,

> Our answer is that we are in positions near the Russian borders purely for the purpose of protecting our own national security in conjunction with our allies. We have the base in Turkey, for example, at the request of the Turkish Government. We certainly have no aggressive purpose in being there. We are not trying to subvert the Turkish Government or to install our system of government there. We are working with the Turkish Government, at its invitation and on a defensive basis, not on an offensive basis.[16]

The Soviet government could and indeed did claim the same purity of motive with respect to its aims in Cuba.

Walter Lippmann noted that we could not act against Cuba by invasion for

> we would have acted on the rule that a possible threat against our security or our interests justifies us in going to war. . . . We cannot go to war even against Castro because of what he may conceivably do in the future. . . . We cannot wage a preventive war against Castro without establishing the rule that a preventive war is legitimate against our military position in Berlin, Turkey, Iran, Pakistan, Thailand, South Vietnam, Taiwan, Okinawa, South Korea, and Japan.

Lippmann recalled that the American claim in the Monroe Doctrine for isolation of the Western Hemisphere was coupled with a renunciation of American interest in the Eastern Hemisphere. "We cannot invoke the Monroe Doctrine without meeting the question of what we are doing all over Europe and Asia."[17]

The Cuba resolution passed the Senate on September 20 by a vote of 86 to 1—Senator Winston Prouty voted no because he felt the resolution did not go far enough—and the House on September 26 by a vote of 384 to 7. It expressed American determination

> to prevent by whatever means may be necessary, including the use of arms, the Marxist-Leninist regime in Cuba from extending by force or threat of force, its aggressive or subversive activities to any part of this hemisphere.

The resolution also stated that the United States was determined to prevent in Cuba "the creation or use of an externally supported military capability endangering the security of the United States."

With the passage of the resolution, Democratic leaders in both the House and Senate denounced jingoistic speeches which, in the words of Representative Emanuel

Celler, "would lead us down the way to war—thermonuclear war."

President Kennedy made it clear that he felt that his powers were sufficient to handle the situation in Cuba without Congressional action, but he felt that the resolution afforded an opportunity for the Congress to let off steam.

Even the passage of the resolution did not quiet the furor completely. At a secret House Republican caucus during the last week in September, the Cuba issue was unanimously described as "the biggest Republican asset" in the coming election.[18] And in late September the *Congressional Quarterly* asked a number of U.S. editors and members of Congress to select the five top issues of the election campaign in their areas. The 208 congressmen and 348 editors from all parts of the nation who replied mentioned Cuba as an issue far more than any other. A *New York Times* analysis on October 14 expressed the opinion that of all the election issues Cuba "appeared likely to sway the most voters."

On October 10, Senator Keating challenged the administration to deny that there were intermediate-range missile bases in Cuba, saying that

> Construction has begun on at least a half dozen launching sites for intermediate range tactical missiles.[19]

But Keating's charges, which came late in the day, caused no immediate reaction either in the Senate or in the press.

Indeed, in spite of the attention paid to Cuba in the press, opinion polls in mid-October showed that the public was not greatly alarmed. The October 13 Gallup Poll noted that "contrary to impressions in some quarters, the American people are no more 'invasion-minded' about Castro's Cuba today then they were immediately after the Bay of Pigs episode." Only one out of four favored sending U.S. armed forces into Cuba, and better than six out of

ten opposed such a move. But the public was far from complacent, for only one out of five favored a hands-off policy.
People were asked what action we should take in regard
to Cuba now, taking everything into account. Ten percent
thought the United States should bomb or invade or carry
out some other belligerent act; 13 percent favored a trade
embargo; 26 percent thought we ought to do something
short of war; and 22 percent thought we should keep
hands off.[20]

Another Gallup Poll, on October 17, showed that fear
of all-out war with Russia deterred people from supporting
the invasion of Cuba: 51 percent thought that if we sent
an invasion force, it would bring war with Russia; 37
percent did not. Among those who felt all-out war with
Russia would be likely if we invaded, 19 percent felt we
should invade anyway, but 69 percent thought we should
not. Even among those who thought it was unlikely that
invasion would bring war, only 36 percent favored invasion
anyway, while 57 percent were opposed.[21]

Such was the state of American public and Congressional opinion in mid-October.

U-2 surveillance of Cuba had been increased during
September. Photographs revealed that batteries of surface-
to-air missiles (SAMs), like those the Soviets had already
supplied to Iraq and Indonesia, were being installed in
several locations on the island. These air-defense missiles
increased the risk of U-2 flights over Cuba. A Soviet SAM
had brought down U-2 pilot Gary Powers over Soviet
territory in 1960. Should a U-2 be shot down over Cuba,
it was feared, the resulting uproar might force the United
States to renounce further intrusions into Cuban airspace,
as had been the case after the Powers incident. U.S. intelligence would then be severely hampered in its effort to
follow the arms build-up.

At a special intelligence meeting on October 4 it was
noted that one area of western Cuba where SAMs were

being installed, the area around San Cristóbal and Guanajay, had not been photographed in nearly a month. A special flight plan, thought to minimize the danger to the U-2, was prepared for the San Cristóbal-Guanajay area and it was approved by the President on October 10.

Poor weather delayed the flight until the 14th. Photographs from the flight were processed and analyzed on Monday, October 15, and by early evening of that day the results were certain. Soviet medium-range missile installations were under construction at San Cristóbal. Along with the beginnings of the construction work, the photographs clearly showed missile trailers, erector-launcher vehicles, fuel trucks, and radar trucks in the surrounding area.

While news of the discovery was quickly communicated to top administration officials, McGeorge Bundy, the President's National Security adviser, decided not to notify the President that night. He knew that Kennedy would immediately ask to see the evidence and that it would take all night to prepare the material for presentation to him. Bundy later wrote the President that his decision to wait until morning was also influenced by his fear that a hastily called meeting in the middle of the night would arouse suspicion and put the Soviets on alert. The President had just returned to Washington at 1:40 Monday morning from a strenuous weekend of campaigning, and Bundy reasoned that a good night's rest would be the best preparation he could have for the crisis. "What help would it be to you," he later wrote the President, "to give you this piece of news and then tell you nothing could be done about it till morning."[22]

After a detailed briefing by the CIA on Tuesday morning, Bundy went to the White House around nine to inform the President who was still in his bedroom with the morning papers. It is clear from public accounts that the President's initial reaction was that which guided his conduct in the weeks ahead. The Soviets had repeatedly assured him that they would not introduce offensive weapons into Cuba, and he was surprised and angered at Khrushchev's deceit. "Privately," writes Arthur Schlesinger, "he was furious."[23]

From the outset, President Kennedy was determined to remove the missiles by one means or another. From the first, he appears to have been convinced that a confrontation was necessary, that some limited warlike action was required. An adviser who saw him later that day felt that there was no doubt in the President's mind that the United States would have to act to remove the bases.[24] The question was not, "Should it be done?" The question was, "How should it be done?"

Robert Kennedy has written:

> He knew he would have to act. The U.S. could not accept what the Russians had done. What that action would be was still to be determined. But he was convinced from the beginning that he would have to do something.[25]

Later in the morning, in the White House Cabinet Room, the top officials of the government met to consider what course of action the United States should take. That meeting continued regularly night and day for the next thirteen days and the group met daily for some six weeks. This group of officials, which the press later dubbed the Ex Comm (Executive Committee of the National Security Council), included Robert Kennedy; Dean Rusk; Robert McNamara; CIA Director John McCone; McGeorge Bundy; Treasury Secretary Douglas Dillon; Theodore Sorensen; Undersecretary of State George Ball and his deputy, U. Alexis Johnson; General Maxwell Taylor, the chairman of the Joint Chiefs of Staff; Assistant Secretary of State for Latin American Affairs Edwin Martin;[26] Deputy Defense Secretary Roswell Gilpatric and Assistant Secretary of Defense Paul Nitze; and State Department Soviet affairs expert Ambassador Llewellyn Thompson.[27] Vice President Lyndon Johnson, Adlai Stevenson and Presidential Assistant Kenneth O'Donnell met with the group from time to time as did elder statesmen Dean Acheson and Robert Lovett.[28] Donald Wilson, deputy director of the U. S. Information Agency, was brought in for the later meetings just before the President's public statement of October 22.[29]

The discovery of Soviet missile installations in Cuba came as a surprise to the U.S. government. Robert Kennedy describes the dominant reaction at the first Ex Comm meeting as one of "stunned surprise" and "shocked incredulity."[30] Increasing Soviet-arms shipments to Cuba had been watched closely. But after careful analysis of all the known facts and of probable Soviet intentions, the U. S. National Intelligence Estimate for September had concluded that the Soviets would *not* introduce offensive missiles into Cuba. The Russians, the estimate argued, had always been cautious in nuclear matters. They had never stationed strategic weapons outside of their own borders. If they had never sent missiles to Eastern Europe, why would they sent them to Cuba, where distance would render supply lines insecure and the volatile character of the regime and its ruler would complicate the problems of control? The estimate concluded that placing offensive missiles in Cuba would not be in the best interests of the Soviet Union. The missiles would be discovered quickly, and discovery would provoke a strong American response. In attributing this line of reasoning to the Soviets, the CIA estimators were assuming that the Soviet planners shared the American estimate of what was in the best interests of Moscow. They were wrong, but at the time it seemed to be a reasonable presumption.

Why *did* the Soviet Union place strategic missiles in Cuba? This question, which puzzled the members of the Ex Comm and U.S. intelligence, has never been answered definitively. It seems unlikely that we will ever know with certainty. But a review of the strategic situation in mid-1962 as well as the probable Soviet estimate of Kennedy's response suggests a reasonable explanation.

Soviet motivation was of more than academic interest

to the men who met in the Cabinet Room of the White House, for their judgment was to influence the decision on an appropriate response to the Soviet move. First, it was suggested that Moscow was attempting a diversionary action, trying to lure the United States into attacking Cuba while the Soviets moved in on Berlin. It was noted that the uproar over the Suez crisis had tended to camouflage the crushing of the Hungarian uprising in 1956. The idea of a diversionary move carried some weight because the Kennedy administration had been obsessed with the prospect of a recurrence of the Berlin crisis. Khrushchev had lifted the ultimatum on Berlin in October 1961, and early in 1962 the Western Allies had set out on a course to probe Soviet intentions on Berlin and Germany. During 1962 the Soviets carried out certain low-level harassments, such as buzzing planes in the Berlin air corridor, but the problem did not reach a state of crisis. On August 18, 1962, Khrushchev renewed his warning that the Soviet Union would sign a separate treaty with East Germany unless the West ended its "occupation" of West Berlin. This new threat was part of a pattern of increasing Soviet pressure on Berlin that developed in the late summer and early fall of 1962. The administration therefore considered Berlin to be the focus of tension in East-West relations and the most dangerous potential flash point. Berlin, it was argued, was the real objective and Cuba merely a side show. In fact, the reverse was the case. Concentration on Berlin may also have been a factor in the administration's failure to see why the Soviets might feel it in their interest to put missiles in Cuba.

Closely related to the diversion theory was the suggestion that the Soviet Union had placed missiles in Cuba to use as bargaining chips. It was speculated that they planned to offer to trade their removal for the removal of American overseas bases that threatened the Soviet Union or even for Berlin itself. But while fixation on Berlin may have led some in the State Department to embrace this explanation, it is difficult to sustain. It seems unlikely that after the war scare of the previous summer over Berlin, the Soviets could have so underestimated the strength of American determination to hold the former German capital. If this explanation had any validity, it seems likely that the removal of NATO bases in Turkey, from which nuclear missiles were aimed at the Soviet Union, would have been considered the object of a bargain.

Neither of these two explanations was very convincing to President Kennedy.

A third explanation, offered at the time by the Soviets and reinforced by Khrushchev in his memoirs, is that the missiles were installed merely to defend Cuba. It could be argued that, after the Bay of Pigs, Castro could not be faulted for his constant claim that the United States was planning another invasion. Indeed, his fears may have been justified. The State Department Desk Officer for Cuba during the Kennedy years was Robert A. Hurwitch. He has said that, even after the Bay of Pigs, "Our objective vis à vis Cuba was the overthrow of the Castro regime, the removal of the Castro regime and its replacement with one that was friendly to the United States and the Western world." The Kennedy administration tried to "institutionalize" the Cuban exile organization so that it could be used as a smokescreen should the occasion for invasion arise, as it almost did during the missile crisis.[31]

Preparation for another invasion seems to have persisted as a theme of the Kennedy administration. Veterans of Brigade 2506, including Hugo Sueiro Rios, now a retired U. S. Army captain, appear to have expected another invasion. After the release of the Brigade from Castro's prisons in late 1962, Sueiro and more than two hundred of his fellow Cubans joined the U. S. armed forces. Interviewed by *The New York Times* on the occasion of the tenth anniversary of the 1961 invasion, Sueiro said.

> We expected to return rapidly to Cuba after the special officers' training course in Fort Benning, Ga.

We were badly mistaken. After President Kennedy was killed, there was a change in the political situation in this country and we were told that another invasion of the island was impossible.[32]

Castro had long been pressing Moscow for additional defense assistance, and the Soviet missiles could be viewed as a powerful deterrent to any hostile U.S. action against the island. Yet this explanation alone hardly seems sufficient. While the survival of the Castro regime was certainly a Soviet foreign policy objective and its desirability was probably a factor in the decision to send the missiles, it could hardly have been an objective of high enough priority to justify abandoning a long-standing policy against stationing strategic nuclear missiles outside of the Soviet Union. Nor could it justify the risk of a major confrontation with the United States. Despite Castro's repeated requests, the tail does not wag the dog in strategic matters affecting the nuclear powers.

Another possible motive, and the explanation most impressive to the President,[33] was that the move was Khrushchev's ultimate test of American will and resolve. According to this theory, which parallels closely that propounded by Dean Acheson and accepted by Kennedy at the time of the Berlin crisis, Khrushchev considered America too soft to fight and was therefore confident that nothing more than a loud protest would result. If Khrushchev was allowed to get away with putting missiles in Cuba, it was claimed, he would make further probes, on Berlin or against the overseas bases. American credibility would suffer as our Allies came to doubt our word, and Soviet influence throughout the world would therefore be enhanced.

In retrospect, it appears likely that such reasoning was a significant factor in the Soviet decision, but it does not appear sufficient to have justified the risk, even as low-level a risk as the Soviets apparently thought they were incurring. A move of a basically military character appears more likely to have been taken for a military reason. But President Kennedy considered that cold-war politics was the most important reason. There are numerous accounts of his determination not to let Khrushchev get away with it, accounts of his feeling that our prestige, and presumably his own, were involved, and his own statement on October 22 emphasized that "our courage" was challenged.

The President told Arthur Schlesinger that he felt that the Soviets had taken the risk in the hope of drawing Russia and China closer together and possibly strengthening the Russian position in the Communist world; in the hope of reopening the Berlin matter after the election in a situation of greater Soviet advantage; and in the hope of severely damaging the U.S. political position in the world.[34]

President Kennedy's concern with prestige appears to have prevented him from appreciating fully the significance of what is generally accepted to be the real source of the Soviet action: the Soviets were taking a bold risk to try to equalize the overwhelming strategic-missile imbalance against them.

During the 1960 campaign, Kennedy and the Democrats came down hard on what they alleged was the coming missile gap, the point where Soviet missile power would overtake and even outstrip our own. Shortly after assuming office, President Kennedy, reversing the policy of President Eisenhower who had resisted military pressure for increased arms expenditures, authorized the expansion of the Minuteman and Polaris missile programs. The Soviets must have viewed this expansion with considerable alarm. Their own ICBM program had been set back when they discovered that their 800,000-pound-thrust satellite-launching rocket was too big for practical use as a weapon. They knew that, in reality, *they* were on the short end of the missile gap. But since U-2 flights over the

Soviet Union had ceased after the Powers incident and because of the acceleration of strategic-weapons development ordered by Kennedy, the Soviets must have concluded that Washington was unaware of the true situation of Soviet inferiority.

Then, in the summer and fall of 1961, an American intelligence breakthrough allowed us to pinpoint Soviet missile sites.[35] The administration decided to make that knowledge public, apparently fearing that if Khrushchev continued to think that we believed in the missile gap, he would be tempted to undertake new adventures, particularly with respect to Berlin. It was a risky course because once the Soviets realized that we were aware of their weakness they would surely increase their efforts. But President Kennedy decided to take that risk.

On October 21, 1961, Deputy Defense Secretary Roswell Gilpatric revealed that the United States was not deceived about the Soviet capacity, and he declared that we had a second-strike or retaliatory capability in strategic weapons that was at least as extensive as that which the Soviets were capable of delivering by striking first. "Therefore," said Gilpatric, "we are confident that the Soviets will not provoke a major nuclear conflict."[36] Other reports at about the same time made clear that the missile gap had failed to materialize and that the United States had an overwhelming preponderance of nuclear power over that of the USSR. Allied governments, including those we knew were penetrated by Soviet intelligence, were briefed secretly on the strategic balance to permit the Soviets to verify through their own intelligence channels the information made public in Gilpatric's speech.[37]

At that time, Soviet missiles were on "soft" sites, many grouped in clusters at fixed above-ground locations. Once these sites had been pinpointed by American intelligence, their usefulness as a deterrent would vanish because they would be vulnerable to an American first strike. Early in 1962, Defense Secretary McNamara announced that the

United States was switching from a counter-city nuclear strategy to a counter-force strategy. The change had nothing to do with humanitarian considerations. Its purpose was to indicate to the Soviets that our nuclear arsenal was now so powerful and so accurate that we could threaten their retaliatory capacity. McNamara's announcement, coming only a few months after the Gilpatric speech, must have created near panic in Soviet military circles. We knew where their missile sites were; now we were switching our strategy to target their missile sites instead of their cities. Soviet military planners probably concluded that we were moving to a first-strike strategy aimed at eliminating their retaliatory capacity. They may have feared that we had already achieved a first-strike capability.

In addition, President Kennedy had told columnist Stewart Alsop, a close personal friend, that he would not hesitate to be the first to use nuclear weapons.[38] This meant that we would not hesitate to use nuclear weapons against aggression by conventional forces, for example, in Europe, where we were outnumbered on the ground.

The existence of increased military influence on the Soviet regime is suggested by Khrushchev's revelation in his memoirs that after the Powers incident in the spring of 1960 he no longer exercised complete control over Soviet policy. The pressure exerted on Khrushchev by the Soviet military to do something to overcome what appeared to them to be a situation of mortal danger must have been substantial.

On the basis of such developments the Cuban move can be seen as a desperate, although ineffective, attempt on the part of the Soviets to redress the strategic balance and to eliminate what they felt was an intolerable threat.

While trying to determine Soviet motives, the Ex Comm also tried to assess the significance for American national security of the Soviet move. The tone of the President's October 22 statement, which gave the impression that Soviet missiles in Cuba presented a new and mortal threat to the United States, has tended to obscure the facts. Ex Comm members differed in their opinions, but many felt that the danger to the nation was not substantially increased. Most significant was the view of Secretary McNamara, which he argued for several days, that Soviet missiles in Cuba did not markedly alter the strategic balance. The Soviet Union already had ICBMs that threatened the United States directly from Soviet territory, and he felt that a few more missiles in Cuba, although they decreased our warning time in case of attack, did not make much difference. "A missile is a missile," McNamara is reported to have said. "It makes no great difference whether you are killed by a missile fired from the Soviet Union or from Cuba."[39]

The Soviets had no first-strike capacity against the United States, no ability to destroy our retaliatory capacity. We were aware of this. We knew, further, that none of their weapons were sufficiently accurate to hit our missile sites, even from Cuba. The Soviet Union could not, therefore, hope to achieve a first-strike capacity by putting a few dozen missiles in Cuba.

Others in the Ex Comm made the point that missiles in Cuba reduced our warning time almost to zero and that missiles coming from the south would escape detection by the American radar net, which was aimed north. It was suggested that our manned strategic bomber force, based largely in the south, would be virtually defenseless.

Although warning time was reduced, the United States was not defenseless. Half of our SAC bombers were on airborne alert at all times and would therefore not be caught on the ground. In addition, the problem of coordinating salvos in a nuclear attack on the United States would be substantial. If the Cuban missiles were released against the United States at the same time as missiles from the Soviet Union, the early arrival of those from Cuba would give additional warning time. If the

Cuban missiles were held back to avoid this, they would be vulnerable on the ground even to conventional American attack. Finally, the American submarine-based deterrent, our Polaris fleet, was and is totally invulnerable.

President Kennedy, however, was less concerned with the military implications of the missiles than with what he felt to be their implication for the global political balance. Theodore Sorensen has written that the President thought that though, in view of all the power the Soviets were capable of unleashing on the United States from bases in the Soviet Union and from nuclear bombers, the missiles in Cuba did not "substantially" alter the strategic balance *"in fact"* but that the balance would have been altered *"in appearance"* and that in such matters involving national will and world leadership, appearances contribute to reality.[40]

In October 1962 the global political balance was overwhelmingly in favor of the United States. Since opposing forces, in international politics as in physics, tend to seek equilibrium, it is hardly surprising that the Soviet Union sought to redress this balance, both in strategic terms and in political terms. As noted above, they could not have hoped to achieve a strategic advantage over the United States by the placement of missiles in Cuba. They could, on the other hand, have hoped for a gain in political advantage. This President Kennedy was not willing to permit.

The balance that the United States accused the Soviet Union of upsetting in October 1962 was, in fact, one of great advantage for the United States. There seems to have been no recognition that this was not a situation that the Soviet Union could tolerate any more than the United States could be expected to tolerate an overwhelming Soviet advantage. President Kennedy was not willing to permit the slightest diminution of the American hegemony and he was willing to risk a nuclear war to maintain it. We were unwilling to permit anything approaching equality even on the political level because we objected to the way in which the Soviets used their power to achieve their ends. They, of course, make the same objections to our use of our power.

It has frequently been maintained over the years since World War II that we can negotiate only from a position of strength. But history in general demonstrates the fallacy of the idea that real negotiations are possible in situations of preponderance. Negotiation, by definition in fact, can occur only when both sides are of relatively equal strength. When one or the other is preponderant, the stronger will see no need to negotiate and the weaker will fear to enter into discussions at a disadvantage. Should the situation in 1962 have moved closer to equilibrium, true negotiation of some of the outstanding international issues might have been possible, although it is unclear whether this was the Soviet intention.

Most members of the Ex Comm came to share the President's view of the unacceptability of the slightest alteration in the political balance of power. Because of its secrecy, President Kennedy thought the Soviet move was designed to confront the United States with a *fait accompli* which might well be revealed by Khrushchev personally in a belligerent speech at the United Nations.[41] The United States might then be forced to the negotiating table or to a summit to deal with Berlin and other issues.

It was noted that the effect on Latin American nations might be devastating and Castro-type insurgencies might be encouraged. Our allies might come to doubt our resolve; the credibility of our commitments might be questioned. This is the rationale, of course, for U.S. policy that carried through into the Johnson and Nixon administrations when it was used to justify American policy in Southeast Asia.

This view of the necessity to protect our credibility, to convince our allies of our resolve, rang rather hollow in 1962 and is even more difficult to sustain now. Our European allies, as even Sorensen has recognized, had lived for years under the threat of Russian missiles within a few miles of their borders. They might well wonder what all the fuss was about. In the eyes of most Western Europeans, Cuba was just not that important. Many Europeans admired Castro and secretly if not openly applauded his ability to thumb his nose at the Yankee tyrant. Europeans had been appalled at the Bay of Pigs and many took seriously Castro's claim that another American invasion was imminent. They might well consider that Soviet missiles in Cuba were not worth a nuclear war. No European interest was at stake in such a war, and Europeans would probably be its first victims. Europeans would not be impressed by the argument that it was important to safeguard the American political hegemony, for Europe at that time was entering a period of increasing resentment of American political, economic, and cultural dominance.

It was feared, Sorensen writes, that if we failed to act, De Gaulle and other leaders might conclude that if we would not act in Cuba, ninety miles from our shores, we could not be counted on to react to a threat farther from home. Yet, both the French and the British had already decided not to place all their eggs in the American basket; both were developing independent nuclear deterrents. Reassuring them, when they obviously would never be fully reassured, seems an insufficient excuse for risking nuclear war.

The need to protect our credibility becomes an even slimmer excuse when we consider the situation in Latin America. Many Latin Americans, in secret and in public, cheered Castro's attacks on "North American imperialism." Despite our success in extracting—through political and economic pressures, and promises of increased foreign aid—resolutions of condemnation of Castro at meetings of the OAS, sympathy for Castro was strong throughout Latin America. Nonintervention in the internal affairs of another state, to which the United States was bound under the OAS Charter, was a sacred credo to the Latin Americans. It had been dishonored, to our great cost, at the Bay of Pigs. Another intervention would not be welcome.

During this period, State Department analysis of the possible reactions of our allies predicted that if the United States took a strong action against Cuba, the Europeans and Latin Americans would turn against us, while if we took a weak action they would turn away from us.[42] This seems a fair presumption and it certainly undermined the credibility argument.

In retrospect, the potential disasters that the Kennedy administration feared might result from the weakening of the American hegemony appear almost innocuous when measured against the possibility of a nuclear exchange. Would it really have been so terrible to have been required to negotiate with Khrushchev to get the missiles out or even to have gone to a summit meeting? The specter of Munich is always raised in such cases, but there is no comparison between the two situations. The weakness of Britain and France militarily in the face of a rearmed Germany in 1938 led to appeasement of Nazi aggression. In 1962 an adjustment in the strategic balance to reduce the *degree* of U.S. preponderance might have lowered East-West tensions without risk of nuclear war.

Would the psychological effect on our Western European allies really have been so severe had we not forced a nuclear confrontation? De Gaulle, for example, was already proceeding with his own nuclear strike force. As a result of the unilateral American decision to force a confrontation over Cuba—which could have led to the nuclear devastation of France over a matter the French considered an exclusively American interest—De Gaulle became more determined to loosen France's ties to the United States. Within several years he was to take France out of NATO.

Would our failure to intervene in Cuba have irreparably weakened our ties with Latin America and led to the rise of Castroism, as the Kennedy administration feared? Again the answer is uncertain. The Kennedy administration was convinced that it could hold back the forces of revolutionary change in Latin America through sponsorship of reform under the Alliance for Progress. This program offered incentives for reform to the ruling oligarchies in the belief that they would be willing to divest themselves of some of their power and share it with the masses of the underprivileged. It is not clear why Kennedy became convinced that this sharing of power would come about willingly. The course of the social revolution in Latin America has been determined much more by internal factors than by anything the United States—or Castro—did or did not do.

The factor that some critics have considered crucial to the President's decision, the threat to the political survival of the administration, is barely touched on in most administration accounts of the Cuban missile crisis.[43] Sorensen writes that during the Ex Comm discussions one of the Republican members passed him a note reading,

> Ted—Have you considered the very real possibility that if we allow Cuba to complete installation and operational readiness of missile bases, the next House of Representatives is likely to have a Republican majority? This would completely paralyze our ability to react sensibly and coherently to further Soviet advances.[44]

Although it is a revealing demonstration of the bipartisan quality of the American foreign policy establishment, this warning appears somewhat naïve. As the Presidential prerogative in foreign policy has grown through usage in the years since World War II, the power of the Congress effectively to influence foreign policy, particularly the war-making power, has lapsed. In large measure, Congress itself is at fault, for it has permitted the Executive too much latitude and it has failed to require strong justifications for questionable national policies. This Congressional permissiveness, which became a political issue only in the late 1960's, was in evidence during the Kennedy administration. Even in 1962, the House, which has in any event no constitutionally prescribed role in making foreign policy, could do little more than throw temporary roadblocks in the way of Presidential initiative in foreign policy. The powers of Congress to influence foreign policy, as was to become only too clear by the end of the decade, are at best minimally negative. Congress can do nothing to force the President to make war if he does not choose to do so; it can do little, as has been demonstrated in recent years, to prevent his making war if he chooses to do so. Which party controls the Congress has little effect on this basic constitutional problem, whose imbalance can be corrected only over the years.

While it ought to have been clear that the election of a Republican House of Representatives would present less of a threat to the survival of the Republic than was presented by a nuclear confrontation, President Kennedy must have taken politics into consideration when he made his decision, particularly with respect to the necessity for the *rapid* removal of the missiles. (Even if the missiles did not affect the military balance, they might have to be removed eventually, but did they have to be out by the end of October?) There does not seem to be any other plausible explanation for the timing. Yet one may question whether the presence of Soviet missiles in Cuba at the time of the election of 1962 would have necessarily ensured a defeat for the administration. By taking a different approach, might the President not have been able to unite the country behind the search for a negotiated settlement?

The main business of the Ex Comm was to recommend what course of action the President should follow to bring about the removal of the missiles. Several courses, of varying degrees of severity and danger, were considered.

The first course, initially favored by Secretary McNamara and a few others, was to do nothing. It was suggested that since the missiles did not alter the strategic balance, we should learn to live with them as we had long expected the Soviets to live with our nuclear missiles almost on their borders. By remaining calm, we could prevent the Soviets from inflating the importance of the matter. It would then be accepted gradually as a not very significant change in strategic deployment which did not affect the United States strategic position. The President rejected this course from the outset.

A related proposal was that advanced principally by Adlai Stevenson. Stevenson suggested a political or diplomatic approach that would bring about the removal of the missiles in exchange for certain agreements on our part. The diplomatic route was also supported on the first day of Ex Comm meetings by McGeorge Bundy, who later changed his position.[45] Sorensen writes that this course of action, which presented fewer risks or drawbacks than any other, was considered by every member of the group at one time or another.[46] The President, however, rejected a political solution from the beginning, and Stevenson was later publicly labeled an appeaser for having urged it.

A third course was indirect military action in the form of a blockade. And finally, direct military action—an airstrike against the missile sites or an invasion—was considered.

At first, the airstrike appealed most to the President. It was thought initially that a so-called surgical strike could eliminate the missiles quickly and cleanly. As the discussion proceeded, however, it became clear that the airstrike would be neither "surgical" nor effective. It could not, the Joint Chiefs argued, be limited to the missile sites. Castro's jet fighters, or even his newly arrived strategic bombers, might retaliate. SAM batteries would fire at American planes. We could not overlook the storage sites of the nuclear warheads. All of these targets would have to be attacked in a massive bombardment. Even then, the Joint Chiefs were not able to assure the President that all the missiles could be knocked out before they could be fired at the United States. Further, it quickly became clear that in the wake of such a massive bombardment, Cuba would collapse politically, socially, and economically; an invasion and eventual U.S. takeover would be necessary.

The additional drawbacks of an airstrike were pointed out by the Attorney General. He argued that a sudden attack without warning on a smaller state by a great power was a violation of our traditions as a nation and would blacken the name of America in the pages of history.

The blockade, too, offered disadvantages from the point of view of the administration's objectives. It would not bring about the removal of the missiles, and it might well give the Russians time to complete installation of the bases. A great deal of time was spent in discussing whether it would be possible to obtain agreement in the OAS to the establishment of a blockade. OAS endorsement would lend an aura of legitimacy to what was essentially an act of war by providing an admittedly transparent legal covering. It was considered important to have this legal covering for the blockade, although an airstrike or an invasion would hardly have been legal either.

Finally, the President, having assured himself that even the airstrike could not guarantee the removal of all the missiles, chose the blockade as an initial limited course of action. At the same time, he ordered final preparations for airstrikes and invasion should those courses become necessary. He also ordered final preparations for an American response to Soviet reactions anywhere in the world. It was expected that in response to our blockade of Cuba the Soviets would blockade Berlin.

On October 22, 1962, at seven o'clock in the evening,

the President revealed to the nation and to the world the presence of Soviet missiles in Cuba and the response he had ordered. His statement bears little relation to the realities of the situation as they were discussed in the Ex Comm during the previous week. The President's statement had a markedly alarmist tone and emphasized in its opening paragraphs the severity and unique character of the threat to the nation. "The purpose of these bases can be be none other than to provide a nuclear strike capability against the Western Hemisphere," Kennedy declared. Yet a Soviet strike capability against the Western Hemisphere, particularly against the United States, already existed, as he himself noted later in his address. But one suspects that the point had already been impressed on most who heard and saw him on television: we were facing a situation of unprecedented danger. Also noteworthy in the President's statement were the emphasis on the clandestine character of the Soviet move, the suggestion of the personal challenge and affront inherent in the Soviet deceit, the suggestion that we could not let the Soviets get away with fooling us in this manner, and the statement that "our courage and our commitments" were challenged.

And so, with President Kennedy's speech, the issue was joined. Khrushchev was, in effect, given a public ultimatum: "Remove the missiles or else," and the "or else" was given weight by a limited act of war, the blockade. Once the affair had been brought out into the open, of course, the factor of prestige mattered more than any other. Khrushchev had dared to challenge the United States. That challenge would be met and the Soviets would be forced to capitulate.

As the world knows, President Kennedy skillfully managed the Cuban missile crisis so that his objectives were achieved without war. Several questions remain: Why did the President force a confrontation in public rather than in secret, thereby dangerously engaging the prestige of both sides? Why was he so insistent that the missiles had to be removed before a certain date? What other course of action might he have followed to remove the missiles with less risk of war? Finally, was the Cuban missile crisis really necessary?

On October 18, two days after President Kennedy learned of the missiles, Soviet Foreign Minister Andrei Gromyko paid a call at the White House. The visit had been arranged some time in advance, and the President, in spite of the almost constant meetings of the Ex Comm, was unwilling to cancel it for fear of arousing suspicion. The President allowed Gromyko to make his presentation without revealing his knowledge of the missiles. The Soviet Foreign Minister talked first of Berlin and assured the President that the Soviet government had no intention of precipitating a crisis over Berlin that would embarrass Kennedy in advance of the elections. But, reiterating Khrushchev's August statement, Gromyko informed the President that after the election, unless there was a settlement, the Soviet Union would sign a separate treaty with East Germany.

Gromyko then brought up the subject of Cuba, emphasizing Castro's fear of invasion. Soviet assistance to Cuba, he insisted, was entirely defensive. Kennedy listened without revealing that he knew otherwise. Then, to avoid any misunderstanding, he sent for and read aloud to the Soviet Foreign Minister the warning he had issued in September against offensive missiles in Cuba.

When Gromyko left the White House, Robert Lovett, a member of the Republican establishment and former Secretary of Defense in the Truman administration whom Kennedy had called in to advise on the crisis, entered the President's office. Dean Rusk and Llewellyn Thompson were with the President. Kennedy asked Lovett if he had been briefed and then said, grinning,

> I ought to finish the story by telling you about Gromyko who, in this very room, not over ten minutes ago, told more bare-faced lies than I have ever heard

in so short a time. All during his denial that the Russians had any missiles, or weapons, or anything else in Cuba, I had the low-level pictures in the center drawer of my desk and it was an enormous temptation to show them to him.[47]

The President's main reason for not confronting Gromyko with the evidence was his desire to avoid alerting the Soviets until he was fully ready to act. New evidence in the form of more detailed photographs was coming in daily, and U.S. military preparations, although they had begun, were not yet complete. President Kennedy also feared that if he let the Soviets know what he knew, Moscow might reply with evasions or threats. It was even conceivable, he feared, that Gromyko might decide to announce the presence of the missiles from the White House steps on leaving. Kennedy believed that the American people should learn of this development from their President, along with his plans for dealing with the situation.[48]

While it is understandable that President Kennedy did not wish to risk premature disclosure by confronting Gromyko with the evidence on October 18, before he was ready to act, why did he not call him back when he was ready to act, four days later? Or, the President could have made a private representation to Khrushchev himself, once American forces were in a position for action.

Apparently President Kennedy rejected the idea of confronting Khrushchev privately with the evidence because of the "danger" that the Soviet leader might seize the diplomatic initiative, mobilize the nonaligned countries and left-wing opinion in the West, and force the United States to "a conference no less disastrous than Munich, in which the President would find himself under the heaviest kind of pressure to trade off NATO bases in Europe for Russian missiles in Cuba."[49] In essence, he was afraid that the pressures for peace might prove overwhelming. Walter Lippmann, among others at the time, criticized this "suspension of diplomacy." If Kennedy had confronted the Russians secretly with the pictures, Lippmann commented, then his action could not be subject to the criticism that a great power had issued an ultimatum before trying to negotiate the issue.[50] A private message to Khrushchev would have given the Russians a chance to back down without humiliation and would have been less risky than a public confrontation. Our intentions would have been made credible by the military preparations then under way, the movement of naval forces into the Caribbean, the dispersal of our SAC bombers from their bases in the southern part of the United States, and the movement of airborne assault troops to bases in Florida. These military movements had been widely reported in the press by the time of the ultimatum, and the Soviets were surely aware of them.

By making his ultimatum public, however, President Kennedy was able to give the impression that a dire threat to the national existence had suddenly arisen. This assured widespread public support for whatever move he might choose to make. But it is likely that President Kennedy could have rallied widespread support for a peaceful solution as well. It will be remembered that, according to the Gallup Poll of October 17, fear of all-out war with Russia deterred Americans from supporting an invasion of Cuba.

What was the reason for President Kennedy's insistence that the missiles be removed so quickly? The official explanation was that installation was proceeding rapidly and we dared not let the missiles become operational. But, if it had been generally agreed that the missiles in Cuba presented not a significant additional military threat, but rather a political threat, the need for haste is unclear. As long as they were removed eventually, the threat would be removed. Considerations of strategy—political if not military—convinced the President that the Russian withdrawal would have to be complete; considerations of prestige con-

vinced him that it would have to be unilateral; and considerations of partisan politics convinced him that the
withdrawal would have to be brought about by the end of
October.

On October 27, on President Kennedy's instructions,
Robert Kennedy called Soviet Ambassador Anatoly Dobrynin to his office. He later described that conversation
in detail:

> We had to have a commitment by tomorrow that those
> bases would be removed. I was not giving them an
> ultimatum but a statement of fact. He should under-
> stand that if they did not remove those bases, we
> would remove them. . . . Time was running out. We
> had only a few more hours—we needed an answer im-
> mediately from the Soviet Union. I said we must have
> it the next day.[51]

None of the published accounts, not even Robert Kennedy's, make clear that the President instructed his brother
to deliver a 24-hour ultimatum, for it was an ultimatum, in
spite of Robert Kennedy's denial. It is conceivable, but it
seems highly unlikely, that Robert Kennedy could have
added the 24-hour deadline on his own initiative. While
a case can be made, and was made in the Ex Comm, that
it was necessary for military reasons to get the missiles
out before they became operational, it seems likely that the
pressure would not have been so intense had the American
election not been imminent.

Another aspect of Robert Kennedy's conversation with
Ambassador Dobrynin has caused speculation. Chairman
Khrushchev's memoirs mention an appeal by Robert Kennedy on behalf of the President for help. Khrushchev
wrote that Ambassador Dobrynin told him:

> President Kennedy implores Chairman Khrushchev to
> take into consideration the peculiarities of the Amer-
> ican system. Even though the President himself is

very much against starting a war over Cuba, an irreversible chain of events could occur against his will. That is why the President is appealing directly to Chairman Khrushchev for his help in liquidating this conflict. If the situation continues much longer, the President is not sure that the military will not overthrow him and seize power. The American army could get out of control.[52]

When Khrushchev's memoirs were first made public, this incident was widely regarded as apocryphal. Such a thing could never happen in the United States. Robert Kennedy would never have said such a thing. The first is probably true. Americans generally reject the possibility of a military coup; but such a suggestion does fit rather neatly into Soviet conceptions of the nature of power in Washington. And it does seem possible that the President's brother might have played on this Soviet conception for his own purposes. He could well have said this or something like it, allowing Dobrynin to believe that the President really feared that the military would get out of hand. This possibility has also been suggested by Elie Abel, who says it was a "deliberate Kennedy gambit designed to hoodwink the Russians into putting more pressure on Castro."[53]

Was there another course of action that President Kennedy might have followed to get the missiles out with less risk of war? In retrospect, the political course proposed by Adlai Stevenson would probably have been successful in bringing about the removal of the missiles, and at much less risk. Essentially, the United States would have had to make a concession to bring this about, but that concession would have been justified in the interest of preserving peace and avoiding the immediate threat of nuclear war.

Stevenson was not one of those who believed that the missiles made no real difference. "No politician," he remarked, "could have missed the significance of Russian missiles in Cuba. We just had to get them out of there."[54] But when the President first showed Stevenson the U-2 photographs and said, "We'll have to do something quickly. I suppose the alternatives are to go in by air and wipe them out, or to take other steps to render the weapons inoperable," Stevenson replied, "Let's not go to an air strike until we have explored the possibilities of a peaceful solution." In March 1965, Stevenson recalled, "I was a little alarmed that Kennedy's first consideration should have been the air strike. I told him that sooner or later we would have to go to the U.N. and it was vitally important we go there with a reasonable case."[55]

On Wednesday, the day after he had received the news of the missiles, the President had been annoyed at what he considered an ambivalent note from Stevenson proposing the dispatch of a high-level courier to Khrushchev and opposing the idea of an initial airstrike.* While acknowledging that we could not be expected to negotiate under the gun, Stevenson's note continued:

> To risk starting a nuclear war is bound to be divisive and the judgments of history seldom coincide with the tempers of the moment. . . . I feel you should have made (sic) it clear that the existence of nuclear missile bases anywhere is negotiable before we start anything. . . . I confess I have many misgivings about the proposed course of action [the airstrike].[56]

At the Friday Ex Comm meeting, Stevenson echoed a suggestion previously made by another member, and by Stevenson himself privately and tentatively to Robert Kennedy earlier, that the United States might want to consider offering to give up our Italian and Turkish

---

* Sorensen, who reports this incident, does not identify Stevenson as the author of the note, but it is clear from the context that it was Stevenson. The Schlesinger and Robert Kennedy accounts, which do refer specifically to Stevenson's proposals, reinforce this impression. Further, the sentiments and style point to Stevenson as the author.

missile bases in exchange for the removal of the missiles in Cuba, since we were planning to close down those bases anyway.

Those missiles were obsolete and highly vulnerable, even to rifle fire, and they were already being replaced by Polaris submarines; on the other hand, the Soviet missiles that would have been removed from Cuba as part of such a deal were far from obsolete and the Soviets had no comparable undersea fleet to replace them. The Italian and Turkish bases were of little value and the Russians were certainly aware of that. Yet Khrushchev had always made such a propaganda point of the aggressiveness of American policy as manifested in the missile bases ringing the Soviet homeland that he could hardly have refused to seize the opportunity to free the Soviet people from this supposed menace.

At that time Stevenson expressed a preference for the blockade (or quarantine, as it was finally called for public relations purposes) over the airstrike, but he pressed for consideration of a diplomatic route. Our negotiating position, as envisaged by Stevenson at that time, might have been based on a proposal for the neutralization of Cuba under international guarantees and U.N. inspection. If Cuba were to be neutralized, not only would the missiles have to be removed, but our naval base at Guantánamo would have to be closed. Cuba's integrity could be guaranteed against invasion and subversion.

The proposal that the United States might agree to give up the Turkish and Italian missile bases was one of the most controversial aspects of the Cuban missile crisis. The missiles in question were first-generation liquid-fueled Jupiter IRBMs with a range of some fifteen hundred miles. Since the range of these early missiles was not sufficient to threaten the Soviet Union directly from American soil, the Eisenhower administration tried to find a place for them in Europe. They were offered to our European allies at the meeting of the NATO heads of government in Paris in

December 1957 to counter the threat to Europe from Soviet missiles. The offer generated little enthusiasm. Fear of inviting a preemptive Soviet attack was strong. In the end, only Italy and Turkey agreed to permit the missiles to be stationed on their soil. (The British had previously agreed to the stationing of a similar missile on British territory.) Eisenhower is reported to have had so little faith in the missiles that he commented to aides that it would have been better to have dumped these missiles into the ocean rather than to dump them on our allies.[57]

At the Saturday Ex Comm meeting, President Kennedy was amused to hear one member* of the group, who had served the previous administration, confirm that the Thor and Jupiter missiles were obsolete and of little military value and that they had been practically forced on our unwilling allies by the Eisenhower administration.[58] Kennedy himself had given instructions for the removal of the Turkish missiles some eighteen months before, as they were to be replaced by the more advanced missiles in our Polaris fleet stationed in the Mediterranean. The State Department had dragged its feet and failed to carry out the President's instructions. Now Kennedy was extremely annoyed to find that the missiles were not only still in place, but that they were being used as a bargaining chip against him by the Russians.

When the so-called second letter from Khrushchev proposed an agreement on these bases in exchange for the removal of the Cuban missiles, Kennedy became concerned. He refused to consider removing the missiles from Turkey during the crisis, yet he recognized that it was a reasonable suggestion and would be so perceived by the public. He "did not want to involve the U.S. and mankind in a catastrophic war over missile sites in Turkey that were antiquated and useless," said his brother.[59] The President pointed out to the State Department that people would

* Probably McCone (AEC Chairman) or Dillon (Under Secretary of State).

consider the Soviet suggestion only fair and that this made our position vulnerable. About twenty-four hours before he was to have gone ahead with the invasion if Khrushchev had not agreed to remove the missiles, Kennedy considered making a public statement about the Turkish missiles. He was concerned that an invasion was such a major step, it would be difficult to explain why he did not avoid this course of action by agreeing to remove the missiles from Turkey—a step which was in the American interest in any event.[60]

When reporters asked why it was wrong for the Soviets to have missiles in Cuba when we had them in Turkey, the official reply was that the American missiles were not put there surreptitiously and that they were put there only after a Soviet threat to attack Europe with nuclear weapons; their mission was defensive, not offensive.[61] Years later, in a discussion of Soviet missiles in Cuba and American missiles in Turkey, Senator Fulbright commented,

> It seems to me there has been an implicit distinction all along that we are good people and do not intend to harm anybody, and they are bad people and they intend harm to us, and this makes all the difference.[62]

Robert Kennedy wrote, "The fact was that the proposal the Russians made was not unreasonable and did not amount to a loss to the U.S. or to our NATO allies."[63] Yet, in the face of this admittedly reasonable proposal, President Kennedy persisted in refusing to negotiate, preferring to force the Soviet retreat at the risk of war rather than even discuss a "not unreasonable" proposal.

By Saturday, Adlai Stevenson had revised his negotiating proposal to exclude the Turkish and Italian bases; he felt that they would draw attention away from Cuba and raise the whole issue of foreign bases.[64] But the President totally rejected Stevenson's program. Some members of the Ex Comm, writes Schlesinger, "felt strongly that the thought of negotiations at this point would be taken as an admission of the moral weakness of our case and the military weakness of our posture."[65] (One can only suggest that there is little hope for a world in which such attitudes govern the decisions of nuclear power.)

Presumably as a result of Stevenson's preference for negotiation rather than confrontation, the President did not have confidence that his U.N. Ambassador would be tough enough to make a forceful presentation of the American position in the United Nations. On the suggestion of Robert Lovett, the President called in John McCloy, the former High Commissioner to Germany, to join Stevenson at the U.N. Dean Rusk was instructed to handle the situation so that Stevenson would not realize that McCloy was being brought in because of lack of confidence in Stevenson. Rusk said that he would make the suggestion in such a way that it would not only be acceptable to Stevenson but would appear publicly to have been his recommendation.[66] The official version was that McCloy, a major figure in the Republican establishment, was being brought in to lend a bipartisan flavor to the presentation at the United Nations.

President Kennedy's fears about Stevenson were groundless. The U.N. Ambassador presented his country's case forcefully at the televised meeting of the Security Council. He publicly challenged the Soviet representative to deny that there were missiles in Cuba and then dramatically and effectively presented the evidence himself in the form of enlargements of the U-2 photographs.

Finally, we can ask whether the Cuban missile crisis was really necessary. On several levels the answer would seem to be no. In military terms, the threat was not sufficient to justify the risk of nuclear war. In political terms, the unwillingness to permit any move away from the overwhelmingly dominant American political position in the world seems unreasonable. A negotiation of the issue and an eventual neutralization of Cuba would probably have resolved the matter with less risk of war, and the results would probably have been of long-term benefit to the United States. A neutralized Cuba would have meant the removal of a political albatross from around the neck of the Kennedy administration and would have freed American policy for a more positive approach to relations with Latin American nations.

President Kennedy was moved to act because of his history of preoccupation with Cuba as an issue; because he feared that his prestige would suffer, that Khrushchev would think him weak; because he permitted vestiges of cold-war thinking to freeze his policy and prevent any flexibility in dealing with the Soviet Union; and because of his fear that the American public would respond to the missiles problem by removing his party or even himself from office.

At the height of the crisis, after the blockade had gone into effect and Russian ships were moving steadily toward the line, President Kennedy discussed the matter with his brother. The Attorney General told him, "I just don't think there was any choice . . . and not only that, if you hadn't acted, you would have been impeached." Robert Kennedy continued, "The President thought for a moment and said, 'That's what I think—I would have been impeached.' "[67]

There is no indication in Robert Kennedy's account of this exchange that it was made in jest or even in a spirit of exaggeration. Did President Kennedy seriously believe that he would have been impeached if he had not acted as he did? If he did think this, he must have been swayed by the strains of the moment into a serious misjudgment. First of all, Congress was not in session, so no matter what he did or failed to do, an immediate Congressional response was impossible. But let us imagine the most unlikely course of events:

Had Kennedy accepted Stevenson's political program

and entered into negotiations with Khrushchev for the removal of the missiles, it is conceivable, but unlikely, that
an extremely hostile House of Representatives would have
been elected in November of 1962. When the new Congress came in the following January, either the negotiations would have been successful, in which case the missiles would already have been removed, or they would still
be going on. Assuming the worst that could happen, a hostile House of Representatives might have entered Articles
of Impeachment against President Kennedy for either
treason or "other high Crimes and Misdemeanors" as spe-
cified in the Constitution, on the grounds that he had failed
to go to war to remove a threat to the national security. The
Senate would then have been required, for only the second
time in our history, to try an impeachment against a President. President Kennedy's defense would presumably have
been that he had preserved the peace and that he was
conducting negotiations to remove a less than mortal threat
to the nation. It is difficult to imagine that the Senate or
the American people could have rejected such a defense.
This scenario may be far-fetched, but it does demonstrate
that if either President Kennedy or his brother thought
that impeachment was a real possibility, he could not have
thought through the matter very carefully.

The political pressures on President Kennedy seemed,
at least to him, to have been substantial. Yet his own actions contributed to them. He had been too specific about
what the United States would and would not tolerate in
Cuba, and his statements reduced his options. With the
Republicans attacking, he moved to more and more belligerent statements, which later made it difficult for him
to handle the problem without appearing to go back on
what he had said in the past. He fell into a kind of trap in
emphasizing a distinction between offensive and defensive
missiles. Basically there was little difference, but his emphasis made it difficult for him not to act when obviously

"offensive" missiles began to arrive in Cuba. Yet even those offensive missiles could be considered defensive in that they were a deterrent to invasion. With missiles in Cuba, the island was no longer at our mercy, because an attack on Cuba would mean a nuclear war in the same way that a Soviet attack on Berlin would mean war. If we expected Khrushchev to live with the Berlin "bone in his throat," it is difficult to say that he should not expect us to live with the Cuban bone in ours. In each case, the situation could be considered an annoyance, but it becomes a life-and-death matter only when one side is determined, at any cost, to wrench out that bone.

Although President Kennedy handled the Cuban missile crisis well once he made it a crisis, his initial decision that he must remove the missiles at all costs, and immediately, is open to serious question. He was moved to that decision largely by considerations of politics, although there is no evidence that he sought to foment a crisis on the eve of the election as the British and even General Eisenhower suspected. But the question remains: Would President Kennedy have withstood the pressures better if it had not been an election year? In any event, the pressures would have been less intense.

Finally, President Kennedy might have fallen back on what has become something of a lost art for Presidents. He might have told the people the truth. Kennedy, whose credibility was much greater than that of his successors, would have had a highly persuasive case to present to the country. He could have told the people that the missiles were not a new and unprecedented threat. By a careful leading of public opinion, he might have made the country understand that the main difference was that we now were in a position similar to that of the Europeans, who had lived for years with Soviet short-range missiles next door. He could have reminded the people that Soviet missiles threatened the United States from the Soviet Union, as our missiles threatened the Russians. Our deterrent was not threatened or reduced. Cuba was not a threat to the United States. While the Soviet Union was a threat, the United States was taking measures sufficient to counter that threat. Had President Kennedy utilized to the fullest his enormous potential for leadership of the nation, he would have been able to convince the people that the most important thing in such a time is to reduce tensions, not to increase them. There would have been some partisan objection. Yet a sober, reasonable, responsible President, who had refused to risk nuclear war unless the republic's survival was truly at stake, would have afforded a sharp and effective contrast to shrill opposition warmongering.

The only conceivable time when national leadership can be justified in risking a nuclear holocaust is in the face of an immediate and overwhelming threat to the very existence of the nation. Even then, a strong argument can be made by those who believe that such a risk is never justified, that it is better to be Red than Dead, that man must always choose life in the hope of ameliorating its conditions. If the survival of the republic can thus be a mixed case, there is no case at all for any other justification for risking nuclear extinction. If all other threats are less than mortal, then the means to counter them must be primarily political; they should be removed by negotiation. This is not to say that one need immediately make concessions. But the primary emphasis should be on willingness to talk rather than insistence on unconditional surrender of the enemy. As Walter Lippmann wrote, there are very great dangers in the suspension of diplomacy.

Six | Counterinsurgency:
The Fatal Illusion

The Cuban missile crisis did not change the basic condition of nuclear stalemate between the United States and the Soviet Union. Indeed, the crisis probably lessened the likelihood, at least for the immediate future, that either of the superpowers would rely heavily on nuclear weapons as instruments of foreign policy. The leaders of both the United States and the Soviet Union felt that they had come uncomfortably close to nuclear war.

From the time he assumed office, President Kennedy was determined to reorient U.S. defense policy away from the exclusive reliance on massive retaliation that had characterized the Eisenhower strategy. A flexible response, Kennedy felt, would be suited to a wide range of Soviet threats. Massive retaliation served as a deterrent to a nuclear attack on the United States, but it was not an effective deterrent to the threat of limited conventional war on the pattern of Korea. Even less was it appropriate in meeting the threat of wars of national liberation, insurgencies in the third world, which, Kennedy felt, would present the major challenge to American policy in the 1960's.

In the tradition of cold-war policy-makers, the new President was determined not to "lose" one square foot of "free world" territory to communism. He therefore saw the possibility of Communist-supported insurgencies in the third world, no matter how remote or insignificant the area, as a threat to the vital interests of the United States —a threat to which we must respond.

Khrushchev's January 1961 speech supporting wars of national liberation had made a profound impression on President Kennedy. He urged his advisers to draw up an appropriate American response to the Soviet threat in this area, and he instructed himself in the theory and practice of guerrilla warfare as expounded by Mao Tse-tung and Che Guevara.

Mao's classic treatment of revolutionary war compares the guerrilla fighter to the fish that swims and thrives in friendly and sustaining waters. Without those waters— the support of the people of the countryside—the fish cannot survive. Thus the key to the struggle for national liberation is the support of the population; political mobilization is the key to victory. In Mao's formulation there are three stages to the revolutionary struggle—the strategic defensive, the stalemate, and the offensive—but Mao concentrates on the first, that of building the base and organizing the people.

In revolutionary war, or people's war, time and will are vastly more important than equipment and supplies. Conventional supplies may be inadequate, but revolutionary spirit will sustain the guerrilla and permit him to escape defeat by even the mightiest concentration of physical power. This is the theory which, in large measure, has been borne out in Southeast Asia in the 1960's.

While Western military strategists plan how to end a

war as quickly as possible, Mao's theory concentrates on how to keep the war going, on the protracted struggle.[1]

Mao has written that countries governed by a legislature are unable, financially or psychologically, to wage a long war of attrition. The democratic nation will tire of the war and then the war's continuation will mean political suicide for the nation's leaders. Thus the revolutionary fighter, who plans for the protracted struggle and who is sustained by his revolutionary faith, will inevitably outlast those who try to suppress revolutionary movements.

The guerrilla must never fight on the enemy's terms. If he does he will always be defeated. Rather, he must adopt unconventional tactics which will enable him to avoid a military decision and live to fight another day. The war must continue, the revolution must continue; compromise raises the possibility of the loss of revolutionary spirit. This theme of endurance and revitalization, important in Mao's thought, was a major component of the Chinese Cultural Revolution of the mid-1960's, in which Mao attempted to restore revolutionary élan through the Red Guards.

Communist theorists regard wars of national liberation as an inexorable element of the historical process. Khrushchev's January 1961 speech followed this pattern. In contrast, American policy-makers tend to view people's wars or insurgencies as the result of Communist conspiratorial activity, which can set off an insurgency wherever living conditions are poor. This view was propounded by the leading counterrevolutionary theorist of the Kennedy administration, Walt W. Rostow, in an address to the graduating class of Green Berets at the U. S. Army Special Warfare School at Fort Bragg, N.C., in early 1961.

The four major crises—Cuba, the Congo, Laos, and Vietnam—faced by President Kennedy when he assumed office, said Rostow, were each the result of the efforts of the "international Communist movement" to exploit the instabilities of the underdeveloped areas. (Cuba differed from the others in that it was a broadly based national insurrection.) Throughout the old world, he continued, old societies were trying to change to gain a position in the modern world and to take advantage of the benefits of technology. This, he said, is a truly revolutionary process, "the revolution of modernization." Power is moving from the social hierarchy to those who command the tools of modern technology. The American purpose, Rostow maintained, is to create truly independent nations, each of which must be permitted to fashion the kind of society it wants. We believe, he claimed, that if independence can be maintained, these nations will choose their own interpretation of the open society, of democracy. We seek nations that will stand up and maintain their independence, and which will move toward human freedom and political democracy in their own time. We seek to protect the independence of the revolutionary process; communism does not. Rather, it seeks to subvert it. The Communists are by the nature of their system driven to violate the independence of states, while we by the nature of ours are moved to support the cause of national independence. "We are struggling to maintain an environment on the world scene which will permit our open society to flourish. . . . Modern societies must be built, and we are prepared to build them." Neither the United States nor any outsider can win a guerrilla war, he concluded, but the whole international community must learn to deter this type of aggression. We must understand that it is aggression in Vietnam, just as it was in Korea. International action must confront this aggression. Then, in a remark that presaged his later advocacy of the bombing of North Vietnam, Rostow said, "Without such international action those against whom aggression is mounted will be driven inevitably to seek out and engage the ultimate source of the aggression they confront." The best way to deal with insurgency, he concluded, is to "prevent it from happening."[2]

This remarkable statement embodies most of the themes that led to deeper and deeper involvement in counterinsurgency activity, particularly in Southeast Asia, under the two administrations Rostow served. Its presumptions are the core of the Kennedy doctrine: the struggle is of a crucial nature, no matter how remote the area or how peripheral to our interests, because these wars are always part of the global Communist challenge. Despite the inherent weaknesses and severe social and economic dislocations that frequently exist in underdeveloped areas, nations can be "built," if only enough Americans are willing to put their energies and efforts to the task. By adopting their tactics, Americans could beat the Communists at their own game. We could and should be involved in these nation-building activities throughout the world. Communism, in essence, has nothing to offer the new nations. Our system is better in all situations and, with U.S. help, all people will see the wisdom of development in the American pattern—the "free world" pattern—rather than the Communist style.

This counterinsurgency doctrine caught the imagination of the Kennedy administration, particularly that of the President and his brother, early in their term of office. Counterinsurgency efforts were based on the following assumptions. In most of the third world, Communists and other left-wing elements seek to aggravate the tensions that arise from local grievances, to turn movements for peaceful change into extremist channels, and, in general, to profit from the strains inherent in the development process. They also attempt to overthrow legitimate governments by subversion and armed rebellions in which the rebels have the support, or at least the acquiescence, of a substantial part of the population.

It was usually said that one rebel guerrilla could tie down ten regular soldiers and that the ratio of regulars to guerrillas would have to be up to 15:1 to assure suppression of the insurgency. In Malaya, an insurgency supported largely by the Chinese elements of the population was put down only after a ratio of 30:1 was reached. But President Kennedy and his counterinsurgency strategists believed that these heavy manpower requirements could be reduced substantially if the local government could gain or regain the confidence of the population by appropriate political, economic, and social measures, and, most important, if the local government could master the techniques of counterinsurgency warfare. This latter task was to be the new mission of the U. S. Special Forces, the Green Berets, to whom President Kennedy devoted a great deal of personal attention.

Organized nineteen years ago, the Special Forces— prior to their adoption by President Kennedy as the new vanguard for counterinsurgency warfare—had been made up largely of East European émigrés. They had been trained to parachute behind enemy lines, should a conventional war with the Soviet Union have broken out in Europe, and organize guerrilla and sabotage teams. Under Kennedy, and over the objections of the Joint Chiefs and the Army traditionalists, the Special Forces were transformed into an elite unit, having special skills and operating outside Army routine. They were to represent, according to President Kennedy's conception, a new breed of Americans who would be able to fight brush-fire wars by using Communist tactics against alleged Communists in jungles throughout the world. Some converts to the counterinsurgency fad even went so far as to suggest that guerrilla warfare was lodged deep in the American tradition. Americans, it was said, had been guerrilla fighters against the British during the American Revolutionary War. And the American suppression of the Philippine Insurrection (1899–1901), one of the least glorious episodes in our history, was cited by Roger Hilsman, an important architect of counterinsurgency strategy, as "one of the most successful counter-guerrilla campaigns in history."[3] The strongest early statement of counterinsurgency theory by the President came on the day after the failure of the Bay of Pigs invasion, when it was inspired largely by a desire to put on a strong front in a moment of clear weakness and misjudgment.

A fuller exposition of American counterinsurgency policy was given by veteran State Department official U. Alexis Johnson in an article in *The Foreign Service Journal* of July 1962. The purpose of the American program, wrote Johnson, was to assist new nations to build the kinds of societies and governments that could sustain themselves, develop in the modern world, and, "above all, remain free from domination or control by Communist forces hostile to us." To this end, we would not seek to build up military force for its own sake or even to promote economic development for its own sake; instead, these programs would be carried out within the context of an overall mission of counterinsurgency.

The basic problem would be to prevent those states we were aiding from being destroyed from within—destruction meaning that they would be taken over by Communists. The United States would have to meet this danger, Johnson wrote, with the "totality" of military, political, economic, social, and psychological resources, both our own and those of the country we were defending. Inherent in this statement is the presumption that the "legitimate government" in such countries is always something to be preserved. A further presumption is that a successful insurgency would produce a government hostile to U.S. interests.

American strategy was to be an all-inclusive attack on the roots of subversion and insurgency, fulfilling the Rostow prescription for stopping the trouble before it starts. The American effort would "in most cases" be one of advice, assistance, and training of administrators, police, paramilitary and military forces. It was noted, however, that there was "no line of demarcation between military and non-military measures" to meet the threat of insurgency. Civic action projects, such as those carried out by the Green Berets, were designed to utilize military forces in a manner likely to strengthen their support among the local population. Thus the Green Berets and their local counterparts built roads, constructed schools, worked at sanitation and flood control, and established communications networks.

In addition to the military, political, economic, social, and psychological measures that were to be "orchestrated" to protect the new nations, a key element of the counter-insurgency effort was the strengthening of local police through AID Public Safety programs. Local police and constabulary forces were considered to be the first line of defense against subversion and political violence. Local police forces were trained in modern technology both in the United States and in their own countries. In addition to training police, the AID program installed systems of village communications and alarms, furnished emergency economic aid to areas under attack, and provided technical guidance in sanitation and transportation.

Counterinsurgency thus aimed at eliminating the conditions required by the insurgents by strengthening the weaknesses in the society, improving internal security, and fostering reforms to alleviate the social ills on which insurgency thrives. In seeking to deny a friendly environment to the insurgents, the policy aims at drying up the friendly sea in which the fish swim. Military countermeasures against the insurgents must be limited and must spare civilian life and property in order to detach the rebels from the population. But, as Alexis Johnson noted in what was surely one of the major understatements of the decade, "Frequently, urgent requirements of an internal defense nature must override a carefully worked out economic development plan."

The role of the U. S. Information Agency in this program is substantial. USIA was founded to act as the propaganda arm of the United States, to tell America's story to the world. Under the counterinsurgency program, the agency took on the task of working abroad for "mutual understanding and a community of interest between the government and the people," or, in non-bureaucratic English, it worked to sell their government to the people of individual countries, a role that it was forbidden by statute to play in the United States.

If a government deserves the support of its people, it will receive that support, and in that case USIA's assistance will be superfluous. If it does not deserve that support, it seems unlikely that any amount of internal propaganda will close the gap. USIA was clearly acting outside the limits of its statutory authority in assuming this role, and the program has been seriously challenged by the Senate Foreign Relations Committee.

In his article, Johnson concluded that the advantage enjoyed by the United States was that "in virtually every country of the earth" we were working in "voluntary and willing partnership" with governments and societies anxious to preserve their independence and to live in peace. "We cannot believe that such ideals can be less attractive than the totalitarian images projected by the advocates of a collectivist order."

There was no discussion in Johnson's presentation of whether the global role of the United States or the pervasiveness of our presence throughout the third world might not hold some disadvantages in the long run.

In many of the newly independent countries there was a residue of anticolonial feeling and a tendency, which the United States deplored, to look for assistance to sources other than the West. There seems to have been little realization that an unwillingness to accept this kind of diversity requires the establishment of a true Pax Americana.

The proponents of counterinsurgency recognized that the transition from colonialism to independence has usually entailed profound political, economic, and social dislocations that have weakened the emerging states. Yet, these "experts" still presumed that whenever and wherever turbulence breaks out, the United States itself is ultimately threatened. Insurgency is considered of one piece, according to the theorists. One of the most strongly held tenets of policy throughout the Kennedy and Johnson administrations was the belief that there was no essential difference between the situation that existed in Vietnam and the earlier insurgencies in Greece, Malaya, and the Philippines.

President Kennedy's espousal of a counterinsurgency strategy was viewed with greater skepticism abroad than at home. One of the most perceptive observations of the deficiencies of the new approach came from John Douglas Pringle writing in *The Observer* (London) on June 4, 1961. He warned of the danger that President Kennedy might decide too quickly that the tough school was right and that the only practical policy was to meet communism on its own terms. In Washington this was called "fighting fire with fire"—a phrase that sent shudders down more cautious backs, for it implied the retaliatory use of subversion, guerrilla warfare and even, if necessary, direct intervention. Pringle noted that while Kennedy's defense policy had been widely and, on the whole, rightly praised, it was also deliberately designed to give him freedom to fight small wars. Already it was fair to say that President Kennedy was less frightened of war than was President Eisenhower, because he was less dependent on nuclear weapons.

> It is extremely doubtful whether the Administration has given sufficient thought to the implications of such a policy. Apart from the obvious dangers of Chinese intervention and nuclear war, it does not seem to have considered the political effects. Even at its most blatant, Communist subversion (as in South Vietnam) works through indigenous groups so that it does not appear to be foreign intervention. But American in-

tervention, even in the modest form of sending specialists to train guerrillas, is bound to appear as imperialism to people who have only recently gained their independence, and so to strengthen the very forces which Communism exploits.

The administration did not appear to have considered whether it could reconcile such a policy (which, in some cases such as the Bay of Pigs, meant breaking international law) with the support of the United Nations against Communist transgression—one of the great strengths of the West. The answer might be that, unfortunately, the United Nations did not loom very large in the plans of the Kennedy administration.

President Kennedy himself was more inclined to look for salvation to the Western community as a whole—a rather amorphous entity which might include Latin America, but which would certainly repel many of the neutrals of Asia and Africa. It was clear to many foreign observers that President Kennedy did not believe in the possibility of cooperation with the Communists, except possibly in the limited fields of disarmament and arms control. Coexistence for him, as for Khrushchev, was at best competitive. Khrushchev, in supporting the cause of wars of national liberation, and Kennedy, in his counterinsurgency program, shared a common belief that they could win the cold war while avoiding nuclear war. Both had the strength given by faith and the limitations of a rigidly held ideology. Khrushchev believed in the inevitability of communism; Kennedy believed that democracy was the destiny of mankind.

In a lighter vein were the observations of former CIA official Robert Amory, who recalled the extreme reaction to Robert Kennedy's insistence that "everybody get Gung-Ho" about counterinsurgency. The Chief of Staff directed that every Army school devote a minimum of 20 percent of its time to counterinsurgency. This reached the Finance

School and the Cooks and Bakers School, "so they were talking about how to wire typewriters to explode . . . or how to make apple pies with hand grenades inside them."[4]

The major weaknesses and limitations of counterinsurgency strategy were that its success depended on the efforts of the government concerned rather than on those of the United States. To the degree that Americans became involved in such an effort, the United States bore the responsibility for the defeat of the insurgency, but at the same time it lacked the power to assure that the programs necessary toward that end were carried out. There was, therefore, a considerable discrepancy between the theory and the reality.

In theory, successful application of counterinsurgency techniques would be possible if a democratically inclined government of a third-world country were threatened by an insurgency movement feeding on local discontent. In an agriculturally based tropical country the rebellion might center on the rural population; in another case, the core of the insurgency might be a discontented urban proletariat, led by left-wing students and intellectuals. The United States, theoretically, would respond to a call for assistance from the beleaguered government with a broad program including military assistance, light weapons, communications equipment, vehicles, civic-action and military training; an internal security or police program that would strengthen the local police; a public information program under USIA to enable the government to communicate more effectively with the people; and a special program of economic aid for the disaffected areas. The American contribution would be accompanied by a heavy diet of advice on political, economic, and social matters from the American embassy.

Careful application of these elements theoretically would enable the assisted country to pull itself together, and the insurgency, if not actually defeated militarily, would wither away.

While this is the theory, the reality may be much more complex. In reality, the country requesting counterinsurgency assistance may be an economically and socially backward nation with little real claim to national unity, with enormous gaps between the wealthy ruling elite and the miserable urban or rural poor, with deep social and religious cleavages, with a heritage of inept government or with little experience at self-government, with a tradition of civil service corruption. The insurgents may not be only Communists or other left-wing radicals but also deeply disaffected workers or peasants, who have little or no stake in the preservation of the status quo and who will respond to any movement that promises a modicum of the social justice that has been denied them by the ruling oligarchy. To the alienated workers and peasants the government the United States seeks to preserve and shore up may represent nothing more than high taxes and usurious interest rates, military conscription and forced labor, and support of the landlords against those who work the land.

The United States may press the local government to ameliorate conditions and relieve grievances to cut the ground from under the appeal of the insurgent movement, but it is the local government that must carry out the programs. The kind of social reform necessary to forestall insurgency would require the ruling oligarchy to share its power and its property with the masses, the very groups that seek to remove it from power.

On the military side, counterinsurgency requires that violence be held to a minimum in order not to widen the gap between the people and the government. Winning the allegiance of the population means that the government must protect them and keep economic and social disruption of the society to a minimum. But what if the country has a long history of bloody civil strife, of betrayals and reprisals? Government forces may be in constant danger of ambush and thus unlikely to act with restraint toward villagers whom they suspect of cooperation with the rebels. In such cases, the government troops may be the scourge of the countryside, sweeping into villages, confiscating rice and chickens without payment, abusing the women, perhaps even burning the huts in an attempt to deny shelter to rebels.

Perhaps the largest loophole in the counterinsurgency policy is its overestimation of the amount of influence the United States can have on the recipient country once a significant commitment has been made. While we think we are going to be able to use the government in power for our purposes, it is actually able to use us for its own ends, and short of liquidating the commitment, there is little we can do but continue to pay the bill.

Even before the escalation of the war in Vietnam, all these built-in weaknesses of the counterinsurgency policy were in operation and were working for its doom. Eventually, its failure in Vietnam led President Kennedy to make major decisions and commitments that radically changed the character of American involvement and gravely deepened the American commitment. In the words of the Pentagon Papers analysis, Kennedy transformed the "limited-risk gamble" of the Eisenhower administration into a "broad commitment" to prevent Communist domination of South Vietnam.[5]

The revelations of the Pentagon Papers and other material on the Kennedy administration's secret activities in Southeast Asia have led some commentators to condemn the motives of President Kennedy and his advisers. In an article, "Kennedy's Private War," by Ralph L. Stavins in *The New York Review of Books*, for example, Kennedy is said to have made a calculated decision for war; it is claimed that he consciously decided "to accelerate the war."[6]

Academicians who are unfamiliar with the tortuous and usually frustrating process of governmental and Presidential decision-making, and are unaware of how limited is the real power of the President to bring about his will despite his great *apparent* power, frequently overestimate the degree to which a given decision or course of action is clear-cut or purposeful. With hindsight, they accuse the leaders of the past of evil motives and Machiavellian schemes when, at the time, the choice may have been between the best of several inadequate alternatives or when, in the absence of a clear decision, the force of bureaucratic inertia may have been permitted to govern the course of policy.

Criticism of the policy followed by President Kennedy in adopting a counterinsurgency strategy, and through it and other actions deepening American involvement in South Vietnam, does not require the imputation of evil motives to the President. Indeed, the true tragedy of the Vietnam experience and of the Kennedy doctrine in general, and the most bitter lesson for the future, is that these policies were undertaken with the *best* of intentions. They were the reflection of American altruism, of the "can do" spirit of America, of all that has traditionally been considered most noble and honorable in the American character.

President Kennedy and others who supported the counterinsurgency policy naïvely believed that with enough good will, with the right kind of assistance, with the right kind of training, we could convert the South Vietnamese government into a strong freedom-loving democracy that would prevail over its enemies. Our policy-makers apparently never considered what might be the limits of American power to affect the course of events in a society alien to our own, of vastly different values and traditions. Throughout the history of the Kennedy administration's deepening involvement, there was a serious gap between what American policy-makers thought was happening and what was really happening. Thus, as the situation went from bad to worse, confusion and despair in Washington increased. Yet no one ever said—or if he did, it is not recorded—"Maybe it just won't work."

The Pentagon Papers analysis notes that the pervasive

assumption on which the Kennedy administration's policy was based was that the inherent weaknesses in Vietnam— ranging from President Ngo Dinh Diem's lack of administrative expertise to the Army's lack of fighting spirit— could be cured "if enough dedicated Americans, civilians and military, became involved in South Vietnam to show the South Vietnamese, at all levels, how to get on and win the war." Defeat was not considered to be within the realm of possibility for the most powerful nation in the world, and it was assumed that the mere introduction of Americans would give the South Vietnamese "the elan and style needed to win."[7]

As the Pentagon Papers analysis notes, the Kennedy strategy was flawed from the outset for political as well as military reasons because it depended for its success on the willingness of the Diem regime to make the required effort. Yet we had no real means of requiring Diem to make that effort. If he could not or would not reform, then "the U.S. plan to end the insurgency was foredoomed from its inception, for it depended on Vietnamese initiatives to solve a Vietnamese problem."[8]

When President Kennedy took office the situation in South Vietnam was grave, and that in Laos was critical, in terms of the U.S. desire to prevent Communist domination of any of the Southeast Asian countries. The Eisenhower administration policy of backing a right-wing element in Laos had collapsed and the Western position was in jeopardy. On the eve of the inauguration, President Eisenhower warned his successor that he might have to send U.S. troops into Laos. But the new President decided to seek a political compromise, to try for a ceasefire rather than to continue to support the rightist elements. This shift in strategy in Laos led Kennedy to feel that he had to make a show of strength in Vietnam, lest the Communists think him weak and too willing to compromise. The disaster of the Bay of Pigs reinforced him in this determination.

Early in his administration, President Kennedy approved a counterinsurgency plan for Vietnam that had been prepared under the Eisenhower administration. It provided for extensive military and social reforms, which, if carried out, it was claimed, would enable the war to be won in eighteen months.[9]

In late March of 1961, only two months after Kennedy had assumed office, the CIA's National Intelligence Estimate provided a grim picture of the situation in South Vietnam. It reported that deterioration of internal security had reached serious proportions with more than one-half of the countryside to the south and southwest of Saigon under Viet Cong control. Saigon itself was encircled and the Viet Cong had begun to move in closer to the city. The Diem government had survived a coup attempt, but the problems that had given rise to the attempt still existed, with increasing feeling in the Army that President Diem was unable to rally the country to carry on the fight against the Communists.[10]

Two weeks after this gloomy picture had been presented, Walt W. Rostow, then McGeorge Bundy's assistant on the White House National Security staff, laid before President Kennedy a memo in which he urged that the United States turn to "gearing up the whole Vietnam operation."[11] Rostow suggested appointment of a full-time "back stop" man (he had in mind the appointment of long-time CIA operative General Edward Lansdale); a visit to South Vietnam by the Vice President; and an increase in the number of troops in the Military Assistance Advisory Group (MAAG), then limited to 685 under the Geneva accords. This last move, Rostow admitted, "involves some diplomacy, unless we can find an alternative way of introducing into Viet-Nam operation a substantial number of Special Forces types." Although the United States was not a signatory of the Geneva agreements, we had pledged not to move to disrupt them. Rostow's suggestion that the United States expand the MAAG mission beyond the

Geneva limit was, therefore, a proposal for a move into new territory that the Eisenhower administration had not seen fit to make.

Throughout March and early April, deterioration of the military situation in Laos occupied much of the attention of the White House. Events in Laos were to have a profound influence on President Kennedy's decisions with respect to Vietnam. The President was being urged to commit American forces to Laos, but the Joint Chiefs, remembering the bitter experience of the Korean War in which Asian troops had fought the American Army to a standstill, were reluctant to agree to a commitment of American ground forces unless the President would authorize in advance the use of nuclear weapons should the Chiefs determine they were necessary. President Kennedy was unwilling to make such an authorization.[12]

By mid-April it was becoming clear that a political solution leading to a neutralized Laos might be possible. (The Geneva Conference on Laos opened on May 16.) By April 20 the Bay of Pigs invasion had turned into a disaster of major proportions for the American position and for the prestige of the new President. On that same day, Kennedy ordered an immediate reappraisal of the situation in South Vietnam and asked for recommendations for action that would "prevent Communist domination of that country."[13] A task force headed by Deputy Defense Secretary Roswell Gilpatric presented its preliminary report on April 27. But with the Laos crisis at its head, the recommendations were quickly strengthened to include a proposal for introduction of a substantial number of American troops for "training" purposes into South Vietnam, "as insurance against a conventional invasion."[14]

President Kennedy—fearful that in the wake of the Bay of Pigs, Khrushchev might think him weak and irresolute—authorized a token introduction of American troops into Laos, and he authorized American military advisers who up until then had been operating secretly in

Laos to shed their civilian disguises.[15]

Turning his attention back to Vietnam, on April 29 President Kennedy approved some of the military recommendations in the Gilpatric task force report including a 100-man increase in the MAAG mission. While this increase appears modest, it is highly significant in that it represented the first real breach of the Geneva accords by the United States and was thus something of a watershed, if not in military, at least in psychological terms. It was felt that the American move could be justified publicly by saying that the other side was similarly violating the agreements, but the President decided that it would be better to keep the whole thing quiet.

The other significant military decision of April 29 was also a major harbinger and a complete departure from the policy of the past. The President authorized a basic change in the role of the MAAG mission in Vietnam. Its responsibilities were expanded to include "authority to provide support and advice" to the Vietnamese Self-Defense Corps and other elements of the local military forces. For the first time, American troops were being placed in situations that would lead to their involvement in combat. This decision marked the beginning of American casualties in Vietnam.

By early May it had been decided that the United States would not make a major military move in Laos, and planning for Vietnam was affected by this decision. The Gilpatric task-force report underwent several revisions to tone down its recommendations for Vietnam policy and to shape it to the President's desires. In such cases, the final recommendations are usually drafted after the President has reviewed the preliminary report and indicated orally the direction in which he wishes to move, or at least the terms in which he desires the alternatives to be posed. The final task-force report was submitted on May 8, and the President's decisions of May

11 were relayed to the government in National Security Action Memorandum (NSAM) #52 of that date. In this secret document the American objectives in South Vietnam were stated more bluntly than they had ever been to the public:

> To prevent Communist domination of South Vietnam; to create in that country a viable and increasingly democratic society, and to initiate, on an accelerated basis, a series of mutually supporting actions of a military, political, economic, psychological and covert character designed to achieve this objective.[16]

The most important decisions made on May 11 were to send approximately four hundred U. S. Green Berets to accelerate the training of the Vietnamese Special Forces; to begin negotiations for a bilateral defense agreement with South Vietnam, although the President authorized no firm commitment without his further review; and, perhaps most significant, to undertake a program of covert actions against North Vietnam and Laos. These included sending agents into North Vietnam to gather intelligence and conduct sabotage and harassment; overflights by CIA planes for leaflet drops; training of South Vietnamese Army troops for ranger raids; and infiltration of American and South Vietnamese teams into Laos to harass bases and lines of communication. The use over North Vietnam of civilian air crews (presumably under the CIA) of both "American and other nationality" in addition to Vietnamese was also authorized.

These covert operations, known as Operation Farmhand, were among the first approved by the secret committee, later known as the 303 Committee, set up by President Kennedy in the wake of the Bay of Pigs disaster to try to assure control of CIA operations. According to one source, the committee was chaired by McGeorge Bundy and, during the Kennedy administration, included Roswell Gilpatric, Alexis Johnson, and Richard Helms.[17]

It is unclear whether the Attorney General, who had been a member of the committee set up to investigate the Bay of Pigs failure, participated actively in the 303 Committee. The 303 Committee was the counterpart for clandestine operations of the Special Group (Counterinsurgency) set up in 1962 under Maxwell Taylor and Robert Kennedy to manage the overt counterinsurgency operations.[18]

The core group for Operation Farmhand was the highly secret Vietnamese First Observation Group organized in 1956 with headquarters at Nha Trang. Originally planned to prepare stay-behind groups in South Vietnam in the event of conventional North Vietnamese invasion, in 1960 the First Observation Group began to undertake combat missions against the Viet Cong. Under the actions approved by President Kennedy on May 11, 1961, the First Observation group was to be greatly enlarged, supported by four hundred U. S. Special Forces, and relieved of its combat mission so that it could concentrate exclusively on clandestine activities in "denied areas," outside Vietnam.

An important factor in Operation Farmhand's air activities was CAT (Civil Air Transport), a Chinese Nationalist flag airline that operates throughout the Far East from headquarters in Taiwan. An outgrowth of the Flying Tigers, CAT is controlled by Mrs. Anna Chennault, widow of the Flying Tiger leader. CAT is identified in the Pentagon Papers by General Lansdale as "a CIA proprietary" which

> provides air logistical support under commercial cover to most CIA and other U. S. Government agencies' requirements. CAT supports covert and clandestine air operations by providing trained and experienced personnel, procurement of supplies and equipment through overt commercial channels, and the maintenance of a fairly large inventory of transport and other type aircraft under both Chinat and U.S. registry.[19]

CAT has a long history of involvement in U.S. undercover operations in the Far East. Among its "notable achievements," Lansdale listed:

> Support of the Chinese Nationalist withdrawal from the mainland, air drop support to the French at Dien Bien Phu, complete logistical and tactical air support for the Indonesian operation, air lifts of refugees from North Vietnam, more than 200 overflights of Mainland China and Tibet, and extensive air support in Laos during the present crisis. . . .

"The Indonesian operation" apparently refers to the CIA-backed attempt to overthrow the Sukarno government in 1958.[20]

Operation Farmhand raids into North Vietnam were largely unsuccessful. The teams were frequently captured as soon as they landed, and the program led to numerous protests to the International Control Commission by the North Vietnamese, who accused the United States and South Vietnam of espionage and "provocative acts" against North Vietnam.

In May of 1961, Vice President Lyndon Johnson paid an official visit to South Vietnam and embraced President Ngo Dinh Diem as "the Winston Churchill of Asia." When Johnson raised with Diem the possibility of the United States sending combat troops to South Vietnam, the South Vietnamese President was cool. No doubt realizing that large numbers of foreign troops would further discredit his regime in the eyes of his people, he wanted combat troops only in the event of a direct North Vietnamese invasion.

But by fall, as the situation deteriorated further, Diem was asking Washington for a bilateral defense pact, a proposal he had previously rejected.

The White House was preoccupied with the Berlin crisis in the late summer of 1961, but Khrushchev's belligerence strengthened President Kennedy in his determination not to show weakness. After the erection of the Berlin Wall had demonstrated the inability of American policy to prevent a major Communist psychological victory, Kennedy was presumably even more receptive to proposals that he make a show of force in Vietnam. But proposals for the introduction of combat troops were again put off, and President Kennedy elected to proceed with the counterinsurgency strategy that had been proposed by Walt Rostow in June: "aircraft, helicopters, communications men, special forces, militia teachers, etc."[21]

By October, Walt Rostow was proposing a 25,000-man SEATO force for Vietnam to guard the Laos border. Other plans called for sending American troops into the Vietnamese Central Highlands. In addition, the President was being urged by some advisers for the first time to commit the United States to the defeat of the Viet Cong as our "ultimate objective," even though this might require a substantial number of American divisions.

Despite the assumption inherent in the proposals of Rostow and others that infiltration or invasion from Laos and North Vietnam was the major threat, a special edition of the CIA's regular National Intelligence Estimate on October 5 reported that "80–90 percent of the estimated 17,000 VC had been locally recruited, and that there was little evidence that the VC relied on external supplies."[22] The NIE also predicted that "the D.R.V. (North Vietnam) would probably not relax its Vietcong campaign . . . to any significant extent" should SEATO troops be introduced.

Faced with this conflicting advice, President Kennedy decided to send his personal military adviser, General Maxwell Taylor, along with Rostow and others, to Vietnam to investigate the situation on the scene. At a National Security Council meeting on October 11, Taylor was instructed to consider three possible strategies: (1) overt intervention "to defeat" the Viet Cong; (2) smaller or covert intervention involving "fewer U.S. combat forces, mainly to establish a U.S. presence" in Vietnam; or (3) stepping up U.S. assistance and training of Vietnamese units, and furnishing more U.S. equipment.[23] According to the analysis in the Pentagon Papers, the President had, in essence, agreed to the third course of action, involving helicopters, tactical air support, and an expansion of the advisory mission, prior to the departure of the Taylor-Rostow mission.[24] The purpose of the mission, therefore, was to determine whether, and in what degree, overtly designated American combat units would be sent.

On completion of his inspection tour, General Taylor cabled the President proposing the introduction of some eight thousand combat troops whose mission could be labeled as American assistance in overcoming the ravages of a recent flood. This ploy, Taylor said, would permit the troops to be removed easily once the flood-relief mission was completed, or, if it were deemed advisable, their mission could be expanded into actual combat operations. Taylor justified the introduction of combat troops largely on propagandistic grounds, recognizing that while they could "exercise little direct influence on the campaign against the VC," they would "give a much needed shot in the arm to national morale."

Taylor recommended this course of action despite what he recognized were its considerable disadvantages: that our strategic reserve was so weak that we could "ill afford" to allow our forces to be pinned down in a "peripheral area of the Communist bloc"; that U.S. prestige would be even more deeply engaged by sending troops than it was at present; that once troops had been sent, "it will be difficult to resist the pressure to reinforce"; and, finally, that tensions might be increased to the point of risking a major war in Asia.

Taylor's initial proposals were opposed by Secretary of State Rusk, who cabled from Japan, where he was attending a conference, that while he attached "the greatest possible importance" to Southeast Asian security, he was wary of a military commitment without reciprocal political reforms by Diem. Rusk cautioned against committing American prestige too deeply on what might be a "losing horse."[25] It is unclear from the documents whether he meant Diem or South Vietnam itself.

Taylor continued to send messages to President Kennedy recommending sending combat troops for purposes both of raising Vietnamese government morale and of demonstrating our determination to "resist a Communist take-over." He considered the presence of American ground troops "essential . . . to reverse the present downward trend of events." While he discounted the risk of our backing into a major war, he did warn President Kennedy that "the U.S. troops may be called upon to engage in combat to protect themselves . . . [and] as a general reserve, they might be thrown into action."[26]

The main evaluation of the Taylor-Rostow report, the Pentagon Papers analysis concluded, put "Saigon's weaknesses in the best light and avoids suggesting that perhaps the U.S. should consider limiting rather than increasing commitments to the Diem regime." It presumed that all the problems could be solved "if enough dedicated Americans become involved . . . [and] if worse comes to worst, the U.S. could probably save its position in Vietnam by bombing the North."[27]

Simultaneously with the submission of General Taylor's recommendations, a CIA National Intelligence Estimate forecast that Hanoi would match any American escalation of the war, but this judgment of the U.S. intelligence community seems to have been discounted by the White House.

The issue posed by the Taylor-Rostow recommendations was pointedly stated in a joint memorandum to the President from Rusk and McNamara on November 11. This memo was probably written at the direction of the President after discussion at a National Security Council meeting to pose the issue more precisely. It began by defining the American interest in South Vietnam in terms of a strongly worded statement of the domino theory.

> The loss of South Viet-Nam would make pointless any further discussion about the importance of Southeast Asia to the free world; we would have to face the near certainty that the remainder of Southeast Asia and Indonesia would move to a complete accommodation with Communism, if not formal incorporation with the Communist bloc . . . The loss of South Viet-Nam to Communism would not only destroy SEATO but would undermine the credibility of American commitments elsewhere. Further, loss of South Viet-Nam would stimulate bitter domestic controversies in the United States and would be seized upon by extreme elements to divide the country and harass the Administration. . . .

These domino-theory conclusions differed from those of the CIA, which was predicting that should a Communist government emerge in South Vietnam only Laos would be affected. The Rusk-McNamara memorandum also failed to consider that small nations which, for reasons of geography and tradition, make "an accommodation" with communism do not necessarily become enemies of the United States. We have for years enjoyed good relations with Yugoslavia and Finland, for example. Burma, while making "an accommodation" with communism, has quite successfully maintained isolation from all foreign influence. Cambodia, under the leadership of Prince Sihanouk in the early 1960's, made a similar accommodation; yet any country, such as this, where Pepsi-Cola can be found in the outlying villages can hardly be said to be entirely removed from American influence.

The fears expressed of the "bitter domestic controversies" that might arise if South Vietnam was lost seem particularly ironic. It is difficult to imagine that they could have approached in intensity those that arose as a result of the actions to prevent that loss.

Rusk and McNamara proposed that the United States should "commit itself to the clear objective of preventing the fall of South Viet-Nam. . . ." and, to that end,

> we should be prepared to introduce United States combat forces if that should become necessary for success. Dependent upon circumstances, it may also be necessary for United States forces to strike at the source of aggression in North Viet-Nam.[28]

The Rusk-McNamara memo attempted to make a clear distinction between two kinds of American forces. The first, which *"Should be introduced as speedily as possible,"** were support troops, such as helicopter companies, reconnaissance aircraft, naval patrols, and intelligence units. The second category would be "larger organized units with actual or potential direct military mission." It was recognized that the second category would pose a more serious problem in terms of both of U.S. domestic reaction and possible matching Communist escalation. The two Secretaries noted that "the ultimate possible extent" of our military commitment in Southeast Asia in the event of overt intervention by Hanoi and Peking would be approximately 205,000 men.

It is difficult to understand how the Joint Chiefs could have underestimated so seriously the number of U.S. forces that would ultimately be required when they knew that the intelligence community was predicting that the enemy would match American escalation. Seven years later the total American commitment on the ground in South Vietnam reached two and one-half times that number *without* overt intervention by Hanoi or Peking.

Rusk and McNamara noted that employment of combat forces posed

---

* Italics in original.

a certain dilemma: if there is a strong South Vietnamese effort, they may not be needed; if there is not such an effort, United States forces could not accomplish their mission in the midst of an apathetic or hostile population.

In addition, Rusk and McNamara felt that openly introducing large numbers of ground troops might risk provoking a Communist breach of the cease-fire in Laos. They also suggested that unless other nations would agree to send troops, it would be "difficult to explain to our own people why no effort had been made to invoke SEATO or why the United States undertook to carry this burden unilaterally."[29] Other material in the Pentagon Papers suggests that these were the President's personal concerns. He also felt that there would be difficulty convincing the people that this was a case of Communist aggression because there was no clear-cut invasion as in Korea. If the United States sent more than advisers, he thought, we would have to have the support of other nations. In addition, Congress was opposed to the introduction of troops.[30]

An additional factor probably influenced Kennedy's decision to hold back on an overt commitment of ground troops. In mid-July 1961, General Douglas MacArthur had visited the President at the White House. MacArthur came for lunch, but Kennedy kept him on for three hours. According to former Presidential Assistant Kenneth O'Donnell, Kennedy emerged from the meeting with MacArthur "somewhat stunned."[31] He spoke admiringly of the retired general who, he said, had been highly critical of the advice the Pentagon had been giving the President. MacArthur "implored the President to avoid a U.S. military build-up in Vietnam" or elsewhere on the mainland of Asia. He regarded the domino theory as "ridiculous in a nuclear age."

Despite these concerns and despite their own reservations, Rusk and McNamara recommended in their November 11 memo the adoption of an unqualified commitment to South Vietnam and the introduction of enough combat troops to do the job. On November 13 President Kennedy accepted all of the recommendations in the memorandum with the exception of the total commitment to preventing the fall of South Vietnam. U.S. troops sent to Vietnam, however, would still be known formally as advisers. In practice, it was difficult to maintain the distinction between the two categories of troops noted in the Rusk-McNamara memorandum. As time went on, the distinction blurred between advisers who engaged in combat and ordinary combat troops. By the time of his death, President Kennedy had sent nearly 17,000 American military men to South Vietnam.

In addition to the military actions approved on November 13, Kennedy also decided to require Diem to make a "concrete demonstration . . . that he is now prepared to work in an orderly way . . . and broaden the political base of his regime. . . ." As to the U.S. role vis-à-vis the Saigon government, instructions to the American ambassador in Saigon noted that "we would expect to share in the decision-making process in the political, economic and military fields as they affect the security situation."[32]

Diem was disappointed at President Kennedy's unwillingness to make a total commitment and objected to the political conditions. So strongly did President Kennedy feel about the necessity of proceeding with his Vietnam program that on December 7 he authorized the American embassy to soften the demands for reform and a share of the decision-making. Thus the commitment made by Kennedy had essentially none of the political quid pro quos suggested by Secretary Rusk. The United States was becoming more deeply involved in South Vietnam—and on Vietnamese terms rather than on American terms.

Documents that have become available to the press indicate that throughout 1962, even after his decision to send "advisers," President Kennedy focused his attention on a counterinsurgency program in Vietnam rather than on a military build-up exclusively. According to an article by Chalmers Roberts in the *Washington Post* on July 1, 1971, a National Security Action Memorandum of January 18, 1962, established the Special Group (Counterinsurgency) "to assure unity of effort and the use of all available resources with maximum effectiveness in preventing and resisting subversive insurgency and related forms of indirect aggression in friendly countries." The "critical areas" assigned to the group for coordination of counterinsurgency efforts were Laos, Vietnam, and Thailand. President Kennedy pressed particularly heavily on the AID program for supporting local police forces, directing AID to give the program greater "autonomy within AID, if this seems necessary . . . to protect it from neglect."

In May the President directed the inauguration of training in counterinsurgency for higher-level officials at the Departments of State, Defense, and Justice, the CIA, AID, and USIA and also for "selected foreign nationals."

The Joint Chiefs, however, continued to discount the utility of the counterinsurgency approach particularly in Vietnam, and felt that if the Viet Cong were not brought under control they could see "no alternative" to the full commitment of U.S. combat ground forces.

Throughout 1962 there were disputes within the administration as to how the counterinsurgency program in Vietnam was faring. Roger Hilsman, Assistant Secretary of State for Intelligence and Research, was optimistic; the CIA less so.

Kennedy's counterinsurgency strategy for Vietnam as developed in early 1962 centered on the building of strategic hamlets. The program was worked out by Robert K. G. Thompson, head of the British Advisory Mission in Saigon. Thompson, a career officer in the British colonial service, had spent much of his career in Malaya, and it was on the basis of his experience in the Malayan Emergency that he devised the plan that the Kennedy administration hoped would be successful in Vietnam.

Thompson felt that the insurgencies in Asia were rooted in the awakening of Asia's rural population to the modern world that had occurred during the Japanese occupation and the anticolonial struggles that followed. To be successful, any program to defeat insurgency must aim "to establish and maintain a free, independent and united country which is politically and economically stable and viable."[33] Since an insurgent struggle is a war for the control of the people rather than for the control of territory, the government must aim to restore its authority and maintain law and order throughout the country.

Another important principle, according to Thompson, is that the government must function according to the law. He recognized that frustration often arises over lengthy and cumbersome legal processes not designed for emergency situations. But if a government does not act according to the law, it forfeits the right to be called a government; it cannot then expect its people to obey the law. The law may be toughened to meet emergency situations, he notes, but each new law must be effectively and impartially applied. Detention, for example, is a controversial policy, yet it is a power that most Western governments have exercised in time of war.

Finally, the government must have an overall plan for defeating the insurgency, a plan that emphasizes the defeat of the political subversion rather than the defeat of the guerrillas themselves. Unless the subversive political organization is eliminated, the insurgency will reappear. Isolation of the population from the guerrillas is the only way to root out the underground political organization that supports and sustains the guerrillas.

As far as Vietnam was concerned, Thompson felt that a serious error had been made after independence in that a large conventional army was established to counter what was presumed to be a conventional military threat from North Vietnam. Political power in the country quickly went to the army, and the government was required to devote much effort to juggling various army commands to retain control and keep possible plotters from growing strong enough to move against civilian rule. Efforts to encourage Diem to broaden the base of his government foundered because real power lay with the army.

Paying and supplying the army was a heavy economic burden on the new nation and required accepting an indefinite amount of American aid. Such dependence on foreign aid is politically and psychologically disastrous for a young country. The Americans were similarly trapped, for there was no easy way to disengage or install a more flexible program of alternative sources of supply of military hardware. Foreign aid, particularly military aid, tended to tie the United States to Vietnam.

Emphasis on the development of the army had meant that all the best young talent had gone into the army, with little left for government administration. Eventually most of the three hundred-odd province and district chiefs were military officers. Further, the army tended to preempt what meager services were available. In a country with insufficient numbers of trained personnel, this left nothing for the civilian side. Military hospitals, for example, refused to treat civilians, yet there were few civilian hospitals. In other areas, such as propaganda, radio, and psychological warfare, the army tended to usurp the functions of the civilian government, although it tried to make amends by promoting civic action. What was happening in Vietnam, Thompson felt, was that a large conventional army, trained to defeat, occupy, and administer a foreign country, was performing those same functions, in the same style, in its own country. The army failed to develop disciplined behavior among the troops, and this tended to negate the effects of civic-action projects. Such emphasis on the military side was an obvious reflection of a misunderstanding of the nature of internal war.

Thompson did not think democracy was necessary or a particularly salable item in the Far East; he felt that it could not make a real contest with communism. People could be convinced, he felt, if the rule of law was established. Only if the government had constructive programs and then delivered the goods, could it get popular support. Security, he believed, must precede the building of the democratic process, and, most important, the determination and capacity to win must be demonstrated to the people.

The strategic-hamlet program planned by Thompson began in early 1962, although preliminary work had been done during the previous two years. Since Vietnamese villages tended to be scattered, with the peasants living near their fields, relocation was necessary. At first it was estimated that some eleven thousand strategic hamlets would be required. Some 50 percent would require only minor regrouping or relocating of houses, 30 percent would require major regrouping (more than half the houses would have to be relocated), and the remaining 20 percent would have to be completely regrouped.

Relocation to the strategic hamlets would isolate the villagers from the Viet Cong so that they could not provide food or recruits to the rebels. The strategic-hamlet program had two main objectives. The first was the protection of the population. In addition to physical defense, barbed wire, and a moat, good radio communication with the district capital and with the other villages would be established. Hamlet militia were to be trained to protect against guerrilla raids. The most important aspect of the program was to be the elimination of the Viet Cong infrastructure, the underground political organization. Until this was done, the hamlet would not be secure and the people could not be expected to declare for the government.

The second objective was to unite the people and involve them in positive action on the government side. Community spirit would be built and a sense of national solidarity promoted. This program was thought necessary because in many remote villages there was little realization that there was a government in Saigon that was ultimately responsible for the fate and welfare of the people.

Many of the military, American and Vietnamese, objected to the strategic-hamlet program on the grounds that it was a defensive strategy, but Thompson contended that its purpose was to secure base areas and then expand.[34]

The techniques proposed by Thompson, like the problem of insurgency itself, were not new. The idea of moving the people off the land and concentrating them in fortified villages so that military operations against guerrillas could be carried on more easily was at least as old as the century. During the Boer War, a substantial British expeditionary force landed in South Africa in 1900, and captured all the major cities. The Boer states were then annexed to the British Crown. Assuming that the war was over, the British commander returned home, leaving mopping-up operations to Lord Kitchener. But the Boers, under such leaders as Jan Christiaan Smuts, continued to fight. They carried on an extensive and well-coordinated guerrilla campaign, attacking outposts and disrupting British communications. Kitchener was unable to control the elusive bands of Boer guerrillas who struck and then disappeared into the countryside. To clear the countryside and break the Boer resistance, the British rounded up the Boer families from their scattered farms and concentrated them in areas that could be more easily defended—hence the origin of the term "concentration camp."

During the first Indochina war, the French more or less successfully employed the technique of regrouping and reorganizing isolated populations so that the people would have no choice but to support the government, and would be unable to sustain the guerrillas moving about the countryside. The French settlements were referred to as "regroupment" camps. (For obvious reasons, after World War II the term "concentration camp" fell into disuse.) The technique was employed in a frontier province in 1946 and later in villages along the Mekong and Bassac rivers in Cochin-China. In 1952 the French regrouped nearly half a million Cambodians from underpopulated areas in Kampot and Takeo provinces. This operation was considered to have been the first significantly successful French use of the technique, which then became the main pillar of the counterinsurgency strategy in the Algerian War. French claims of success for this technique may have been premature and the example was not the best. The Cambodians are atypical among the peoples of Indochina in that they have a strong sense of national identity centered on loyalty to their king. They also have a 2000-year history of animosity to the Vietnamese, who comprised the majority of the rebels in Cambodia during the period of the regroupment. The regroupment technique *was* successful in helping to break the back of the Algerian revolution, which achieved political success in spite of a successful military suppression of the insurgency by the French.

According to the Pentagon Papers, despite optimistic reports of progress, the strategic-hamlet program in Vietnam "failed dismally" as had similar programs attempted by the French in Vietnam. Some of the reasons for the failure are suggested by Asian affairs expert Milton Osborne, who concluded that the Malayan experience on which Thompson based the strategy was not comparable to the situation in Vietnam.[35] In Malaya, as in Cambodia, the insurgents were ethnically different people with no long history in the country. The Malayan rebels were a Chinese minority who were divided in their loyalties between Communists and non-Communists. The nucleus of the insurgency was the 500,000-Chinese community, particularly in the squatter settlements that had sprung up during the Japanese occupation. Since these were not permanent settlements with long histories, resettlement was not strongly resisted by the people.

Thus, in Malaya, an alien population with little social cohesion was uprooted and transferred to new locations. In Vietnam, on the other hand, under the strategic-hamlet program, the attempt was made to "resettle established communities with very strong ritual ties to the soil which they had occupied over periods at times exceeding one, and sometimes even two, hundred years."[36] The villagers were being removed from lands which bore the graves of their ancestors, sites to which they had strong religious ties. Further, in Vietnam the villagers were not ethnically separate from the supporters of the government, as was the case in Malaya. In Malaya, many of the Chinese squatters were miners or industrial workers rather than farmers, and thus not attached to the land.

Other differences were the relatively small number of people resettled in Malaya as compared with Vietnam, and the dissimilarity in the agricultural pattern. Once the resettlement had been accomplished in Malaya, it was possible to deny food to the guerrillas, but in the rich Mekong Delta it was practically impossible to deny food supplies to the insurgents; they helped themselves from the fields.

In addition, the extent of the insurgency was much greater in Vietnam. Osborne notes that the official rate of terrorist incidents against the government during the period of the strategic-hamlet program was a hundred government and civilian casualties per day and some five hundred violent incidents per week. In Malaya at the height of the Emergency these figures averaged less than seven per day.

But, Osborne concludes, the qualitative difference between the Malayan and Vietnamese insurgencies was more important than the quantitative difference. He is highly critical of the decision to embark on the program, claiming that sufficient information was available at the time to indicate the inapplicability of the Malayan experience. He was left with the "uncomfortable feeling that too many important political decisions were made on the basis of hope and supposition rather than on the basis of careful analysis of fact."[37]

Most counterinsurgency experts agree that in any case the Diem government pushed resettlement at much too rapid a pace. The Vietnamese National Assembly endorsed the strategic-hamlet program in April of 1962, and only eight months later, in December, Diem announced that 4,077 hamlets had been completed of a total of over 11,000 to be built and that 39 percent of the population, or more than five million people, were living in these hamlets. In Malaya it took two years to resettle only 66,000.

In retrospect, President Kennedy's decisions of November 13, 1961, seem momentous. At the time, they apparently did not. So much attention had been focused on the issue of whether to send ground combat troops to Vietnam at that time that the strengthening of combat support troops and the expansion of the role of the advisory mission came "almost by default," without real assessment of the long-term consequences.[38]

But these decisions indicate that President Kennedy accepted in principle the necessity of preserving South Vietnam as an anti-Communist state, although he was unwilling to make a formal public commitment to that goal. He was determined to pursue, at least through 1963, a counterinsurgency strategy rather than a purely military strategy. This was a compromise that took account of public and Congressional reluctance to support a heavy military commitment.

Yet the distinction between the two approaches was more semantic than real. The President felt that he was doing the right thing but that it could not be explained well enough to the public, so that it would support the program. Apparently he never considered using his position as President to attempt to convince the nation of the wisdom of the course of action he felt was in the national interest. He preferred to follow an equivocal, devious course, rather than to lead the nation in the direction he felt it should go. And it apparently never occurred to President Kennedy or to his advisers that carrying out, by these somewhat devious means, policies with which the nation was probably not in sympathy, and would probably not support, was a perversion of the democratic process.

The administration did not learn until after the overthrow of President Diem on November 1, 1963, how seriously the situation in Vietnam had deteriorated. It was misled by optimistic reports of the success of the strategic-hamlet program and to some extent by its own wishful thinking.

But it was already clear by the summer of 1963 that Diem was unwilling and perhaps unable to govern the country in a manner that would permit American programs to be carried forward. A serious crisis with the Buddhists broke out in midsummer, culminating in the famous raid on the pagodas by Diem's American-trained Special Forces. World attention to the raids and the subsequent suicides by fire of Buddhist monks made the American commitment to Diem less and less defensible to the American people.

The step-by-step complicity of the U.S. government, including President Kennedy himself, in the plot to overthrow Diem has been documented. Although the United States did not instigate the coup, it was kept informed and went along with every step, even assisting the plotters with information as to the disposition of forces loyal to Diem. We know that the United States Embassy had also promised the generals that we would not interfere to prevent the success of a coup. A major CIA operative worked so closely with the plotters that he was actually present in the room with them when the coup was launched. It is clear that the coup would never have occurred had the generals not been certain of U.S. backing.

The documents make clear that the decision to support the overthrow of Diem was not made on the spur of the moment but was a thoroughly conscious policy of the United States government. The chief exponent of the coup was newly appointed Ambassador Henry Cabot Lodge, who arrived in Saigon at the time of the raid on the pagodas. While President Kennedy gave Lodge considerable discretion in managing the day-to-day dealings with the plotters, his every move was in response to detailed guidance from Washington. On August 29, 1963, when the coup attempt was considered imminent, a cable from Secretary Rusk to Lodge gave the ambassador detailed instructions that had been approved at a National Security Council meeting. Lodge was told that the United States "will support a coup which has a good chance of succeeding but plans no direct involvement of U.S. armed forces." This particular language, which recalls that used by President Kennedy at the time of the Bay of Pigs, permits the use of CIA agents, who are not considered members of the U.S. armed forces. Lodge was authorized to announce, at his own discretion, the suspension of American aid to the Diem government. The plotters had asked for this suspension as a demonstration that the United States supported their efforts. It was considered "the green light."

On August 30, in a private cable to Lodge, President Kennedy said that he had given his "full support" to the instructions of the previous day and added, "we will do all that we can to help you conclude this operation successfully."[39]

The August coup plan was aborted by the generals themselves, but the plotting continued with the full knowledge of Washington. It is clear from the record that in the weeks and months leading up to the coup that finally did succeed on November 1, President Kennedy gave Lodge broad authority. It is also clear that Kennedy kept very close control over the American involvement and understood exactly how specific he would have to be to overrule any action by his ambassador. In the final days, he did not overrule him.

While the murders of Diem and his brother were not part of the plot, the record indicates that while Lodge had arranged specific American protection for the plotters should they fail, he made no similar arrangements for Diem beyond a somewhat vague telephone offer to "do anything for your personal safety."[40]

The decision to support the overthrow of Diem was the second and most significant watershed in the Vietnam involvement under President Kennedy. Indeed, a strong case can be made that no other move in the whole story, except perhaps the full-scale build-up that began in 1965, was as important.

In deciding to remove Diem, who had been the pillar of American policy in Southeast Asia for nine years, the United States inserted itself perhaps irrevocably into the Vietnamese struggle. We became, to a large extent, morally as well as politically responsible for the future of the Vietnamese government. There is no evidence that any thought was given in the Kennedy administration to the long-term consequences of Diem's disappearance.

President Kennedy apparently assumed as he deepened American involvement that the United States, with its enormous power, would be able to control the situation; that the generals would be more malleable as instruments of American policy than Diem had been; and that, with the military in control, the war would continue and there would be no danger of a secret deal with Hanoi. The accession to power of the generals removed the fear, prevalent in the Kennedy administration, that Saigon might make peace with Hanoi under the terms of which the United States would be asked to leave Vietnam. This possibility was clearly unacceptable to Washington.

But with the exception of Ho Chi Minh, there was no personality of any stature in Vietnam to serve as a replacement for Diem. For all his faults, Diem had been regarded by his people as a genuine nationalist.

Repugnance over the necessity to accept foreign aid is a greatly undervalued factor in most discussions of American foreign policy, and in particular in discussions of our involvement in Vietnam. The term "My-Diem," American-Diem, commonly used in the early 1960's by Vietnamese peasants to refer to any government official, demonstrated how clearly Diem was linked in the minds of the ordinary Vietnamese with foreign control. Yet he was considered less a tool of the foreigners than the succession of military nonentities who followed him.

Washington has always failed to recognize the subtle psychological twist by which the recipients of our aid are more likely to hate us for it than to be grateful. When Secretary McNamara went to Vietnam and tried to bolster the prestige of General Nguyen Khanh by holding his hand up in front of the crowd and the cameras, the effect on the Vietnamese population was almost certainly the opposite of what was sought.

The political vacuum after the death of Ngo Dinh Diem drew the United States more and more deeply into Vietnamese affairs on every level. Political chaos followed the coup, and the counterinsurgency program, particularly the strategic-hamlet program, collapsed. Yet, there was apparently no thought in Washington that this might be an excellent opportunity for the United States to begin disengagement. It was typical of the mentality that governed the Kennedy administration, and which continued under President Johnson with the same advisers, that the chaos became one more challenge to the American "Can do" spirit, one more problem for the master problem-solvers, one more managerial task for the experts.

In all of this, President Kennedy and his advisers were never aware of the intellectual and nationalist arrogance that characterized the counterinsurgency policy: the American concept of national security alone defines the role of "friendly countries." Upheavals in such countries may turn against the interests of the United States and, consequently, the interests of "freedom"; therefore, insurgencies must be suppressed. But if the friendly country is less than efficient in suppressing insurgencies, then the United States is justified in taking any course, even the overthrowing of that friendly government in the interest of assuring that the struggle will be pursued. For, after all, it is our interests, not theirs, that matter.

Arthur Schlesinger saw President Kennedy shortly after he had received the news that the coup had taken place and that the Vietnamese President and his brother lay dead of assassins' bullets. Schlesinger described him as "somber and shaken. I had not seen him so depressed since the Bay of Pigs. No doubt he realized that Vietnam was his great failure in foreign policy, and that he had never really given it his full attention."[41]

In a bitter historic parallel, twenty-one days later the American President, and five years later *his* brother, lay dead of assassins' bullets.

Seven | Sufficient Beyond Doubt: The Arms Race

In the opinion of many knowledgeable observers within the government and without, there was in early 1961 an opportunity to halt the arms race with the Soviet Union. Even if competition between the nuclear superpowers could not be ended, these observers thought there might be a period of stability in which each side would accept that its strategic forces were sufficient to destroy the other and, therefore, to deter any attack. It was hoped that each side would realize that a further expansion of these forces would yield little additional advantage, that expansion would only stimulate the other side to "catch up," resulting in an increase in the size and sophistication of nuclear arsenals, and therefore in the danger of war by accident or miscalculation, without any increase in security for either side.

Shortly before John F. Kennedy took the oath of office as President of the United States, Soviet and American scientists met in Moscow at a Pugwash Conference. These unofficial conferences, named after the Nova Scotia summer residence of their founder, Cleveland industrialist Cyrus Eaton, periodically brought together disarmament experts from around the world. At the Moscow meeting, V. V. Kuznetzov, a high official in the Soviet Foreign Office, met with Walt Rostow and Jerome Wiesner, who was to become President Kennedy's science adviser. Kuznetzov expressed concern about the furor over defense policy during the recent Presidential campaign, and he warned the Americans that should the new administration embark on a massive arms build-up, the Soviet Union would not stand idly by.[1] There seemed to be a suggestion that the Soviets were seeking a reduction of tensions and a respite from the arms race. Further gestures were forthcoming and they reinforced that original impression. Khrushchev sent President Kennedy an unusually warm congratulatory message on his inauguration and, a few days later, freed two American Air Force officers who had been held prisoner in the Soviet Union.

But Kennedy was apparently more impressed by Soviet words than by Soviet actions. Khrushchev's speech of January 6, 1961, declared the Soviet government's faith in the inevitable victory of socialism through wars of national liberation. Arthur Schlesinger reports that Kennedy regarded this statement as the "authoritative exposition of Soviet intentions" and that it "alarmed Kennedy more than Moscow's amiable signals assuaged him."[2]

Such a reaction indicates a lack of understanding of the special role of propaganda, particularly expressions of optimism, in Communist states. Euphoric or belligerent statements such as Khrushchev's may be the result of domestic as well as international factors. Frequently, too, they are used as smokescreens to mask serious conciliatory gestures. To a significant extent, Kennedy seems to have taken Khrushchev at his word—a mistake the Soviet leader did not make about the new American President.

For various reasons, President Kennedy chose not to take the Soviet overtures seriously. He moved early in his administration to increase significantly the American strategic arsenal—a decision that doomed any immediate chance for agreement on a nuclear test ban and led directly to the Soviet decision to resume testing in the fall of 1961.

Before discussing President Kennedy's fateful decisions and the factors that led him to them, it is important to establish the framework that has governed thinking about defense policy in the nuclear era. Once both the Soviet Union and the United States had acquired the ability to attack each other with nuclear missiles, it became apparent that there could be no effective physical defense against such an attack. Since then, both sides have relied on what are essentially psychological defenses. Strategies of mutual deterrence are, in reality, a competition in the accumulation of arms in such a way as to convince the opponent that the risk of attack is not worth taking. In theory, as long as each side can maintain the ability to inflict an unacceptable degree of damage on the other, even after absorbing an initial attack, deterrence will work.

The strategy of deterrence, however, suffers from both psychological and technical defects. In the first instance, it is always necessary to maintain the credibility of the deterrent. The potential enemy must be convinced that the weapons of mass destruction will be used, even though all sane men might agree that their use could mean the end of life on earth. There is, to a large extent, a built-in absurdity in the proposition that to defend "freedom" or, alternatively, "communism" each side must be able and willing to initiate what might well become mutual annihilation. Thus, to maintain credibility, each side is constantly under pressure to exercise various forms of nuclear saber rattling, to exercise what John Foster Dulles referred to as brinkmanship. In a situation of mutual threat, each side fears above all else the dangers of demonstrating weakness, for insofar as the enemy perceives weakness he will be tempted to take advantage. Thus at regular intervals, each side must produce a sufficient number of alarms, of threatening gestures, and of shoutings in the wings to convince the enemy of his determination to stand fast. If he cannot completely convince the enemy, at least he must instill a measure of doubt as to his intentions. The enemy will not attack if he is uncertain as to the response. This situation, as Jerome Frank has pointed out, leads both the United States and the Soviet Union "to indulge in essentially irrational gestures in an effort to demonstrate their resoluteness."[3] But if such gestures are taken seriously, they may do more than deter aggression; they may stimulate a reaction. Thus, inherent psychological pressures are constantly at work to destabilize the balance of terror.

The second major defect in the strategy of deterrence is the inexorable march of technological development. The opponents in the nuclear-arms race are never content to rely only on existing stockpiles for deterrence. They live in constant fear that the other side might be on the verge of a major technological breakthrough that would give it an overwhelming advantage. A major breakthrough would neutralize the deterrent, that is, make possible an attack that would wipe out the enemy's retaliatory force. Because of the fear that the enemy may be on the verge of a breakthrough—and one can never be sure that he is not—each side is moved to ever-greater efforts in research and development of new weapons. And, as has been amply demonstrated in recent years, success in research and development leads almost inevitably to purchase and deployment of the new weapon. If something works well, why not use it?

We cannot be sure that the Soviets are not installing successful Defense A; therefore, we must develop Offense B to protect our deterrent by being sure that we can penetrate Defense A—which may, in fact, not exist. Yet, if we are capable of developing Offense B, we must assume that they too are capable of doing so, and therefore we must develop Defense C to avoid that danger. Strategic theorists refer to this pattern as the action-reaction phenomenon, and many assert that it is the primary fuel of the arms race. George Rathjens of MIT, one of the soundest analysts of these matters, has written that uncertainty about the intentions of the adversary "may well be the most powerful stimulant of the arms race."[4] Thus it is usually considered that increased knowledge of the opponent's intentions and abilities increases the security of both sides and reduces the chances of the outbreak of nuclear war. Conversely, rising uncertainty and secrecy tend to produce a reaction or indeed an overreaction and to decrease the security of both sides, both of which are then moved to further reactions. Lack of information also increases the chance for war, particularly the chance for a preemptive strike by the side that fears the adversary is about to achieve a first-strike capability, the ability to wipe out the enemy's retaliatory force.

These powerful psychological factors were at work in the early part of 1961 when President Kennedy was considering his first defense budget. But they were not alone in influencing his decisions.

Every President is subject to constant pressure from the military services to develop and purchase new weapons. The Air Force, for example, is the strongest military lobby on Capitol Hill and has many powerful and articulate friends in both the Senate and the House. It has also developed, particularly since World War II, a powerful civilian constituency, carefully cultivated through a highly successful public relations effort.

The Pentagon routinely supplies to Congressional offices a map of the United States that illustrates, in shadings from white to black, the importance of the aerospace industry to the economy of each of the fifty states. Only one or two of the states are white or light gray, indicating the presence of little or no defense-related industry.

President Kennedy was determined to deny the Air Force its longed-for new bomber, the B-70, which he felt was not needed, and he therefore felt he could not deal harshly with its other requests without political repercussions.

An additional factor was the Skybolt missile, a kind of airborne Polaris. Skybolt was an air-to-ground missile designed to be fired from the American B-52 and the British V bomber. As a strategic weapon, it was competing with the Polaris and Minuteman systems for funding. The Air Force strongly backed continuation of the Skybolt program because, in essence, it provided a means of prolonging the effective life of the B-52 bomber force.

Dr. Herbert York, former Director of Defense Research and Engineering in the Pentagon, reports that there was general agreement that the Skybolt was a dubious program from the very beginning. But President Kennedy felt that, for reasons of Air Force politics, he could not kill both the B-70 bomber program and the Skybolt program at the same time. As he put it, he needed the Skybolt to shoot down the bomber.[5] There is a real question—and the British were absolutely convinced—that the Kennedy administration continued to encourage the British to accept and count on the Skybolt missile even though we knew it was no good and would most likely be canceled at a later date. When it was canceled, the American decision precipitated a major crisis in Anglo-American relations and a domestic crisis for the British government.

To some extent Kennedy was a prisoner of his own campaign rhetoric, which had accused the Republicans of permitting the development of a missile gap.

Since 1954 the Eisenhower administration had been concerned about the possibility of a missile gap, as it was known that the Soviets were ahead of the United States in the development of large rockets. The Soviet lead was confirmed in 1957, when they became the first nation to develop a rocket sufficiently powerful to place a satellite in orbit. By 1959, however, the post-Sputnik panic had largely dissipated. U-2 flights over the Soviet Union had produced evidence that while the Russians might have more missiles than the United States, there would be no gap in deterrence, that is, it made no difference in the strategic balance.

Yet, despite the evidence, the tendency of planners in the military to try to provide for the worst possible occurrence led to the claim that a missile gap might develop in the 1960's.

Robert Amory, a former CIA official, has indicated how the idea of this potential missile gap developed.[6] Once the Soviet Union had demonstrated through the Sputnik launch the capacity to build a missile of very high thrust, American planners made projections, on the basis of their knowledge of the Soviet industrial potential, of the Soviet capacity to build numbers of similar missiles for use as ICBM's. These projections assumed that the Soviet ICBM design would be frozen at the very first missile. From this projection, they calculated the time when the Soviets would have one-hundred missiles, then five-hundred, then thousands. By comparing these projections with American plans—when we would have the equivalent number of missiles—a *potential* missile gap was developed. Those who sought justification for increased arms spending as well as those who sought political profit ignored the "potential" part of it, and the alarm spread.

In fact, rather than proceeding from their first ICBM design, the Soviets concentrated on intermediate-range missiles (IRBM's), which were a threat to Western Europe but not to the United States directly. They made a similar decision with respect to strategic bombers. While they clearly had the capacity to do so, the Soviets never developed a long-range bomber comparable to our B-52. Instead, they concentrated on medium-range bombers that threatened Europe. But the *possibility* that the Soviets might develop a long-range bomber was seized upon by the U. S. Air Force as requiring American development of a new generation of bombers beyond the B-52.

These Soviet decisions to concentrate in their strategy on a threat to Western Europe were apparently the result of their belief that, as far as the United States was concerned, Western Europe was a hostage. Soviet planners must have felt that the President of the United States would not permit Paris or Rome to be demolished for the sake, for example, of keeping Iran out of Soviet control. This analysis was probably correct, although the Kennedy administration spent much time and energy trying to convince the world to the contrary. In this respect, the Soviets were rather more sophisticated than we in determining what were the vital interests of the United States. Washington, on the other hand, has always attempted to give the impression that each of the nations around the world to which we are "committed" under the alliances negotiated in the mid-1950's by John Foster Dulles is of equal importance to the security of the United States.

It was already clear by 1960 that the missile gap was a fallacy. Yet, as it became a major issue in the heat of the Presidential campaign, the outgoing administration, despite the personal prestige of President Eisenhower and his assurance that our defenses were adequate, was hard pressed to defend its policies. Democrats accused the Republicans of niggardliness, of placing a budgetary limitation on defense, and of being unwilling to surpass that limitation no matter the threat. Candidate Kennedy pledged that as President he would submit to no such arbitrary restriction: the missile gap would be eliminated, no matter the cost.

By the time of Kennedy's inauguration, press reports were beginning to deflate the missile-gap rhetoric. The prestigious Institute for Strategic Studies in Britain, which issues annual estimates of the military balance between the nuclear powers, reported that the USSR had about thirty-five operational ICBM's and some two hundred long-range bombers.[7] Just after Kennedy's inauguration, the Republican Policy Committee, anxious to disprove Democratic claims that under Republican stewardship defenses had been slighted, revealed the major components of the American strategic force. It included two Polaris submarines, each with sixteen missiles, and sixteen Atlas ICBM's, including a number in firing position. (The Atlas was a liquid-fueled missile, usually stored horizontally above the ground in coffinlike concrete casings. Before the Atlas could be fired, it had to be fueled and then raised to firing position.) According to the Republican Policy Committee position paper made public by the then Congressman Melvin Laird, the United States also had over six hundred B-52 strategic bombers, fourteen hundred B-47 medium-range bombers, fourteen aircraft carriers (at that time the Soviets had none), eighteen wings of tactical aircraft, sixty Thor IRBM's in England, thirty Jupiter IRBM's being installed in Italy and fifteen planned for Turkey.[8] At the beginning of 1961 the United States had a total of over two thousand nuclear delivery vehicles, or enough to destroy the Soviet Union ten times.

The existence of this missile gap in reverse, with the Soviet Union on the short end, was quickly discovered by the new Secretary of Defense, Robert McNamara. To the embarrassment of the White House, McNamara revealed the true situation to the press in early February. The White House quickly denied McNamara's statement and insisted that there was a missile gap, but when President Kennedy was asked about it during his February 8 news conference, he had to fall back on the explanation that "no study had been concluded" in the matter. Somewhat disingenuously the President added, "Of course, it is my hope that the

United States is fully secure. I will be pleased if that is the result [of the study]." It would be "premature," he concluded, to say whether or not a missile gap existed.

Actually, no study was required to learn the true state of affairs. The matter of the missile gap is handled with the utmost delicacy in both the Sorensen and Schlesinger accounts of the Kennedy Presidency. Sorensen in essence admits that no gap existed yet justifies President Kennedy's arms build-up by saying that it "helped make certain that no gap would ever subsequently open."⁹ This begs the question, as such reasoning can be used to justify any policies and any levels of arms spending.

Schlesinger, too, admits that no gap existed and confirms that "the White House staff . . . wondered whether the new budget was not providing for more missiles than the national security required."

President Kennedy came into office determined to increase America's arms spending because he considered our defenses inadequate. This consideration had led to his inflated campaign rhetoric, which in turn became a factor reinforcing his own inclinations and making it less likely he would maintain the Eisenhower defense budget levels. He seemed to feel it would be easier to convince the nation of the need for increased arms spending if the people continued to fear a coming missile gap.

Like most American Presidents, and most Americans, John F. Kennedy believed implicitly in the idea of negotiation from strength. Despite substantial evidence over the years that agreements and détente more often spring from situations of near equilibrium than from situations of preponderance, phrases such as "We arm to parley"— a Churchill saying much admired by Kennedy—remain for the most part unchallenged. Theodore Sorensen writes that "Kennedy believed in arming the United States to provide bargaining power and backing for disarmament talks and diplomacy."¹⁰ This statement raises more questions than it answers. Does the need for "bargaining power" suggest that we should build unnecessary weapons systems in order to have something which can be sacrificed with no effect on our basic posture? Was President Kennedy's approach to disarmament that we needed more, even though our preponderance was clear? What is the meaning of massive armaments as "backing for . . . diplomacy"? Are there diplomatic goals we seek to achieve by threat?

In a similar sophistic vein, Arthur Schlesinger, Jr., in a book prepared for the Kennedy campaign, wrote: "only by showing that we can stay in the arms race as long as they, can we convince the Russians of the imperative need for arms control. But we will arm in order to disarm."[11] As I. F. Stone has pointed out, it is nonsense to suggest that we need to demonstrate to the Soviets, who have less than half our resources, that we can match their arms expenditures.[12] There are those who believe that we can, and should, force the Soviet Union into bankruptcy through the arms race, but there is no evidence that President Kennedy shared this view.

His own views do not seem to have changed in their essential features from those he had formulated as a student when he wrote a thesis on British armaments policy prior to World War II. In this 1940 study, *Why England Slept*, John Kennedy blamed the pacifist mood of the British public for Britain's failure to rearm in time to ward off Munich. He was impressed with what he felt to be the weakness of democracy in the face of challenge. Democracy's great failing, he wrote, is that it is

> essentially peace-loving; the people don't want to go to war. . . . the hatred of war is, in this day of modern warfare, a great disadvantage. . . . The plans have to be made years in advance, and it is extremely difficult to get support for this in a democracy.[13]

He felt that the public must be aroused to understand the dangers that confront it. Only then, in a democratic society, would the people support increased arms spending. In a dictatorship, arms programs can be carried on despite public hostility;

> in a democracy the cry of "war-monger" will discourage any politician who advocates a vigorous arms policy. This leaves armaments with few supporters. . . . There is no lobby for armaments as there is for relief or for agriculture.[14]

Today that situation is almost entirely reversed and this turning in the American democracy was greatly accelerated during Kennedy's Presidency.

Finally, Kennedy complains in his youthful study, "When the decision must be whether it will be peace or war, the fundamental instinct of man against war binds the hands of democratic leaders."[15] He appears to have felt that a democratic society would be better able to meet challenges if only it were not so democratic.

These words were written more than twenty years before Kennedy assumed the Presidency, yet they lend insight into the tendency toward inflated and alarmist rhetoric, particularly where matters of national security were concerned. In his Inaugural Address, Kennedy spoke of "defending freedom in its hour of maximum danger." One has difficulty finding the world-shaking situation at the beginning of 1961 that might have justified that characterization. In his statement after the Bay of Pigs invasion, he said, "we face a relentless struggle in every corner of the globe. . . . No greater task faces this country. . . ." During the Berlin crisis, he told the American people, "the threat is world-wide," and called for a massive fallout-shelter program. In his Cuban missile-crisis statement, he exaggerated the extent to which Soviet missiles in Cuba increased the danger to the United States. In dealing with the Vietnam problem, he resorted to a secret war and dissimulation because he

realized the American people would not support his policy
if conducted openly.

In his Inaugural Address, President Kennedy touched,
perhaps less than consciously, upon many of the psychological elements that propel the arms race. Speaking
of the Soviet Union, he said, "We dare not tempt them
with weakness. For only when our arms are sufficient
beyond doubt can we be certain beyond doubt that they
will never be employed."

When this classic statement of the strategy of deterrence is examined against the background of the nuclear
arms race, it is clear that at least as strong a case can
be made to the contrary. The increasing sophistication of
nuclear technology and the related technologies of missiles and radars tend to make it more rather than less
likely that ultimately these weapons will be employed.
Warning time and therefore reaction time become shorter
and shorter. An example of the problems that arise is the
"Hair-trigger vs. stiff-trigger problem." The nuclear missiles in our retaliatory force must be ready for launch
within minutes. A considerable degree of automation is
therefore required; manual controls are too cumbersome
for the nuclear age. Yet, as that automation is perfected,
how does one maintain this delicate state of readiness,
this hair trigger, and still keep the trigger stiff enough to
prevent an accidental launch or a launch by mistake? How
does one allow time for the President himself to make
the fateful decision?

President Kennedy in his Inaugural Address also
took note of the pressures that tend to escalate the arms
race. Both sides are

> overburdened by the cost of modern weapons, both
> rightly alarmed by the steady spread of the deadly
> atom, yet both [are] racing to alter that uncertain
> balance of terror that stays the hand of mankind's
> final war.

Ironically, as he considered his first defense budget, President Kennedy raced to alter that balance.

Apart from his rhetorical commitment to overcome the missile gap and his long-standing personal belief in the need for high levels of arms expenditures, President Kennedy's decisions were influenced by the views of those military figures who rejected the Eisenhower administration's massive-retaliation strategy. Exclusive reliance on strategic nuclear weapons, Kennedy felt, induced a kind of Maginot-line psychology; the strategy might never be used but it inhibited consideration of any alternative courses of action. He was determined to expand conventional forces to escape what he considered to be a trap and to permit the nation to wage less-than-total war.

Two Chiefs of Staff of the Army, Generals Matthew Ridgway and Maxwell Taylor, and a Deputy Chief, General James Gavin, had resigned from the service after unsuccessful efforts to preserve the capacity of the Army to wage conventional or limited war. All three subsequently wrote books making clear their then heretical positions. Of particular interest are the views of General Maxwell Taylor, who became President Kennedy's personal military adviser and later chairman of the Joint Chiefs of Staff.

In *The Uncertain Trumpet*, Taylor outlined what he called a strategy of flexible response, under which the United States would be able to fight a limited war. He defined limited war as a conflict short of general war in which the United States forces would use atomic weapons "as required to achieve national purposes."[16] This prospect is only slightly less chilling when one realizes that he sees limited war as the alternative to general war in which massive salvos of nuclear weapons would be employed at the outset.

Taylor wrote that without a substantial capacity to wage limited war the United States would be increasingly vulnerable to "atomic blackmail and attrition-type aggressions."[17] He did not discuss whether the existence of this capacity might lead to a more aggressive diplomatic posture and a greater willingness to risk war to gain our diplomatic ends.

Central to Taylor's thesis is the presumption that the Soviet Union is at the bottom of most of the difficulties the United States will face in the world. For some years, he wrote, it had been predicted that with nuclear deterrence the Soviet Union would undertake a rising level of provocations. These could be met only by an increase in our conventional forces. Taylor places great faith in the ability of conventional forces to resist "Communist aggression." He dismisses as a myth the claim that "our side" would be outnumbered in manpower and as proof adds up the available world manpower to show that the forces of the "free world," in which he included SEATO, Iran, Japan, and South Vietnam, would outnumber the Communists. This seems a rather pedantic theoretical exercise, as it is difficult to imagine the kind of war in which the manpower of those nations would be utilized in a united front. Where would they be deployed? In Europe against the Soviet Union? On the Asian mainland? Taylor grants that China's enormous manpower reserves would give her an advantage in the Far East, but concludes that "much of the Communist Chinese manpower is unusable because of logistic limitations."[18] The belief that "logistic limitations" would neutralize the massive manpower of China—a belief that operated throughout the early 1960's—led to the unrealistic estimates by American planners of Chinese and North Vietnamese ability to respond to American escalation of the war in Southeast Asia. This led in turn to grave miscalculations of the numbers of American troops that would be required on the ground in South Vietnam.

Maxwell Taylor feared that our inferiority to the Soviet Union in conventional strength would lead to the loosening of the bonds of our alliances and would "increase the trend toward neutralism and compromise among the weak."[19]

He lamented the downgrading of the Jupiter missile,

which the U.S. Air Force did not want and which had therefore been foisted on our Western European allies. The Jupiter had originally been designed as a mobile IRBM, to be set up on railroad cars or barges. Its conversion to non-mobile status increased the reluctance of our allies to accept it, as the stationary Jupiters made inviting targets for Soviet missiles trained on Western Europe. Taylor's solution was to revive the mobile-Jupiter concept and allocate the missile to the Army as a mobile field weapon. He also favored "rapid deployment of [Jupiters] overseas into areas within range of important Soviet targets."[20]

In calling for his flexible-response strategy, Maxwell Taylor advocated a firm U.S. policy to make clear that we would be prepared "to respond anywhere, any time, with weapons and forces appropriate to the situation. Thus, we would restore to warfare its historic justification as a means to create a better world upon successful conclusion of hostilities."[21]

Taylor accepts the existence of a missile gap and calls for *"heroic measures"** to overcome it. He also calls for the deployment of an anti-missile missile system (ABM), for "we can no longer rely with reasonable confidence upon our ability to deter general war but must make indispensable preparations to assure survival in an atomic war initiated deliberately by the Soviets or growing out of a mistake or accident." On the basis of such reasoning, when Taylor was again in high position in the Kennedy administration, American military planners began turning their attention to strategies of damage limitation and damage denial rather than pure deterrence. Emphasis began to shift from deterring nuclear war to surviving a nuclear attack.

Like Kennedy, Taylor saw the United States in peril because of foreign threats. "Somehow it must be

* Italics in original.

made clear to our citizens that the nation will face a serious crisis beginning about 1961." The military balance would then lean "dangerously" in favor of the Communists "unless we take drastic action now." If the public could be convinced of the coming crisis it would accept the necessity for fundamental change in our attitudes toward national security requirements and would support the higher taxes needed for increased defense expenditures. But despite his alarmist predictions and cries for action, Taylor envisaged at most a military budget of between $50 billion and $55 billion a year for five years. He felt that once the "gap" was closed, budgets need not be as high.[22] Eight years later the military budget reached almost $80 billion, even without the adoption of all of Taylor's program.

Within a few days of his inauguration, President Kennedy began to prepare the nation for a build-up of both strategic and conventional arms. His State of the Union Message on January 30 painted an alarming picture. Domestic problems, he told the nation,

> pale when placed beside those which confront us around the world. No man entering upon this office . . . could fail to be staggered upon learning—even in this brief 10-day period—the harsh enormity of the trials through which we must pass in the next four years. Each day the crises multiply. Each day their solution grows more difficult. Each day we draw nearer the hour of maximum danger. . . .

We must strengthen our military tools, he continued, for "we are moving into a period of uncertain risk and great commitment." Already he had directed an increase in air-lift capacity to enable our conventional forces to respond "to any problem at any spot on the globe at any moment's notice." He had also stepped up the Polaris submarine program and accelerated "our entire missile program."

In his defense message to Congress on March 28, the President revealed in greater detail his plans for the build-up. The Polaris program would be "greatly expanded and accelerated." Planned procurement of the Minuteman missile for the current year would be increased by two-thirds and Minuteman production capacity doubled. "To meet our own extensive commitments," he directed the build-up of our conventional forces, for "we must be ready now to deal with any size of force, including small externally supported bands of men. . . ."

The White House staff and the Pentagon clashed over the need for the arms build-up. The President's science adviser, Jerome B. Wiesner, led the fight with the Pentagon against increasing the level of strategic forces. (Wiesner, now President of MIT, has been closely involved for many years in national security questions, and is a vigorous and articulate opponent of the arms race.) Nearly ten years after the event, he revealed at a Senate hearing some of the influences at work during the crucial weeks of decision in 1961. His remarks illustrate how the arms race is propelled by fear, both of the enemy and of forces within our own society, and how fear and suspicion have, over the years, led both sides to forfeit opportunities to limit the arms race. Wiesner stated:

> In 1961 at the start of the Kennedy administration, we had the opportunity to attempt to freeze the ballistic missile forces at the relatively low levels established by President Eisenhower. Soon after President Kennedy took office, we learned that the Soviet missile force was substantially smaller than earlier estimates which provided the basis for the so-called missile gap. We learned, in fact, that the United States probably had more missiles than the Soviet Union, a somewhat surprising and reassuring fact. At the time

some persons, including me, proposed holding down the U.S. missile levels in the expectation that if the United States showed restraint, the Soviet Union could be persuaded to do the same and that in any event a force of 200–400 missiles . . . would be a mighty deterrent against any likely Soviet strategic force.[23]

At the beginning of Kennedy's administration, the major American ICBM was the huge Titan II missile. With a so-called storable liquid propellant, it was a quick-reaction-time missile which could be launched directly out of a silo. It was, however, very expensive; a squadron of nine Titan II's cost several hundred million dollars.[24]

Secretary McNamara was proposing an increase in the number of the smaller, less expensive Minuteman missiles rather than continued emphasis on the Titan II. The Eisenhower administration, which had begun development of the Minuteman in 1957, had not finally determined how many Minutemen were required. Because this type of missile used solid fuel, it could be stored indefinitely in firing readiness in underground silos and launched on about one minute's warning to previously programmed targets. In underground silos, it was less subject to destruction than were the more vulnerable Titans.

At the beginning of the Kennedy administration the Air Force wanted three thousand new Minuteman missiles and some requests went as high as ten thousand. McNamara recommended a total Minuteman force of 950 missiles (later increased to one thousand) and a Polaris submarine fleet of forty-one boats, each with sixteen missiles. "The explanation given by Secretary McNamara for his recommendation," reports Wiesner, "was that because the Air Force recommended 3,000 Minuteman missiles, 950 was the smallest number Congress would settle for."[25]

President Kennedy, apparently unwilling to try to encourage Soviet restraint by insisting on American restraint, endorsed McNamara's recommendations. Kennedy's desire to head off Air Force pressure to develop a new bomber was presumably a factor in this decision, but in terms of the effect on the strategic-arms race, he would probably have been better advised to agree to the bomber rather than the missiles. The bomber would have appeared to the Soviets less threatening and probably would have provoked less reaction.

Schlesinger tries to shift the responsibility from the President to the Secretary of Defense by suggesting that President Kennedy "was not prepared to overrule" McNamara, as though the hapless President was so ill informed that he dared not challenge his Defense Secretary's judgment.[26] If such were the case, Kennedy could be accused of having allowed a usurpation of authority no President should ever permit. It is more likely, however, that President Kennedy did make this decision himself, and had he not had his own reasons for it, would have been willing to overrule McNamara.

Wiesner's testimony and Schlesinger's statement both suggest a failure of leadership on the part of the President. No President should ever accept an adviser's judgment as to what the Air Force, and under their pressure the Congress, will accept with respect to a policy which he himself feels is unwise. It is the President's responsibility to convince Congress and the people, to the best of his ability, of the necessity for the right course of action. Congress, in any event, cannot force the President or the executive branch of the government to undertake any program or spend any money against his wishes. In recent years Presidents have repeatedly refused to respond to Congressional authorizing legislation which "directed" them to carry out specific programs, and they have rejected such "directions" as improper infringements of the executive prerogative. The Kennedy administration fully understood this and indeed successfully resisted Air Force-inspired Congressional pressure to build the B-70 bomber.

In approving the new strategic-force levels, President Kennedy appears to have been operating in the pragmatic fashion that so characterized his political style. Compromise is the essence of political life, and in dealings with Congress, particularly with respect to weapons systems, a certain amount of "log-rolling" is unavoidable.

In 1961 the Air Force and its vocal civilian constituency were kept reasonably satisfied with nearly one thousand Minuteman missiles. The Navy was not too unhappy with forty-one Polaris boats; they had wanted forty-five. The Army, which, for the moment, was kept out of the missile business by Kennedy's decision against deployment of an ABM system, was compensated by the substantial expansion of its conventional forces, particularly from the time of the Berlin crisis.

But while some degree of accommodation with such interservice rivalries and domestic political pressures is always unavoidable if government is to function at all, the truly gifted political leader knows instinctively what he can compromise on and what he must not. In authorizing a new step in the strategic-arms race, President Kennedy failed to make that subtle distinction.

His personal belief in the need for increased arms spending made it unlikely that he would resist the traditional military pressures that act on any President. Further, his inflated campaign statements—although it is likely he believed them at the time—put him in a position where it would have been embarrassing to reverse directions, even if he had wanted to do so. He seems to have been blind to the price he was paying for his policy.

President Kennedy achieved his goal of a substantial expansion of both our strategic- and conventional-force capabilities. By late 1961, at the time of the presentation of the fiscal 1963 defense budget, the size of our strategic forces was all but determined and the pattern set for most of the decade of the 1960's. But the price for these decisions was high and, to a considerable extent, the future was mortgaged to support an extravagant view of the U.S. role in the world. Jerome Wiesner, who was privy to all the information that led to these decisions, has said that he believes that "the failure to reach agreement on a nuclear test ban and the resumption of nuclear testing by the Soviet Union in the fall of 1961 were direct consequences of this buildup on our part."[27]

I. F. Stone, who has dissected President Kennedy's defense-policy decisions in his usual brilliant and devastating manner, finds it "difficult to believe decisions which cost so many billions—and were so profitable to the arms industry—were merely the result of intramural bureaucratic bargaining and appeasement." But, it does appear that these momentous decisions were more the consequence of petty trade-offs within the bureaucracy, of bureaucratic inertia, and of the personal policies of President Kennedy than of any sinister conspiracy to profit the arms industry. In a certain sense, one prefers to think there is a conspiracy at work in these matters; that, at least, suggests a sense of purpose. It is something one can grab hold of, oppose, and perhaps eventually destroy. How much more difficult is the reality, where the pragmatist with no larger goal or vision to guide him may become the prisoner and eventually the victim of the contending special interests. John F. Kennedy was such a pragmatist.

The new round of Soviet and American testing in the atmosphere in 1961 and 1962 was followed by the limited-test-ban treaty in 1963. Although President Kennedy regarded the test-ban treaty as one of the most important achievements of his administration, it was much less significant than it appeared to the public. The psychological significance of the treaty was much greater than its technological and political significance. Indeed, its acceptance by the military demonstrated that the treaty did not at all impede the progress of arms development, particularly American arms development.

The 1962 American test series included testing of an ABM warhead, essentially the only element in an ABM system that requires testing in the atmosphere. This success paved the way for the vigorous underground-testing program that followed the 1963 treaty. Successful development of an ABM warhead led to pressure by 1968 for American deployment of an ABM system and thus to a whole new cycle of action and reaction in the arms race.

The Soviet Union, too, continued its missile development at a rapid pace, but the comment of one who has been intimately involved in weapons development for many years is illuminating. In his highly instructive though discouraging account, *Race to Oblivion: A Participant's View of the Arms Race*, Dr. Herbert York has written:

> I have not attempted to assess the causes of the strategic arms race and I have not tried to apportion the blame for its existence. Rather, I have examined many of the separate steps by which it has reached the incredible situation now facing us, and I have found in the majority of those cases that the rate and scale of the individual steps has, in the final analysis, been determined by unilateral actions of the United States. . . . The reaction typically far outran the cause.[28]

Those who would hold down the arsenals of nuclear weapons are hard pressed to refute the mistaken though superficially plausible assumption that more military hardware automatically means more security for the United States. This sentiment is usually expressed in terms similar to those used by John F. Kennedy in one of his 1960 campaign speeches when he said, "If we are to err in an age of uncertainty, I want us to err on the side of security."[29] The question remains: What is true security? Which will give us greater security: unchecked spiraling of the arms race, with the constant fear that the other side may achieve a significant breakthrough, achieve a first-strike capability that would threaten the adversary's retaliatory capacity; or does true security lie in an agreement to limit the levels of arms development?

As we contemplate the legacy of the Kennedy arms-build-up decisions, it is clear that Americans have had differing ideas about how to achieve the same end: security. On the one hand, we have sought, bilaterally and through international organizations, agreements by which the arms race might be controlled. On the other hand, we have sought superior military force. In recent years, more often than not, these two courses of action have proved incompatible. President Kennedy, like many of his predecessors and many of his contemporaries, failed to appreciate this fact. As I. F. Stone has noted, "Kennedy as President, like Kennedy as Senator and candidate, tried to ride two horses at once in two opposite directions, rearmament *and* disarmament."[30]

It is clearly no longer possible to have it both ways, to maintain a force superior to that of the Soviet Union and at the same time to expect them to enter into an arms-control agreement with us that will preserve our superiority. With our security—and theirs—assured through mutual deterrence, it is necessary now to take some calculated risks on the side of trust, to forgo an additional spiral of the arms race in the hope of providing the Soviets with the incentive to do likewise.

Throughout the whole history of armaments the pattern has been the same. What man's ingenuity has invented, his ambition and his curiosity have eventually led him to use. To some extent, psychological barriers inhibit the use of the more uncontrollable of weapons. Poison gas was not employed by either side during World War II because of fear of enemy retaliation, although both sides manufactured it and included it in their arsenals. Yet slowly over time the psychological barriers are broken down, at first so subtly that the public is left unaware. Thus in Vietnam in the 1960's, so-called non-lethal riot-control agents were used extensively by American forces. The gas may not have been as poisonous as that used at Ypres, but the least that can be said is that a moral vacuum exists when a gas grenade is rolled into a bunker and the victims are shot when they are driven to the surface.

Gas, napalm, defoliants, herbicides, destruction of crops, burning of villages, free-fire zones, and forced re-location of the population are all said to be justified as methods of warfare "more humane" than wholesale slaughter. In a world environment of increasing deperson-alization, there is little moral difference between wholesale destruction by incendiary bombing and wholesale destruc-tion by atomic bombardment. And the world that will tolerate the slaughter of hundreds of thousands of Ben-galis in East Pakistan is preparing itself psychologically for more and greater Hiroshimas.

Some have suggested that ever-increasing stocks of weapons are the result of a sinister conspiracy of a military-industrial complex. In reality the workings of the system are much more subtle; they involve the labor and academic communities as well as industry and government. During the last decade, largely as a result of the arms build-up begun by President Kennedy, the workings of this system have become institutionalized and its pressures self-gen-erating.

During his brief administration, President Kennedy made three basic defense-policy decisions that profoundly affected the arms race, the role of the United States in the world, and the role of the defense establishment in Ameri-can life. He greatly expanded our strategic forces; he built up conventional forces for the express purpose of per-mitting intervention in small wars; and he authorized reorganization of the Pentagon to control the defense industry in new ways. Of these momentous decisions the third is little studied and little appreciated.

Former Defense Secretary Robert McNamara is widely praised for having built an efficient, orderly structure out of chaos. Only now do we begin to question whether such efficiency and rationalization of the structure and operation of the Pentagon is truly in the national interest. A smoothly functioning monolith may be less controllable than an organization whose own inefficiencies were a kind of check on its excesses. For all the problems created by interservice rivalries, at least those rivalries provided an informal system of checks and balances; the Army, Navy, and Air Force each worked vigorously to control the other two services.

As a result of McNamara's reorganization—which President Kennedy authorized and encouraged, and for which he is ultimately responsible—a new industrial management, the most important in the United States, was created. As Seymour Melman has pointed out, this management, with an annual turnover of over $40 billion, controls resources greater than those of any other single firm. "The confluence of economic decision power of this sort at the same nexus in society where peak political and military decision power reside is understood elsewhere in the world as a characteristic of the Soviet type of society."[31]

Vested interests have developed. And the defense establishment can be counted on to look after its own interests—interests that may not necessarily coincide with those of the nation as a whole. Control of its pervasive influence requires constant attention and vigilance by both government and citizen.

The march of technological progress is inexorable. We are so rich and so powerful as a nation, so talented and inventive as a people, that our science and technology are more dynamic and more productive than those of other nations. We are the constant source of new ideas, new inventions, new approaches. Whether the problem is insurgencies in the third world or assured penetration of the enemy's missile defenses, we constantly seek the new and ingenious application of our superior resources that will enable us to accomplish our purposes. We rarely ask whether we are not attempting the impossible, or whether we ought to be doing it just because it is within the realm of possibility. In his obsession with the management of the problem, with the operational aspects, President Kennedy was perhaps the supreme example of the American character. We are imbued with the spirit of limitless possibilities.

Limits and restraint have not heretofore been part of the American tradition. Never as a people have we been accustomed to operating in a closed system. We have always moved onward toward the new frontier when the available land and resources were exhausted and when the neighbors began to crowd too close. It is not without significance that John F. Kennedy found in the phrase "new frontier" a symbol for his conception of America. But this conception was already out of date by 1961. We are no longer a frontier society with limitless space; we can no longer pick up and move away from the problems that confront us.

In the international area as well, the oceans no longer protect us from the world. In the nuclear-missile age, man lives a quarter of an hour from oblivion. Under these conditions, crusades are no longer possible. Ideological confrontations must yield to the search for new paths of accommodation.

John F. Kennedy was the last President who could have used the New Frontier as his slogan. In this sense, his Presidency was the apogee of the American frontier mentality. It was an ending rather than a beginning. His successor, in attempting to pursue to a conclusion the course in Southeast Asia set by Kennedy, guided the ship of state into turbulent and dangerous waters. For a time it appeared that the ship might founder, but in 1968 it became clear that we would survive, and that our salvation would be found in the inherent wisdom of the people themselves to make the proper choice, to reject the wrong course, and to begin, however slowly, to turn the nation away from war.

In 1968, for the first time, Americans began to consider the question of national priorities, to reconsider where the true national interest lay. They began to perceive that there are limits even to American power, to its ability to bring about the results we seek. There are limits, for example, to its ability to assure the survival of a non-Communist government in Saigon. And Americans began to perceive that success for the American purpose in Southeast Asia mattered less than success in meeting our problems at home; that there are limits to our moral energy as well as to our economic resources.

That perception is changing the nature of American politics. This process of change is continually impeded and frustrated by the rigidities and unresponsiveness of the system and by uninspired national leadership in both parties. Yet public opinion polls confirm that, in most cases, the people are ahead of their government in their willingness to liquidate unwise foreign commitments. This public will is slowly beginning to be reflected in electoral results, as in the 1970 Congressional election and in the rejection at the polls of candidates whose view of foreign policy is extremist.

There are indications, as yet barely visible, that the people, particularly the people of Middle America, will respond to those who speak and appeal to the best in them, and that they will, in the end, reject the leadership of those who appeal to the darker sides of the human spirit.

The tragedy of John F. Kennedy was as much in his life as in his death. While he had an ability to touch and move men almost unequaled by any public figure in the modern era, perhaps in much of history, he himself, because of his political beliefs and political approach, failed to understand his own potential for leadership and accomplishment. He approached politics as a series of problems to be understood, managed, and solved.

What is the problem in the 12th ward? We will correct it. What is the problem with the House Ways and Means Committee? We will do what is necessary to get that bill to the floor. What is the problem in northeast Thailand? We will send a team from the RAND Corporation to determine what counterinsurgency programs are needed to restore government control. What is the problem with urban terrorism in Brazil? We will send American policemen under a CIA program to teach them to use radios and tear gas to manage the problems of internal security.

Kennedy approached the American people in the same way. Ironically, the words for which he is best remembered are the least typical of his political style: "Ask not what your country can do for you: Ask what you can do for your country." These words evoked a surge of inspiration and enthusiasm not only in the United States but throughout the world. They symbolized all that was best in the American political tradition: that the people themselves shall participate, shall serve themselves and each other under enlightened leadership. Yet President Kennedy himself did not really believe those words. Rather, he dedicated himself to accomplishing everything *for* the people, without accomplishing *through* the people; without understanding that leaders can do little for the people unless they first call upon the people to do for themselves.

John F. Kennedy was brought up in the modern version of noblesse oblige, the spirit passed on to his children by former Ambassador Joseph P. Kennedy. That spirit was described in a tribute to his father by Senator Robert Kennedy:

Through no virtues and accomplishments of our own, we had been fortunate enough to be born in the

United States under the most comfortable conditions. We, therefore, had a responsibility to others who were less well off. . . . There were wrongs which needed attention. There were people who were poor and who needed help; mentally ill who needed assistance. And we had a responsibility to them and to the country.[32]

This sense of social conscience and public spirit that Ambassador Kennedy instilled in his children had admirable altruistic and philanthropic results. But it led to an elitist conception of government, a conception that dominated the Presidency of John F. Kennedy. Kennedy and his advisers were the cream of the crop, the brightest, the most successful, the most gifted and talented; their judgment of what was best for America must, therefore, be right.

Most of President Kennedy's fateful mistakes were made not in spite of his virtues but because of them; and those failures raise the question of whether Americans have been taught to cherish the wrong virtues. As *The Wall Street Journal* has noted about the Kennedy administration:

> They were mistakes of too much vigor and too little restraint, too much grace and too little earthiness, too much eloquence and too little thoughtfulness, . . . too much flexibility and too little patience, too much brilliance and too little common sense.
>
> The virtues of the Kennedy Administration were the virtues of the intellectual as opposed to those of the common man, the virtues of a high civilization rather than a democratic one.[33]

This approach to government suggests that the people are incapable of judgment, incapable of appreciating the dangers that their leaders, with their supposed superior wisdom, see clearly. It posits that the people must be saved—albeit in spite of themselves. John F. Kennedy did not really have that trust in the people which is the foundation of the American democratic spirit. As Adlai Stevenson said, "The people are wise. Wiser than the politicians think."

It would seem that Stevenson was right and Kennedy was wrong. As a result of their adventures in globalism, Americans, for the first time in one hundred years, have had to face an overwhelming moral issue with deep political and social ramifications. They began facing it in 1968 and they are now beginning to turn the nation in new directions.

Senator Eugene McCarthy has observed that the last time America was called upon to face an issue of this nature the upheaval was so great that it led to civil war, the social and political consequences of which still await final resolution. Changing the nation's course away from a foreign policy of overcommitment and freeing the American economy—and through it much of American society —from dependence on the military-industrial state structure created to support that foreign policy will be no less difficult, no less lengthy, and no less of a challenge to the character of the American people.

Sources

UNPUBLISHED MATERIAL

John F. Kennedy Library, Oral History
Collection. Interviews with:

Dean Acheson
Robert Amory
Charles E. Bohlen
Sir Alec Douglas-Home
Gilbert Harrison
Robert A. Hurwitch

U. Alexis Johnson
George F. Kennan
Robert Lovett
George Smathers
Llewellyn Thompson
Herbert York

GOVERNMENT DOCUMENTS

Congressional Record

Kennedy, John F. *Public Papers of the Presidents of the United
States: John F. Kennedy.* Washington: GPO, 1962–64.
Volumes in the series, 1961–63.

The Pentagon Papers. New York: Bantam, 1971.

Truman, Harry S. *Public Papers of the Presidents of the United
States: Harry S. Truman.* Washington: GPO, 1948.

U. S. Senate. 87th Cong., 1st Sess., *Report No. 994, Final Report of the Committee on Commerce, Freedom of Information,* Part I, "The Speeches of Senator John F. Kennedy,
Presidential Campaign of 1960." Washington: GPO, 1961.

U. S. Senate. 86th Cong., 2d Sess., *Report No. 1761, Hearings
before the Committee on Foreign Relations,* "Events Relating to the Summit Conference." Washington: GPO, 1960.

U. S. Senate. 91st Cong., 1st Sess., *Report No. 91–129,* "National Commitments." Washington: GPO, 1969.

U. S. Senate. 91st Cong., 2d Sess., *Hearings before the Committee on Foreign Relations on S. 3544,* "Arms Control and
Disarmament Act Amendment 1970." Washington: GPO,
1970.

U. S. Senate. 91st Cong., 2d Sess., *Hearings before the Subcommittee on Arms Control, International Law and Organization of the Committee on Foreign Relations,* "ABM,
MIRV, SALT, and the Nuclear Arms Race." Washington:
GPO, 1970.

BOOKS

Abel, Elie. *The Missile Crisis.* Philadelphia and New York: Lippincott, 1966.

Bell, Coral. *Negotiation from Strength.* New York: Knopf, 1963.

Bloomfield, Lincoln P., and Amelia C. Leiss. *Controlling Small Wars: A Strategy for the 1970's.* New York: Knopf, 1969.

Bohlen, Charles E. *The Transformation of American Foreign Policy.* New York: Norton, 1969.

Bowles, Chester. *Promises to Keep: My Years in Public Life, 1941–1969.* New York: Harper & Row, 1971.

Brandon, Henry. *Anatomy of Error.* Boston: Gambit, 1969.

De Gaulle, Charles. *The Complete War Memoirs of Charles de Gaulle.* Vol. I, *The Call to Honor.* New York: Simon & Schuster, 1964.

Dulles, Allen W. *The Craft of Intelligence.* New York: Harper & Row, 1963.

Eisenhower, Dwight D. *Waging Peace.* Garden City: Doubleday, 1965.

Fall, Bernard. *Anatomy of a Crisis.* Garden City: Doubleday, 1969.

Frank, Jerome D. *Sanity and Survival: Psychological Aspects of War and Peace.* New York: Vintage, 1967.

Greene, Lt. Col. T. N., ed. *The Guerrilla and How to Fight Him.* New York: Praeger, 1962.

Heath, Jim F. *John F. Kennedy and the Business Community.* Chicago: University of Chicago Press, 1969.

Heren, Louis. *No Hail, No Farewell.* New York: Harper & Row, 1970.

Hilsman, Roger. *To Move a Nation: The Politics of Foreign Policy in the Administration of John F. Kennedy.* Garden City: Doubleday, 1967.

Institute for Strategic Studies. *The Soviet Union and the NATO Powers: The Military Balance.* London: ISS, 1960.

Johnson, Haynes, *et al. The Bay of Pigs.* New York: Norton, 1964.

Johnson, Haynes, and Bernard M. Gwertzman. *Fulbright: The Dissenter.* Garden City: Doubleday, 1968.

Kennedy, John F. *Why England Slept.* Garden City: Dolphin-Doubleday, 1962; original edition, 1940.

Kennedy, Robert F. *Thirteen Days: A Memoir of the Cuban Missile Crisis.* New York: Signet-NAL, 1969.

Khrushchev, Nikita. *Khrushchev Remembers.* Boston: Little, Brown, 1970.

Kirkpatrick, Lyman B., Jr. *The Real CIA.* New York: Macmillan, 1968.

Lippmann, Walter. *The Coming Tests with Russia.* Boston: Little, Brown & Co., 1961.

Lippmann, Walter. *The Communist World and Ours.* Boston: Little, Brown & Co., 1959.

Newfield, Jack. *Robert Kennedy: A Memoir.* New York: E. P. Dutton & Co., 1969.

Newhouse, John. *De Gaulle and the Anglo-Saxons.* New York: Viking, 1970.

Nixon, Richard M. *Six Crises.* Garden City: Doubleday, 1962.

Osborne, Milton. *Strategic Hamlets South Vietnam.* Data Paper No. 55, Southeast Asia Program, Department of Asian Studies. Ithaca, New York: Cornell University, 1965.

Rathjens, George W. *The Future of the Strategic Arms Race.* New York: Carnegie Endowment for International Peace, 1969.

Reston, James. *Sketches in the Sand.* New York: Knopf, 1967.

Rostow, Walt W. *The Stages of Economic Growth: A Non-Communist Manifesto.* Cambridge University Press, 1960.

Rostow, Walt W. *The View from the Seventh Floor.* New York: Harper & Row, 1964.

Schlesinger, Arthur M., Jr. *A Thousand Days: John F. Kennedy in the White House.* Boston: Houghton Mifflin, 1965.

Schlesinger, Arthur M., Jr. *Kennedy or Nixon: Does It Make Any Difference?* New York: Macmillan, 1960.

Sorensen, Theodore C. *Kennedy.* New York: Harper & Row, 1965.

Steel, Ronald. *Pax Americana.* New York: Viking, 1967.

Stone, I. F. *In Time of Torment.* New York: Random House, 1967.

Strausz-Hupé, Robert, *et al. A Forward Strategy for America.* New York: Harper & Bros., 1961.

Taylor, Maxwell D. *The Uncertain Trumpet.* New York: Harper & Bros., 1959–60.

Thompson, Robert. *Defeating Communist Insurgency*. London: Chatto & Windus, 1966.

York, Herbert. *Race to Oblivion: A Participant's View of the Arms Race*. New York: Simon & Schuster, 1970.

ARTICLES

Allison, Graham, Ernest May, and Adam Yarmolinsky. "Limits to Intervention," *Foreign Affairs*, Vol. 48, No. 2 (January 1970).

Alsop, Stewart. "Kennedy's Grand Strategy," *Saturday Evening Post*, March 31, 1962.

Alsop, Stewart. "The Lessons of the Cuban Disaster," *Saturday Evening Post*, June 24, 1961.

Bernstein, Victor, and Jesse Gordon. "The Press and the Bay of Pigs," *Columbia University Forum*, Fall 1967.

Dwiggins, Don. "Guatemala's Secret Airstrip," *The Nation*, January 7, 1961.

Horelick, Arnold L. "The Cuban Missile Crisis: An Analysis of Soviet Calculations and Behavior," *World Politics*, Vol. XVI, No. 3 (April 1964).

Johnson, U. Alexis. "Internal Defense and the Foreign Service," *Foreign Service Journal*, July 1962.

Melman, Seymour. "Three Decisions and Three American Crises." (Mimeo.)

Murphy, Charles J. V. "Cuba: The Record Set Straight," *Fortune*, September 1961.

O'Donnell, Kenneth. "LBJ and the Kennedys," *Life*, August 7, 1970.

Rostow, Walt W. "Guerrilla Warfare in Underdeveloped Areas," *The Marine Corps Gazette*, January 1962.

Souyris, Capt. André. "An Effective Counter-guerrilla Procedure," *Revue de Defense Nationale* (France), June 1956, as translated in *Military Review*, Vol. XXXVI, No. 12 (March 1957).

Stavins, Ralph L. "Kennedy's Private War," *New York Review*, July 22, 1971.

Steel, Ronald. "Endgame," *New York Review*, March 13, 1969.

Stone, I. F. "Theatre of Delusion," *New York Review*, April 23, 1970.

NEWSPAPERS

Christian Science Monitor
Daily News (New York)
Los Angeles Times
Miami Herald
Le Monde (Paris)
New York Herald Tribune
New York Post
New York Times
Observer (London)
St. Louis Post-Dispatch
Sunday Times (London)
Washington Post
Washington Star

Notes | All quotations from John F. Kennedy as President, unless otherwise indicated, are taken from *Public Papers of the Presidents of the United States: John F. Kennedy* (Washington, D.C.: Government Printing Office), volumes in the series 1961–1963. Interviews in the Kennedy Oral History Collection of the John F. Kennedy Library are cited as JFKL/OHC.

CHAPTER ONE

1. JFK *Public Papers.*
2. U. S. Senate, 91st Cong., 1st Sess., *Report No. 91–129,* "National Commitments" (Washington: GPO, 1969), p. 29. It is noteworthy that, in the list of outstanding U.S. foreign defense commitments deriving both from treaties and from statements and agreements made by the executive branch, the original agreement with Spain is not included, indicating that it is not considered a "commitment," but the 1963 declaration "upgrading" the agreement is included. The list is printed in U. S. Senate, 90th Cong., 1st Sess., "U.S. Commitments to Foreign Powers," *Hearings before the Committee on Foreign Relations on S. Res. 151* (Washington, D.C.: GPO, 1967), pp. 52–71.
3. Charles E. Bohlen, *The Transformation of American Foreign Policy* (New York: Norton, 1969), p. 87.
4. *Public Papers of the Presidents of the United States: Harry S Truman* (Washington, D.C.: GPO, 1948).
5. The United States is not formally a member of CENTO—called the Baghdad Pact until Iraq defected—but we have been its most active supporter. In 1957 Congress passed a Joint Resolution stating that "the independence and integrity of the nations of the Middle East" were "vital to the national interest."
6. Theodore C. Sorensen, *Kennedy* (New York: Harper & Row, 1965), p. 295.

7. JFKL/OHC, interview with George F. Kennan.

8. Quoted in Jack Newfield, *Robert Kennedy: A Memoir* (New York: E. P. Dutton & Co., 1969), p. 42. Newfield also relates (on p. 264) the following incident. After the 1968 Indiana primary was won by Senator Robert Kennedy, Senator Eugene McCarthy appeared on television with the statement that it didn't really matter who had come in first, second, or third. "'That's not what my father told me,' Kennedy said to the television. 'I always thought it was better to win. I learned that when I was about two.' Then he laughed."

9. Arthur M. Schlesinger, Jr., *A Thousand Days: John F. Kennedy in the White House* (Boston: Houghton Mifflin, 1965), pp. 675–6.

10. JFKL/OHC, interview with U. Alexis Johnson.

11. James Reston, *Sketches in the Sand* (New York: Knopf, 1967), p. 477.

CHAPTER TWO

1. Dwight D. Eisenhower, *Waging Peace* (Garden City: Doubleday, 1965), p. 521.

2. Richard M. Nixon, *Six Crises* (Garden City: Doubleday, 1962), p. 352.

3. Eisenhower, p. 523.

4. *Ibid.*, pp. 536–7.

5. *Ibid.*, p. 613.

6. U.S. Senate, 87th Cong., 1st Sess., *Senate Report No. 994, Final Report of the Committee on Commerce, Freedom of Information*, Part I, "The Speeches of Senator John F. Kennedy, Presidential Campaign of 1960" (Washington, D.C.: GPO, 1961).

7. Emphasis added.

8. Schlesinger, *op. cit.*, pp. 72–3.

9. JFKL/OHC, interview with Dean Acheson.

10. Schlesinger, *op. cit.*, p. 228.

11. Haynes Johnson *et al.*, *The Bay of Pigs* (New York: Norton, 1964), p. 34.

12. Eisenhower, p. 614.

13. Text printed in *Congressional Record*, Vol. 107, p. 364.

14. Weapons available to Castro's forces and to the assault force have been tabulated in Lincoln P. Bloomfield and Amelia C. Leiss, *Controlling Small Wars: A Strategy for the 1970's* (New York: Knopf, 1969), pp. 139–42.

15. Schlesinger, *op. cit.*, p. 164.

16. At that time, Rusk was Assistant Secretary of State for Far Eastern Affairs.

17. Sorensen, p. 295.

18. Schlesinger, *op. cit.*, pp. 231, 233.

19. Lyman B. Kirkpatrick, *The Real CIA* (New York: Macmillan, 1968), p. 183.

20. JFKL/OHC, interview with Senator George Smathers. The conversation about the possibility of assassinating Castro is not placed in time in the Smathers interview. From the context, it appears that it took place in 1961, probably prior to the Bay of Pigs. By early 1962 President Kennedy was tired of hearing from his friend Senator Smathers on the subject of what to do about Cuba. "George," the President told him, "I love to have you over. I want to have you over. But I want you to do me a favor. I like to visit with you. I want to discuss things with you. But I don't want you to talk to me any more about Cuba." On a later occasion, when they were having dinner in the White House— a dinner Smathers says was actually being prepared by the President himself—Smathers raised the matter of Cuba again and the President blew up. "Now, dammit," he exploded, slamming his fork down in his plate so hard that the plate cracked, "I wish you wouldn't do that. Let's quit talking about this subject!" Smathers says that from that point on they talked no more about Cuba.

21. Roger Hilsman, *To Move a Nation: The Politics of Foreign Policy in the Administration of John F. Kennedy* (Garden City: Doubleday, 1967), p. 31.

22. Allen W. Dulles, *The Craft of Intelligence* (New York: Harper & Row, 1963), pp. 168–9.

23. Schlesinger, *op. cit.*, p. 247.

24. Kirkpatrick, pp. 192–3.

25. Schlesinger, *op. cit.*, p. 248.

26. Hilsman, *op. cit.*, p. 31.

27. Schlesinger, *op. cit.*, p. 246.

28. *Ibid.*, p. 250. Emphasis added.

29. Haynes Johnson, p. 68.

30. Sorensen, p. 302.

31. *Ibid.*, p. 297.

32. Schlesinger, *op. cit.*, p. 250.

33. Sorensen, p. 296.

34. Schlesinger, *op. cit.*, p. 242.

35. January 7, 1961.

36. Schlesinger, *op. cit.*, pp. 252, 256–7.

37. Chester Bowles, *Promises to Keep: My Years in Public Life, 1941–1969* (New York: Harper & Row, 1971), pp. 326–8.

38. The Fulbright memo is discussed in Haynes Johnson and Bernard M. Gwertzman, *Fulbright: The Dissenter* (Garden City: Doubleday, 1968), pp. 174–5; and in Schlesinger, *op. cit.*, p. 251.

39. The President's failure to ask for the views of his Secretary of State on this important occasion is interesting. It may indicate that Rusk had already communicated them privately to the President, which would be in line with Rusk's apparent conception of his role as Secretary of State: the President's principal adviser on foreign affairs rather than a spokesman for the State Department position.

40. Johnson and Gwertzman, p. 177.

41. Schlesinger, *op. cit.*, p. 252.

42. Stewart Alsop, "The Lessons of the Cuban Disaster," *Saturday Evening Post,* June 24, 1961. This article, written only two months after the event, is largely supported by later accounts.

43. Johnson and Gwertzman, p. 178.

44. Sorensen, pp. 296–7.

45. *Ibid.*, p. 306.

46. Schlesinger, *op. cit.*, pp. 257–8.

47. *Ibid.*

48. *Ibid.*, p. 258.

49. *Ibid.*, p. 259.

50. Sorensen, p. 295.

51. Text printed in *The New York Times,* June 2, 1966.

52. Schlesinger, *op. cit.*, p. 261; JFKL/OHC, interview with Gilbert Harrison.

53. Text printed in *The New York Times*, April 4, 1961.
54. It was never explicitly stated, but it is presumed that there was one condition under which the United States would have moved directly: in case of an attack on our naval base at Guantánamo.
55. Haynes Johnson, pp. 75–6.
56. *Ibid.*, p. 85.
57. *Ibid.*, p. 70.
58. Kirkpatrick, p. 198.
59. Charles J. V. Murphy, "Cuba: The Record Set Straight," *Fortune*, September 1961.
60. Kirkpatrick, p. 202.
61. Interview in the *Washington Star*, July 20, 1965.
62. Schlesinger, *op. cit.*, p. 294.
63. Haynes Johnson, p. 112.
64. JFKL/OHC, interview with Robert Lovett.
65. Sorensen, p. 304.
66. JFKL/OHC, interview with Robert Amory.
67. Bowles, *op. cit.*, p. 444.
68. Schlesinger, *op. cit.*, p. 276.
69. Stewart Alsop, "The Lessons of the Cuban Disaster."
70. Graham Allison, Ernest May, and Adam Yarmolinsky, "Limits to Intervention," *Foreign Affairs*, Vol. 48, No. 2, (January 1970), p. 246.
71. Johnson and Gwertzman, p. 178.
72. Schlesinger, *op. cit.*, p. 276.

CHAPTER THREE

1. Interview in the *Christian Science Monitor*, June 3, 1959.
2. Later evidence appears to indicate that, while President Eisenhower had given general approval to the U-2 program, he was probably not aware that there was a plane in the sky over the Soviet Union on the eve of his meeting with Khrushchev—a classic example of the ability of bureaucratic inertia to impede diplomacy. See U. S. Senate, 86th Cong., 2d Sess., *Senate Report No. 1761, Hearings before the Committee on Foreign Relations*, "Events Relating to the Summit Conference" (Washington, D.C.: GPO, 1960).

3. Intelligence satellites later gave the United States access to the same kinds of information, such as the location of missile-launching sites, that the U-2 program had provided.

4. Walter Lippmann, *The Communist World and Ours* (Boston: Little, Brown & Co., 1959), p. 13.

5. Walt W. Rostow, *The View from the Seventh Floor* (New York: Harper & Row, 1964), p. 29

6. *Ibid.*, pp. 30.

7. Schlesinger, *op. cit.*, p. 302.

8. *Ibid.*, p. 303.

9. Walter Lippmann, *The Coming Tests with Russia* (Boston: Little, Brown & Co., 1961), pp. 28–9.

10. JFKL/OHC, interview with Ambassador Llewellyn Thompson.

11. The *New York Times*, June 4, 1961.

12. John Newhouse, *De Gaulle and the Anglo-Saxons* (New York: Viking, 1970), p. 123.

13. Some of the President's advisers were critical of the short duration of the proposed meeting—two days—noting that, although the American President can commit his government, Khrushchev would need time to consult with Moscow before he could alter his positions. See James Reston's column in the *New York Times*, May 30, 1961. Such concerns, which also arose during the brief Johnson-Kosygin summit meeting in Glassboro, N.J., in 1966, are an ironic commentary on the policy-making process in the "totalitarian" Soviet Union as opposed to that in the "democratic" United States.

14. Robert Strausz-Hupé, *A Forward Strategy for America* (New York: Harper & Bros., 1961), pp. 38–9.

15. *Ibid.*, pp. 43–4.

16. Discussion summarized in Schlesinger, *op. cit.*, pp. 349–59.

17. Charles de Gaulle, *The Complete War Memoirs of Charles de Gaulle*, Vol. I, *The Call to Honor* (New York: Simon & Schuster, 1964), pp. 3–4.

18. Schlesinger, *op. cit.*, p. 351.

19. JFKL/OHC, interview with Ambassador Llewellyn Thompson.

20. JFKL/OHC, interview with George F. Kennan.

21. Bernard Fall, *Anatomy of a Crisis* (Garden City: Doubleday, 1969), p. 23.

22. Hilsman, *To Move a Nation*, pp. 93–4.
23. Schlesinger, *op. cit.*, p. 337.
24. Schlesinger, *op. cit.*, p. 333.
25. Quoted by Schlesinger, *op. cit.*, p. 339.
26. Schlesinger reports that Khrushchev agreed to consider a cease-fire a priority matter (*op. cit.*, p. 368). But when one considers that there was no real movement in the Laos negotiations for nearly a year after Vienna, it is evident that the summit was not a positive step.
27. Schlesinger, *op. cit.*, p. 373.
28. U. S. Senate, 91st Cong., 2d Sess., "ABM, MIRV, SALT and the Nuclear Arms Race," *Hearings before the Subcommittee on Arms Control, International Law and Organization of the Committee on Foreign Relations* (Washington, D.C.: GPO, 1970), p. 395.
29. Ronald Steel, *Pax Americana* (New York: Viking, 1967), pp. 100–1.
30. Coral Bell, *Negotiation from Strength* (New York: Knopf, 1963), p. 198.
31. Schlesinger, *op. cit.*, p. 348.
32. The *New York Times,* June 6, 1961.
33. Schlesinger, *op. cit.*, pp. 347–8.
34. JFKL/OHC, interview with Ambassador Llewellyn Thompson.
35. JFKL/OHC, interview with George F. Kennan.
36. JFKL/OHC, interview with Sir Alec Douglas-Home.

CHAPTER FOUR

1. Bell, p. 223.
2. See Sorensen, pp. 589–90.
3. Schlesinger, *op. cit.*, pp. 380–1.
4. JFKL/OHC, interview with Dean Acheson.
5. Quoted in Schlesinger, *op. cit.*, p. 381.
6. JFKL/OHC, interview with Robert Amory.
7. The *New York Times*, June 16, 1961.
8. *Ibid.*
9. *Congressional Record*, Vol. 107, pp. 10328–34.
10. June 23, 1961.
11. June 24, 1961.
12. Sorensen, p. 558.

13. The *New York* Times, July 8, 1961.
14. Jim F. Heath, *John F. Kennedy and the Business Community* (Chicago: University of Chicago Press, 1969), pp. 30, 99.
15. Schlesinger, *op. cit.*, p. 391.
16. *Sunday Times*, August 6, 1961.
17. *Ibid.*, July 21, 1961.
18. *Ibid.*, July 30, 1961.
19. July 30, 1961, on ABC's "Issues and Answers," text in *Congressional Record*, Vol. 107, pp. 14222–5.
20. Schlesinger, *op. cit.*, p. 395.
21. August 20, 1961.
22. The *Sunday Times*, August 27, 1961.
23. June 30, 1961.

CHAPTER FIVE

1. Robert F. Kennedy, *Thirteen Days: A Memoir of the Cuban Missile Crisis* (New York: Signet-NAL, 1969), p. 128.
2. *Ibid.*, p. 33.
3. *Ibid.*, p. 39.
4. JFKL/OHC, interview with Robert A. Hurwitch.
5. Hilsman, *To Move a Nation*, pp. 170–1.
6. He lost to Senator Birch Bayh.
7. *Congressional Record*, Vol. 108, p. 18360.
8. *Ibid.*, p. 18538.
9. Kennedy's September 4 statement is reprinted in remarks of Senator Engle, *Congressional Record*, Vol. 108, p. 18648.
10. *Congressional Record*, Vol. 108, p. 18522.
11. *Ibid.*, pp. 18644–52.
12. *Ibid.*, p. 18676.
13. Included in remarks of Representative Fascell in *Congressional Record*, Vol. 108, p. 18676.
14. *Congressional Record*, Vol. 108, p. 18731.
15. *Ibid.*, p. 18825.
16. *Ibid.*, pp. 20024–5.
17. The *Washington Post and Times Herald*, September 18, 1962.
18. Tom Wicker in the *New York Times*, October 1, 1962.
19. *Congressional Record*, Vol. 108, p. 22957.

20. *St. Louis Post-Dispatch*, October 14, 1962.
21. *Los Angeles Times*, October 17, 1962.
22. Bundy's memo to the President is quoted in Sorensen, p. 673.
23. Schlesinger, *op. cit.*, p. 802.
24. All accounts agree on the President's reaction.
25. Robert Kennedy, p. 33.
26. Incorrectly identified in Robert Kennedy's book as "Edward" Martin.
27. Thompson replaced Charles Bohlen, who left after the first day to take up his new post as ambassador to France. Bohlen's departure had, of course, been announced in advance, and although the President desired his counsel, Kennedy felt that a last-minute delay in the departure from Washington of one of the nation's leading experts on Soviet affairs might arouse suspicion.
28. Acheson reports that he removed himself from the group a few days later because he felt that one who was not an officer of the United States government ought not to be involved in making such momentous decisions.
29. Wilson's chief, Edward R. Murrow, was gravely ill.
30. Robert Kennedy, pp. 24, 27.
31. JFKL/OHC, interview with Robert A. Hurwitch.
32. The *New York Times*, April 11, 1971.
33. Sorensen, p. 678.
34. Schlesinger, *op. cit.*, p. 811.
35. Satellite photos and highly placed spies provided vital information. According to former CIA official Robert Amory, Soviet missile production information from Col. Oleg Penkovsky was "uniquely valuable." (JFKL/OHC.) In 1971 CIA Director Richard Helms revealed that in 1962 the U.S. had "a wealth of information on Soviet missile systems [from U-2 photos and] a number of well-placed and courageous Russians who helped us." (*Washington Post*, April 15, 1971.) Penkovsky was arrested in October 1962 and later executed.
36. The *New York Times*, October 22, 1961.
37. Hilsman, *To Move a Nation*, pp. 163–4.
38. Stewart Alsop, "Kennedy's Grand Strategy," *Saturday Evening Post*, March 31, 1962.

39. Hilsman, *To Move a Nation*, p. 195.
40. Sorensen, p. 678.
41. *Ibid.*
42. *Ibid.*, pp. 681–2.
43. The analysis of I. F. Stone in this as in so many cases has stood the test of time. See *In Time of Torment* (New York: Random House, 1967), pp. 18–27. Ronald Steel in *New York Review*, March 13, 1969, has also emphasized this factor.
44. Sorensen, p. 688.
45. Elie Abel, *The Missile Crisis* (Philadelphia and New York: Lippincott, 1966), p. 53.
46. Sorensen, p. 683. All accounts agree that most members of the Ex Comm changed positions at least once during the week.
47. JFKL/OHC, interview with Robert Lovett.
48. Sorensen, pp. 689–90.
49. Abel, p. 61.
50. Lippmann column in *St. Louis Post-Dispatch*, October 25, 1962.
51. Robert Kennedy, pp. 108–9.
52. Nikita Khrushchev, *Khrushchev Remembers* (Boston: Little, Brown, 1970), pp. 497–8.
53. The *Washington Post*, January 4, 1971.
54. Abel, p. 60.
55. *Ibid.*, p. 49.
56. Sorensen, p. 695. For discussion of Stevenson's proposals, see also Schlesinger, *op. cit.*, pp. 806–11.
57. Newhouse, p. 23.
58. Sorensen, p. 696.
59. Robert Kennedy, p. 95.
60. JFKL/OHC, interview with Ambassador Llewellyn Thompson.
61. The *Christian Science Monitor*, October 25, 1962.
62. U. S. Senate, 91st Cong., 2d Sess., "Arms Control and Disarmament Act Amendment 1970," *Hearings before the Committee on Foreign Relations on S. 3544* (Washington, D.C.: GPO, 1970).
63. Robert Kennedy, p. 94.
64. Schlesinger, *op. cit.*, p. 810.

65. *Ibid.*
66. JFKL/OHC, interview with Robert Lovett.
67. Robert Kennedy, p. 67.

CHAPTER SIX

1. See discussion in E. L. Katzenbach, Jr., "Time, Space, and Will: The Politico-Military Views of Mao-Tse-tung," in Lt. Col. T. N. Greene, ed., *The Guerrilla and How to Fight Him* (New York: Praeger, 1962).
2. Walt W. Rostow, "Guerrilla Warfare in Under-developed Areas." This speech by Rostow has appeared in several forms in different collections. The quotations are from *The Marine Corps Gazette*, January 1962.
3. Roger Hilsman, "Internal War: The New Communist Tactic," in Greene, ed., *The Guerrilla and How to Fight Him.*
4. JFKL/OHC, interview with Robert Amory.
5. *The Pentagon Papers* (New York: Bantam, 1971), p. 79.
6. Ralph Stavins, "Kennedy's Private War," *New York Review,* July 22, 1971.
7. *Pentagon Papers*, p. 84.
8. *Ibid.*, p. 86.
9. Schlesinger, *op. cit.*, p. 541.
10. *Pentagon Papers*, p. 86.
11. *Ibid.*, p. 119.
12. Hilsman, *To Move a Nation*, pp. 129, 133.
13. *Pentagon Papers*, p. 88.
14. *Ibid.*, p. 89.
15. Hilsman, *To Move a Nation*, p. 134.
16. *Pentagon Papers*, p. 126.
17. Stavins, *op. cit.*
18. *Washington Star*, June 25, 1971.
19. *Pentagon Papers*, p. 137.
20. See Schlesinger, *op. cit.*, p. 532.
21. *Pentagon Papers*, p. 95.
22. *Ibid.*, p. 98.
23. *Ibid.*, p. 99.
24. *Ibid.*, p. 103.
25. *Ibid.*, pp. 101–2.
26. *Ibid.*, pp. 141–2.

27. *Ibid.*, p. 104.
28. *Ibid.*, pp. 150–1.
29. *Pentagon Papers*, p. 107.
30. *Ibid.*, p. 108.
31. Kenneth O'Donnell, "LBJ and the Kennedys," *Life*, August 7, 1970.
32. *Pentagon Papers*, p. 107.
33. Robert Thompson, *Defeating Communist Insurgency* (London: Chatto & Windus, 1966), p. 51.
34. Diem told Thompson that the traditional Vietnamese way is that successful generals are always retired. (*Ibid.*, p. 59).
35. The development of the technique is described in Captain André Souyris, "An Effective Counter-guerrilla Procedure," *Revue de Defense Nationale* (France), June 1956, as translated in *Military Review*, Vol. XXXVI, No. 12 (March 1957), pp. 860–90.
36. Milton Osborne, *Strategic Hamlets South Vietnam: A Survey and Comparison*, Data Paper No. 55, Southeast Asia Program, Department of Asian Studies (Ithaca, N.Y.: Cornell Univ., 1965), p. 54.
37. Osborne, p. *viii*.
38. *Pentagon Papers*, p. 113.
39. *Ibid.*, pp. 162, 173.
40. *Ibid.*, p. 232.
41. Schlesinger, *op. cit.*, p. 997.

CHAPTER SEVEN

1. Schlesinger, *op. cit.*, p. 301.
2. *Ibid.*, pp. 302–3.
3. Jerome D. Frank, *Sanity and Survival: Psychological Aspects of War and Peace* (New York: Vintage, 1967), p. 141.
4. George W. Rathjens, *The Future of the Strategic Arms Race* (New York: Carnegie Endowment for International Peace, 1969), p. 24.
5. JFKL/OHC, interview with Dr. Herbert York.
6. JFKL/OHC, interview with Robert Amory.
7. *The Soviet Union and the NATO Powers: The Military Balance* (London: Institute for Strategic Studies, 1960).

8. *Congressional Record,* Vol. 107, pp. 1227–37.
9. Sorensen, pp. 612–3.
10. *Ibid.,* p. 602.
11. Arthur M. Schlesinger, Jr., *Kennedy or Nixon: Does it Make Any Difference?* (New York: Macmillan, 1960), p. 42.
12. *The New York Review,* April 23, 1970.
13. John F. Kennedy, *Why England Slept* (Garden City: Dolphin-Doubleday, 1962; original edition, 1940), pp. 222–3.
14. *Ibid.,* p. 223.
15. *Ibid.,* p. 228.
16. Maxwell D. Taylor, *The Uncertain Trumpet* (New York: Harper & Bros., 1959–60), pp. 7–8.
17. *Ibid.,* p. 136.
18. *Ibid.,* p. 138.
19. *Ibid.,* p. 139.
20. *Ibid.,* pp. 141–2.
21. *Ibid.,* pp. 145–6.
22. *Ibid.,* pp. 178–9.
23. U. S. Senate, 91st Cong., 2d Sess., "ABM, MIRV, SALT, and the Nuclear Arms Race," p. 395.
24. JFKL/OHC, interview with Dr. Herbert York.
25. U. S. Senate, "ABM, MIRV, SALT, and the Nuclear Arms Race," p. 396.
26. Schlesinger, *op. cit.,* pp. 499–500.
27. U. S. Senate, "ABM, MIRV, SALT, and the Nuclear Arms Race," p. 396.
28. Herbert York, *Race to Oblivion: A Participant's View of the Arms Race* (New York: Simon & Schuster, 1970), p. 237.
29. Quoted in Sorensen, p. 612.
30. *New York Review,* April 23, 1970.
31. Seymour Melman, "Three Decisions and Three American Crises." (Mimeo.)
32. Read at the elder Kennedy's funeral mass by Senator Edward Kennedy. Text in *New York Times,* November 21, 1969.
33. January 21, 1971.

Index

About the Author

LOUISE FITZSIMONS is a foreign affairs analyst who has worked in recent years in the United States Senate. She was Foreign Affairs Officer of the United States Embassy in Paris, associate editor of Research and Publications at the Carnegie Endowment for International Peace, foreign affairs consultant to the State and Defense Departments, and has worked in the public and private sectors of atomic energy affairs. She has traveled extensively behind the Iron Curtain and in Vietnam, and now lives and works in Washington, D.C., and in New Haven, Connecticut.